2/09

PLANT NAMES
E

Botan .... *g*

A HORTICULTURE BOOK

Horticulture Publications, Boston, Massachusetts
First published in the US in 2005 ISBN 1-55870-747-6
Copyright © David & Charles 2005

Horticulture is a subsidiary of F+W Publications Inc. Company
Distributed by F+W Publications Inc.
4700 East Galbraith Road, Cincinnati, OH 45236
1-800-289-0963

Printed in italy by legoprint
for Horticulture Publications, Boston, Massachusetts

Visit our website at www.hortmag.com

Commissioning Editor Mic Cady
Art Editor Alison Myer
Production Director Roger Lane

Produced for David & Charles by
OutHouse Publishing
Winchester, Hampshire SO22 5DS, UK
Compiler Julia Brittain
Editor Sue Gordon
Designer Dawn Terrey

CONTENTS

FOREWORD

Any visit to a foreign country is enhanced by the possession of a little local knowledge. If you speak a few words of the language, it is always easier to get what you want. So it is with a visit to the world of plants: a basic understanding of botanical Latin makes the gardener, new or experienced, more comfortable in his understanding of the natives.

Latin names are nothing to be afraid of. They may be unfamiliar at first but, as soon as a few words are mastered, the desire for more knowledge will be kindled. The classical languages from which nomenclature is derived are the roots of many other languages. Once one moves on from the initial unfamiliarity, many terms will seem more logical and their meaning often becomes obvious.

Plant names tell many stories, both factual and imaginary. They are a fascinating catalogue created by those that discovered the plants and the botanists who tried to fit those plants into the infinite jigsaw of the plant world. The names given to the plants are valuable information to the

ARBUTUS UNEDO

VALERIANA PHU

gardener; often descriptive and cultural but also a historical record of where a plant fits into the history of our gardens.

Botanical Latin is a living, evolving language. Names change as we learn more about the plants we discover and cultivate. These name changes are often an annoyance to the gardener but a joy to the botanist who has come closer to fitting a piece of the jigsaw into the right position. The most magical property of the language is its international application, a passport for gardeners and plantsmen everywhere to communicate, regardless of their native tongues.

Plant names are fun. Modern cultivar names add a familiar dimension to the classical roots of the language. In our gardens they introduce a host of characters into the border, regardless of their place in history. You will find the famous, the infamous and the improbable sharing the same bed right outside your window.

Andrew McIndoe

MYRTUS COMMUNIS

INULA HELENIUM

About this book

The framework of *Plant Names Explained* is an alphabetical listing, giving translations of many of the descriptive terms (specific epithets, see page 11) that form part of Latin plant names. Often an example of a relevant plant name accompanies the translation; many of these will be familiar garden plants. Some specific epithets (e.g. *angustifolius*, narrow-leaved) are more common than others, occurring in the names of a number of plants. These are picked out in the listing as '**Common descriptive terms**', each accompanied by several plant examples illustrating use of the term.

Once translated into English, specific epithets often reveal useful information about the plant such as its color, native habitat or country of origin. For general interest and easy reference, the book features a series of '**What's in a Name?**' panels, each listing a selection of these Latin descriptive terms with their meanings. These panels are grouped by theme such as shape, plant uses, colors or habitat.

Genus names (see page 11) often derive from the names of notable people, or from Greek, Latin or other ancient languages. For example, *Aubrieta* is named for Claude Aubriet,

a French botanical artist, while *Chrysanthemum* is from the Greek words for 'gold flower'. The book features a series of '**Genus Names**' panels (pale green) explaining the derivation of some of the main genus names beginning with each letter of the alphabet.

Sometimes it is useful to look up the Latin name of a plant of which you know only the common name, for example foxglove, snowdrop or beech. Another letter-by-letter series of panels answers the question 'What's the Latin name?' Herbs, fruits and vegetables are listed in separate '**What's the Latin Name?**' boxes on pages 47, 169, and 113 respectively.

Modern plant names include a whole world of cultivar names (see pages 13–14). These can be useful, funny or just plain fascinating. Selected foreign cultivar names, such as *Philadelphus* 'Manteau d'Hermine' or *Prunus* 'Amanogawa', are translated in a series of alphabetical 'Cultivar names' panels: '**Foreign Expressions**'. A selection of the more quirky English cultivar names are highlighted in a similar alphabetical series called '**Strange but True**'. A third letter-by-letter series of panels is '**Personal Names**', featuring plants such as *Narcissus* 'Jenny',

Rhododendron 'David' and *Lonicera periclymenum* 'Sweet Sue'. Other cultivar names highlight people or places, artists or foods, or are named for special occasions such as birthdays or anniversaries (useful when thinking about gifts). Examples of these are listed in themed '**Cultivar Names**' panels scattered through the book.

For a full list of all the above alphabetic and thematic panels in the book, see pages 8–9.

Any attempt to condense the enormous subject of plant naming into a book of this size may leave some readers feeling disappointed by what has had to be omitted. However, *Plant Names Explained* is intended as a book to dip into for interest and for fun, rather than as an all-encompassing reference manual. For a scholarly, comprehensive and in-depth study of botanical names, refer to the standard work, *Botanical Latin*, by William T. Stearn (Timber Press, 2004). A great linguist and eminent botanist, Stearn spent his life researching the naming of plants and meticulously tracing the origins of many plant names.

While every effort has been made to provide accurate and up-to-date information, plant naming is an increasingly complex business, with names changing all the time. New cultivars appear every year in various parts of the world, while others become unavailable. The publishers therefore cannot accept responsibility for names that may have changed or been incorrectly recorded, or for plants that either are not available locally or are no longer in commerce. We would be very happy to hear from readers should they encounter any inaccuracies.

PRIMULA VERIS

Where to find ...

DECIPHERING PLANT NAMES

The naming of plants is an enormous, complex and often confusing subject, but one that can be every bit as useful and entertaining to gardeners as to botanists and taxonomists. Intended for gardeners and anyone with a passing interest in plants, *Plant Names Explained* sets out to demystify botanical nomenclature and brings to life a subject that can often seem somewhat bewildering.

Why botanical Latin?

Correct botanical naming gives every plant a unique label, so that it can be accurately identified in any language: these names can be used and understood anywhere in the world. Our internationally accepted system of botanical Latin – now well over 200 years old – has become even more valuable in recent decades, as widespread travel and electronic communication have made the world ever smaller. Many of us travel widely and see unfamiliar plants in the gardens, parks and countryside of the places we visit. The nursery trade itself has become increasingly internationalized. The Internet enables us to converse across the world at the touch of a key. It has also become a very useful means of tracking down elusive plants. The system of binomial nomenclature gives us a ready-made tool to ensure that the names of the plants we see, or want to buy, or are eager to identify correctly, are immediately recognizable anywhere.

When visiting a nursery in Japan that specializes in perennials, I had no trouble identifying the plants because their names were clearly written in botanical Latin as well as in Japanese. On another occasion I was walking in a nature reserve in Slovakia with the reserve botanist. Our only method of communication was botanical Latin – accompanied by a bit of smiling and hand waving – but it was surprising how much information we managed to convey to each other.

All countries have common names for their native plants. These names are often delightfully descriptive, with many plants having a range of quirky

Bluebells and bluebells

The common name 'bluebell' shows how, in an international context, sometimes only a botanical name makes it clear which plant we mean. In England the bluebell is *Hyacinthoides non-scripta*, a bulb that makes sheets of blue in the woods in spring. In Scotland the bluebell is *Campanula rotundifolia*, a small summer flower of open grassland known in England as a harebell. In the United States the Virginia bluebell is a pretty perennial, whose showers of lilac-blue bells carpet the woods: its botanical name is *Mertensia virginica*. To Australians, a bluebell is the climber called *Sollya heterophylla*, which dangles its little sky-blue bells among its neighbours.

and charming colloquial names. However, sometimes these names can be ambiguous or obscure (see 'Bluebells and bluebells', below left). This may be because the same common name means one plant in one place but elsewhere refers to an entirely different plant, or it may be because the local name is very local indeed, perhaps known only in a dialect that is restricted to a very small area. Plants that occur in different countries or different regions may acquire a number of names, and confusion soon arises.

Carl Linnaeus

For centuries, Europe's men of science and learning communicated in Latin. Plant descriptions were written in a form of Latin, which evolved as a special language of botanical terms, taking in names from Greek, Arabic and other sources. In the 18th century, when many new plant and animal discoveries were being made, the right man appeared in the right place at the right time. Carl Linnaeus (1707–1778) was a professor of medicine at the respected University of Uppsala in Sweden. The life's work of this great naturalist was to bring order into the system of naming all living organisms. His detailed and orderly approach enabled him to build a system of classifying plants according to particular botanical details, giving each plant two names: the genus (plural: genera) and the species.

The binomial system

This binomial ('two names') system, which Linnaeus set out in his book *Species Plantarum* (1753), gained wide acceptance and was the foundation of modern botanical nomenclature. In a binomial plant name, the genus comes first (always with an initial capital letter), followed by the species name (in lower case). The names are usually written in italics: for example *Bellis perennis* (*Bellis* – genus, *perennis* – species) for the common daisy. Many genus names tell us nothing about the

Linnaeus's choice

Linnaeus often named plants for his friends – sometimes very aptly. He chose *Tillandsia* for his colleague Elias Til-Landz, who had a horror of water and once took a 2,000-mile journey overland from Finland to Sweden rather than sail across the Gulf of Bothnia. What are tillandsias? Mosses or air plants, which take their moisture from the air and require no water!

plant. More often they are adapted from another language, or were chosen to honor a particular person. The second name, the specific epithet, usually does say something about the plant. Sometimes it describes a structural detail (which may be clear only to botanists) or it indicates the plant's place of origin – either habitat or locality – or its habit of growth; thus *Bellis perennis* means perennial daisy.

The 'What's in a Name?' features in this book highlight the meanings of hundreds of descriptive terms like this. The information contained in specific epithets of plants can be very useful to those trying to grow them. For example, it's no good planting *Euphorbia palustris* in dry gravel, as *palustris* means marsh-loving. The specific epithet of *Geranium saxatile* tells us that this plant grows among rocks; likewise, *Geranium pratense* prefers meadows, while *Geranium sylvaticum* likes woods. Place-names can also give an indication of the geographical origin of the plant: *Geranium pyrenaicum* grows in the Pyrenees, and *Crocus corsicus* is from the Mediterranean island of Corsica. Many other epithets describe the shape of the leaves (*latifolius*, broad-leaved), the habit of growth of the plant (*humilis*, dwarf) or the color of its flowers (*albiflorus*, white-flowered).

A further category is the specific epithet that commemorates a person, such as one of the great plant hunters. If you know the area of the world in which the plant hunter worked, you have a good idea of the plant's country, or even region, of origin. Thus many plants named for George Forrest and Reginald Farrer come from China, including the winter-flowering, scented shrub *Viburnum farreri*. The climbing *Clematis florida* var. *sieboldiana* comes from Japan, where Philipp von Siebold was collecting plants, while the epithet *douglasii*, in honour of David Douglas, usually indicates a plant that originally hailed from North America.

The gender issue

The genus name is a noun and the specific epithet a qualifying adjective. Botanical nomenclature is sourced mainly from classical Latin and Greek, where words have different endings for different genders – masculine, feminine and neuter. The specific epithet normally takes the gender of the genus name.

Latin generic names ending in -*us* are mostly masculine (as in *Helleborus foetidus*), those ending in -*a* are feminine (*Campanula alpina*), and those ending in -*um* are neuter (*Trillium grandiforum*). A notable exception is that most trees are feminine (*Prunus incisa, Fagus sylvatica*). Names derived from Greek are masculine if the ending is -*on* (*Platycodon grandiflorus*) and those ending in -*is* and -*ins* are feminine, as are -*ix* and -*odes* and -*oides* (*Bellis rotundifolia, Larix decidua*).

The most common endings for specific epithets that are Latin adjectives are: -*us* (masculine), -*a* (feminine), -*um* (neuter) – e.g. *floridus*; -*er* (masculine), -*ra* (feminine), -*rum* (neuter) – e.g. *niger*; -*is* (masculine and feminine), -*e* (neuter) – e.g. *brevis*. Certain epithets are the same in all genders, for example *simplex, praecox, tenax, repens, bicolor*, etc. Where a specific epithet denotes a person, the ending is usually -*ii* for a man (*Epimedium davidii*) and -*ae* for a woman (*Rosa banksiae*). In this book, specific epithets are listed in their masculine singular form (*angustifolius, niger* etc.)

Those responsible for naming plants have not always got it right. Sometimes insufficient information was available when plants were first discovered and described. For example, the shocking pink Guernsey lily, *Nerine arniensis*, (*sarniensis* means from Guernsey) originally came from South Africa, but it is thought that the ship carrying the bulbs from the Cape was wrecked and the bulbs were washed ashore in Guernsey, where they naturalized. *Scilla peruviana* comes not from Peru, but the western Mediterrean.

In the wild, plants sometimes occur that vary slightly from the type species, perhaps in color or habit. These are known as subspecies (subsp.). The Eastern European variation of the common primrose, which has purplish-pink flowers, is named *Primula vulgaris* subsp. *sibthorpii*. Even smaller differences are described as varieties (var.) or sometimes forms (f.). There are selections of the British native beech, *Fagus sylvatica*, that have narrower leaves than the type, with lobed and cut edges: these are known as *Fagus sylvatica* var. *heterophylla* (*heterophylla*, with diverse leaves).

Some plants are known to be hybrids between two species – either as a result of deliberate breeding, or occurring naturally where the two species grow together. Their 'hybrid epithet' is preceded by a multiplication sign, as in *Helleborus* × *nigercors*, a hybrid between *Helleborus niger* and *Helleborus argutifolius*. In the much rarer case of a hybrid between two genera (a bigeneric hybrid), a multiplication sign precedes the 'genus' name: × *Fatshedera lizei* is a bigeneric hybrid between *Fatsia japonica* and *Hedera hibernica*.

Cultivar names

The binomial system of genus and species works well for wild plants, but for cultivated plants – that is, forms of the species that have been selected and brought into cultivation, or deliberately hybridized in gardens and nurseries – a third name is necessary. This is known as the cultivar name, 'cultivar' being an abbreviation of 'cultivated variety'. The accepted way of writing a cultivar name is to place it within single quotation marks, not in italics, and with initial capital letters, as in *Bellis perennis* 'Dresden China'.

In the past, descriptive forms of Latin were used in cultivar names and many of these are still in use. However, since 1959, when the International Code of Nomenclature was established, it has not been permissible to Latinize

Plants for Amelia

It is fun to find plants that share a name with friends or members of your family. My little granddaughter is named Amelia and I was delighted to find 11 plants with 'Amelia' in their cultivar name, ranging from a pine tree called 'Amelia's Dwarf' to a rose 'Amelia Louise', and from an osteospermum called 'Sunny Amelia' to a pretty little yellow viola 'Amelia'. This seems the best one to grow in my garden.

Much fun can be had finding plants to commemorate people and special occasions: see the alphabetical 'Personal Names' panels in this book for a few examples of the many 'name' plants.

new cultivar names. So *Bellis perennis* 'Alba Plena' for the double white form would not be acceptable as a new name nowadays.

Cultivar names come in their thousands. Quirky or informative, useful or intriguing, named for people, gardens, cities, colors or even food – a wide selection of examples features in special panels distributed throughout the book. An increasing number of cultivar names are from non-English-speaking countries, and translations of some examples of those are included here too. Knowing the meaning of a foreign name can make it easier to remember. Some excellent new clematis are being introduced from Poland and Estonia, and it may be helpful to know that *Clematis* 'Blekitny Aniol' is Polish for 'blue angel' and *Clematis* 'Sinee Dozhd' Russian for 'blue rain'. Most English-speaking gardeners also need help to decipher the many Japanese plant names. The delicate, early-flowering *Prunus incisa* 'Kojo-no-mai' becomes a 'must have' plant when you know its wonderfully evocative translation: 'dance in the ancient castle'.

Trade designations

With the introduction of Plant Breeders' Rights (PBR), cultivar names of a different kind are being registered in ever increasing numbers. Many of these are in a meaningless code that is useful in international commerce but is not suitable for marketing the plant locally.

Newer roses often bear these rather strange cultivar names – for example 'Auscat', for the rose that is usually known as Winchester Cathedral (the prefix 'Aus' indicates that the rose was bred in UK by David Austin Roses). For everyday purposes it therefore became necessary to use a more attractive and understandable selling name, or trade designation. This name is written without quotation marks, starts with a capital letter, and is shown in a different font, as in *Rosa* WINCHESTER CATHEDRAL ('Auscat'), with the trade designation first and the cultivar name following it in brackets.

What's in a name? Three plantsmen

Tolmiea menziesii 'Taff's Gold', a North American woodland plant, is the only plant I know that carries the names of three noted plantsmen. William Fraser Tolmie was a botanist working in the Vancouver area in the 1830s. Archibald Menzies travelled as a surgeon-botanist with Captain Vancouver on his expedition to find a passage between the North Pacific and the Atlantic. Stephen Taffler, a modern plantsman with a passion for all variegated plants, was immediately attracted by the plant's gold-splashed leaves and introduced it as a garden plant.

Tolmiea menziesii 'Taff's Gold' is commonly known as the pick-a-back or piggyback plant, referring to its curious habit of producing little plantlets along its leaf veins. Related to heucheras, it is perfectly hardy but is also successful as a houseplant.

Changing names

Changes in long-established names are a nuisance for everyone and may seem difficult to justify – especially where a familiar name changes to something that is hard to remember and to spell, and even more difficult to pronounce. However, there are usually good reasons for the change. The 'principle of priority', as it is known, has established that the first written description of a plant is taken as its valid name. Familiar names can therefore sometimes fall from grace as new information comes to light from ever more obscure places around the globe. Herbaria in libraries in the former Soviet Union are now being studied by experts and we are having to accept earlier names for some plants familiar to generations of gardeners. The 'new' name may mean nothing to us and may be very difficult for many of us to pronounce – try saying *Allium przewalskianum* quickly.

Another reason for name changes is that modern scientists are able to detect ever more minute differences (and similarities) in plant characteristics. This means that sometimes plants must be separated out into a new genus: our old friend *Senecio* 'Sunshine' became *Brachyglottis* 'Sunshine', while the once-familiar genus *Cimicifuga* has disappeared into another genus, *Actaea*. As for the florists' chrysanthemum, it was despatched to a new genus called *Dendranthema*, only to be returned to *Chrysanthemum* a few years later. Occasionally taxonomists run out

of names and resort to using an anagram of an existing one: the genus *Saruma* has been created from the closely related *Asarum*.

The following pages contain something for everyone. Skip from name to intriguing name, pausing to take in the riches and the oddities of the world of plant names. What plants would make a good wedding present? Who was Miss Willmott? Where does *Verbena bonariensis* come from? And how could there possibly be a plant named *Allium paradoxum* var. *normale*, or one called *Quisqualis indica*? Dip into *Plant Names Explained* for the answers to hundreds of questions like these. You will find it useful, absorbing and fun.

Jane Sterndale-Bennett

Pronunciation: be bold

Pronouncing Latin names flusters many gardeners needlessly. Remember that we are quite used to saying many of them: *Aquilegia* and *Antirrhinum*, *Primula* and *Rhododendron* cause us no problems. Courage is the best principle: just have a go. Say the word aloud several times to hear how it sounds. In most cases the stress is placed on the second or third syllable. There is often no wrong or right way: ask three taxonomists, and you may well get three different versions. Never mind; we can all enjoy saying 'silly bum' for *Silybum marianum*, the milk thistle.

A

a- without *(e.g. acaulis,* stemless)

abbreviatus shortened

abies; abietinus fir; resembling a fir
  Picea abies

abnormis abnormal
  Ranunculus abnormis

abrotanifolius with leaves
  like *Artemisia abrotanum*
  (southernwood)
  Geranium abrotanifolium

abscissus cut off

absconditus hidden

absinthoides like *Artemisia*
  absinthium (wormwood)
  Erodium absinthoides

abyssinicus from Ethiopia (formerly
  Abyssinia)

acaciiformis shaped like *Acacia*
  Eucalyptus acaciiformis

acadiensis from Nova Scotia,
  Canada

acalycinus without (or apparently
  without) a calyx
  Liquidambar acalycina

acanth-, acantho- spiny, thorny
  Onopordum acanthium

acanthifolius with leaves like
  Acanthus
  Carlina acanthifolia

acanthos a prickle or thorn

acephalus without a head

acer, acris, acre sharp, pointed,
  piercing
  Sedum acre

acerbus bitter

acerifolius with leaves like *Acer,*
  maple-leaved
  Viburnum acerifolium

aceroides like *Acer* (maple)

acerosus needle-shaped

acerus without wax

acetabulosus cup-shaped,
  concave
  Ballota acetabulosa

CARLINA ACAULIS

acetosus, acetosellus sour, acid
   Oxalis acetosella
   Pelargonium acetosum
acicularis like a pin or needle
   Eleocharis acicularis
acidus sour, acid
aciformis needle-shaped
acinaceus like a scimitar
acinosus like grapes
   Phytolacca acinosa
acis something pointed
aconitifolius with leaves like
   Aconitum
   Ampelopsis aconitifolia
acraeus living on the heights
   Euryops acraeus
acris, acre see *acer*
acro- the tip or extremity
   of something
   Rhododendron acrophilum

acta the seashore
   Festuca actae
actino- radiating (see below)
actinophyllus with radiating leaves
   Schefflera actinophylla
actinosus full of rays; glorious
aculeatus prickly
   Ruscus aculeatus

COMMON DESCRIPTIVE TERMS
acuminatus tapering to a narrow
   point
Gladiolus acuminatus
Lonicera acuminata
Magnolia acuminata
Rheum acuminatum
Tulipa acuminata

---

acus a needle or pin
acutatus sharpened
   Helichrysum acutatum
acutiflorus with sharply pointed
   flowers
   Calamagrostis × *acutiflora*
acutifolius with sharply pointed
   leaves
   Salix acutifolia
acutiformis in the shape of a point
   Carex acutiformis
acutissimus very sharp
   Quercus acutissima
acutus sharpened, made pointed
   Carex acuta
adamantinus hard like steel

Aaron's beard *Hypericum calycinum*
Aaron's rod *Solidago*; *Verbascum thapsus*
Abele *Populus alba*
Aconite *Aconitum* or *Eranthis*
Adam's needle *Yucca filamentosa*
Adder's tongue *Erythronium americanum*
African daisy *Arctotis*
African lily *Agapanthus*
African marigold *Tagetes erecta*
Alder *Alnus*
Alder buckthorn *Rhamnus frangula*
Alexanders *Smyrnium olusatrum*
Alexandrian laurel *Danae racemosa*
Alfalfa *Medicago sativa*
Alkanet *Anchusa*; *Alkanna tinctoria*; *Pentaglottis sempervirens*
Allspice *Calycanthus*
Almond *Prunus dulcis*
Alpenrose *Rhododendron ferrugineum*

Alumroot *Heuchera*
Alyssum, Sweet *Lobularia maritima*
Angel's fishing rod *Dierama pulcherrimum*
Angel's tears *Narcissus triandrus*
Angel's trumpets *Brugmansia*
Angelica *Angelica archangelica*
Angelica tree *Aralia spinosa*
Apple *Malus domestica*
Apple of Peru *Nicandra physalodes*
Apricot *Prunus armeniaca*
Arborvitae *Thuja*
Arum lily *Zantedeschia aethiopica*
Ash *Fraxinus*
Aspen *Populus tremula*
Aster (China) *Callistephus*
Atlas cedar *Cedrus atlantica*
Autograph tree *Clusia major*
Avens *Geum*
Azalea *Rhododendron*

adeno- gland
adenocarpus with glandular (or sticky) fruits
   Helichrysum adenocarpum
adenogynus with a sticky ovary
   Rhododendron adenogynum
adenophorus bearing glands
   Adenophora bulleyana
adenophyllus with glands on the leaves, or with sticky leaves
   Oxalis adenophylla
adiantoides like *Adiantum* (maidenhair fern)
admirabilis admirable, wonderful
adnatus growing together

adpressus lying flat, fitting close to
   Cotoneaster adpressus
adscendens ascending
adsurgens rising, standing up
   Phlox adsurgens
aegypticus, aegyptiacus Egyptian
   Hypericum aegypticum
aemulus emulating, comparable to
   Dryopteris aemula
aeneus copper or bronze
aequalis equal
   Phygelius aequalis
aequiformis uniform
aequinoctialis equinoctial; from equatorial (tropical) regions

aequipetalus with equal petals

aequitrilobus with three equal lobes

aerius aerial

aeruginosus blue-green (the color of verdigris)
   Rhododendron campanulatum subsp. *aeruginosum*

aesculifolius with leaves like horse-chestnut
   Rodgersia aesculifolia

aestivalis, aestivus of summer
   Adonis aestivalis
   Leucojum aestivum

aethiopicus, aethiopis Ethiopian; also used to mean South African
   Zantedeschia aethiopica

aetnensis from Mount Etna, Sicily
   Genista aetnensis

aetolicus from Aetolia, Greece

COMMON DESCRIPTIVE TERMS

affinis related to
   Dryopteris affinis
   Fritillaria affinis
   Gentiana affinis
   Jasminum officinale f. *affine*
   Persicaria affinis
   Pulmonaria affinis
   Tricyrtis affinis

---

affixus attached to

afghanicus from Afghanistan
   Dionysia afghanica

afoliatus without leaves

CULTIVAR NAMES
Food and Drink

ASTILBE 'LOLLIPOP'

CAMELLIA HIEMALIS 'SPARKLING BURGUNDY'

CARYOPTERIS × *CLANDONENSIS* 'SUMMER SORBET'

DAHLIA 'CAFÉ AU LAIT'

HOSTA 'GUACAMOLE'

HEUCHERA 'PLUM PUDDING'

IRIS SIBIRICA 'BUTTER AND SUGAR'

IRIS 'SMOKED SALMON'

MALUS DOMESTICA (APPLE) 'SCOTCH DUMPLING'

MENTHA ARVENSIS 'BANANA'

PAPAVER ORIENTALE 'WATERMELON'

PELARGONIUM 'TURKISH COFFEE'

PENSTEMON 'SOUR GRAPES'

POTENTILLA FRUTICOSA 'PEACHES AND CREAM'

PRIMULA AURICULA 'OLD MUSTARD'

PULMONARIA 'SPILLED MILK'

RANUNCULUS REPENS 'BUTTERED POPCORN'

RHODODENDRON SARGENTIANUM 'WHITEBAIT'

ROSA GINGER SYLLABUB ('HARJOLLY')

RUDBECKIA HIRTA 'MARMALADE'

SALVIA MERJAMIE 'MINT-SAUCE'

SAXIFRAGA 'BLACKBERRY AND APPLE PIE'

SCABIOSA ATROPURPUREA 'CHILLI SAUCE'

SEDUM 'STEWED RHUBARB MOUNTAIN'

SEMPERVIVUM 'JELLY BEAN'

SISYRINCHIUM 'RASPBERRY'

CULTIVAR NAMES
Colors: Red

ASTILBE CHINENSIS 'VISION IN RED'

ATHYRIUM NIPONICUM VAR. *PICTUM* 'RED BEAUTY'

BEGONIA 'RED UNDIES'

BERBERIS THUNBERGII F. *ATROPURPUREA* 'RED CHIEF'

BUDDLEIA DAVIDII 'ROYAL RED'

CANNA INDICA 'RUSSIAN RED'

CORYLUS MAXIMA 'RED FILBERT'

ENKIANTHUS CAMPANULATUS 'RED BELLS'

ESCALLONIA 'RED ELF'

EUONYMUS EUROPAEUS 'RED CASCADE'

HEBE 'RED EDGE'

HELLEBORUS × *HYBRIDUS* 'RED LADY'

HEMEROCALLIS 'LITTLE RED HEN'

ILEX VERTICILLATA 'WINTER RED'

IRIS SIBIRICA 'MELTON RED FLARE'

LATHYRUS LATIFOLIUS 'RED PEARL'

LAVANDULA STOECHAS 'KEW RED'

LEPTOSPERMUM SCOPARIUM 'RED DAMASK'

LONICERA PERICLYMENUM 'RED GABLES'

MALUS DOMESTICA (APPLE) 'RED FALSTAFF'

MALUS × *ROBUSTA* 'RED SENTINEL'

NYMPHAEA 'PERRY'S BABY RED'

PELARGONIUM 'RED BLACK VESUVIUS'

PERSICARIA MICROCEPHALA 'RED DRAGON'

PHOTINIA × *FRASERI* 'RED ROBIN'

SEMPERVIVUM 'RED SPIDER'

COMMON DESCRIPTIVE TERMS

africanus; afer, afra, afrum
African, from Africa
Agapanthus africanus
Artemisia afra
Cyclamen africanum
Salvia africana

---

agathos good

agathosmus smelling good, fragrant
Buddleia agathosma

agavifolius with leaves like *Agave*
Eryngium agavifolium

agavoides like *Agave*
Echeveria agavoides

ageratifolius with leaves like *Ageratum*
Achillea ageratifolia

ageratoides like *Ageratum*

ageraton not growing old; not withering readily
Ageratum houstonianum

agglomeratus gathered into a head

aggregatus added or collected together; in a cluster
Eucalyptus aggregata

agrarius of land or fields

agrestis rural, rustic; of fields

agrius wild

agrostis grass

ailanthifolius with leaves like *Ailanthus*
Juglans ailanthifolia

aizoon ever-living
Sedum aizoon

akebioides resembling *Akebia*
    Clematis akebioides
alaris on the wing; axillary

COMMON DESCRIPTIVE TERMS
alatus winged
Euonymus alatus
Gladiolus alatus
Nicotiana alata
Passiflora alata
Thunbergia alata

---

albanus, albanicus from Albania
    Geranium albanum
albescens becoming white, whitish
albicans whitish
    Hebe albicans
albicaulis white-stemmed
albidus white
    Nymphaea 'Albida'
albiflorus, albiflos white-flowered
    Geranium albiflorum
albifrons with white foliage or fronds
    Lupinus albifrons
albispinus with white thorns
albocereus white-waxy
    Fargesia albocerea
albomaculatus white-spotted
    Zantedeschia albomaculata
albopictus white-painted
    Begonia albopicta
albopilosus with white hairs
albosinensis Chinese white
    Betula albosinensis

albospicus with white spikes
albomarginatus white-edged
albotomentosus white-woolly
    Stachys albotomentosa
albovariegatus white-variegated
albulus whitish
    Carex albula

COMMON DESCRIPTIVE TERMS
albus white
Cornus alba
Dictamnus albus
Nymphaea alba
Phlox paniculata 'Alba Grandiflora'
Populus alba
Rosa 'Alba Semiplena'
Veratrum album

VERATRUM ALBUM

CULTIVAR NAMES
Personal Names
A

KNIPHOFIA 'ADA'
ROSA 'ADAM'
PRIMULA AURICULA 'ADRIAN'
ROSA × *FRANCOFURTANA* 'AGATHA'
ROSA 'AGNES'
HEMEROCALLIS 'ALAN'
ROSA ALEC'S RED ('CORED')
PELARGONIUM 'ALEX'
RHODODENDRON 'ALEXANDER'
CALLUNA VULGARIS 'ALEXANDRA'
PRIMULA AURICULA 'ALF'
RHODODENDRON 'ALFRED'
DIANTHUS 'ALICE'
PRIMULA AURICULA 'ALICIA'
ROSA ALISON ('COCLIBEE')
CROCOSMIA 'ALISTAIR'
SEMPERVIVUM 'AMANDA'
VIOLA 'AMELIA'
NEMESIA 'AMÉLIE'
HEBE 'AMY'
ROSA ANABELL ('KORBELL')
CHRYSANTHEMUM 'ANASTASIA'
ROSA 'ANDREA'
FUCHSIA 'ANDREW'

PELARGONIUM 'ANGELA'
TULIPA 'ANGÉLIQUE'
PRIMULA AURICULA 'ANGIE'
CLEMATIS 'ANITA'
SALVIA × *SUPERBA* 'DEAR ANJA'
MAGNOLIA 'ANN'
CLEMATIS ANNA LOUISE ('EVITHREE')
HEDERA HELIX 'ANNA MARIE'
HELIANTHEMUM 'ANNABEL'
IRIS 'ANNABEL JANE'
RHODODENDRON 'ANNABELLA'
HYDRANGEA ARBORESCENS 'ANNABELLE'
VERBENA 'SILVER ANNE'
CALLUNA VULGARIS 'SISTER ANNE'
CALLUNA VULGARIS 'ANNEMARIE'
POTENTILLA FRUTICOSA 'ANNETTE'
VERBASCUM 'ANNIE MAY'
ROSA 'ANTONIA'
RHODODENDRON 'ANTONIO'
VIOLA 'ARABELLA'
PRIMULA AURICULA 'UNCLE ARTHUR'
ASTER NOVI-BELGII 'AUDREY'
PELARGONIUM 'AUGUSTA'
PRIMULA AURICULA 'AVRIL'

aleppensis, aleppicus from Aleppo, Syria
  Geum aleppicum
aleuticus from the Aleutian Islands
  Adiantum aleuticum
alexandrinus from Alexandria, Egypt
algeriensis from Algeria
  Salvia algeriensis

algidus cold
  Primula algida
alienus alien, foreign
  Quercus aliena
aliformis wing-shaped
alleghaniensis from the Allegheny Mountains in the eastern USA
  Betula alleghaniensis

alliaceus like *Allium* (onion)

allo- diverse, different, other

alnifolius with leaves like *Alnus* (alder)
   Clethra alnifolia

alnoides resembling *Alnus* (alder)
   Betula alnoides

aloides like Aloe

aloifolius with leaves like *Aloe*
   Yucca aloifolia

alpestris growing just below the alpine zone
   Ranunculus alpestris

alpicola an inhabitant of the alpine zone
   Primula alpicola

COMMON DESCRIPTIVE TERMS

alpinus alpine, growing in the Alps or in the alpine zone
Aquilegia alpina
Clematis alpina
Dianthus alpinus
Eryngium alpinum
Lychnis alpina
Papaver alpinum

---

altaclerensis from Highclere in Hampshire, UK
   Ilex × *altaclerensis*

altaicus from the Altai Mountains in southern Siberia/Kazakhstan
   Primula altaica

alternatus alternate

alternifolius with alternate leaves
   Buddleia alternifolia

althaeoides like *Althaea* (hollyhock)
   Convolvulus althaeoides

alticola hill dweller

alticomus with foliage high up

altifrons with tall foliage or fronds

altipendulus hanging high

altissimus very tall
   Ailanthus altissima

altus tall
   Sedum altum

alutaceus leathery
   Rhododendron alutaceum

alveatus, alveolatus hollowed out, channeled

alyssifolius with leaves like *Alyssum*
   Phlox alyssifolia

alyssoides like *Alyssum*
   Halimium alyssoides

amabilis lovely
   Kolkwitzia amabilis

amanus from the Amanus mountain range in Turkey
   Origanum amanum

amaranthoides like *Amaranthus*

amarellus rather bitter

amarissimus very bitter
   Salvia amarissima

amarus bitter

amarylloides like *Amaryllis*
   Haemanthus amarylloides

amazonicus from the Amazon
   Eucharis amazonica

COMMON DESCRIPTIVE TERMS

americanus American

Agave americana

Erythronium americanum

Fraxinus americana

Lysichiton americanus

Sorbus americana

Tilia americana

amethystinus violet-colored

  Festuca amethystina

ammophilus sand-loving

amoenus lovely, pleasant

  Felicia amoena

amomum an aromatic shrub

  Cornus amomum

amphi- both

amphibius amphibious, growing in water and on land

amplexicaulis clasping or encircling the stem

  Persicaria amplexicaule

amplexifolius with leaves that clasp or encircle the stem

ambiguus doubtful or uncertain

  Consolida ambigua

ambly- blunt

amblyanthus with blunt flowers

  Indigofera amblyantha

amblyphyllus blunt-leaved

ambrosioides like ambrosia, the food of the gods

amentaceus like a catkin (*amentum*)

COMMON DESCRIPTIVE TERMS

amurensis from the area of Heilong Jiang (the Amur river), on the Russian/Chinese border

Adonis amurensis

Dianthus amurensis

Maackia amurensis

Papaver amurense

Vitis amurensis

amygdaleus of an almond tree

amygdalinus, amygdaloides
  almond-like
    Eucalyptus amygdalina
    Euphorbia amygdaloides

amylaceus starchy

an- without

ana- up

anatolicus from Anatolia, Turkey
    Dianthus anatolicus

anceps with two edges
    Lythrum anceps

ancyrensis from Ankara, Turkey
    Crocus ancyrensis

andinus from the Andes
    Prumnopitys andina

androgynus hermaphrodite
    Semele androgyna

anemoniflorus anemone-flowered
    Paeonia officinalis 'Anemoniflora
    Rosea'

aneurus without nerves

anglicus English
    Sorbus anglica

anguilliformis eel-shaped

anguinus snakelike

angularis, angulatus angular, with
  angles
    Geranium sylvaticum
    'Angulatum'

angulosus with angles or corners
    Allium angulosum

angustatus narrowed
    Cornus angustata

COMMON DESCRIPTIVE TERMS

angustifolius narrow-leaved

Elaeagnus angustifolia
Fraxinus angustifolia
Galanthus angustifolius
Hoheria angustifolia
Lavandula angustifolia
Phillyrea angustifolia
Pulmonaria angustifolia
Typha angustifolia

LEAF CHARACTERISTICS

acutifolius with sharply pointed leaves

adenophyllus with glands on the leaves, or with sticky leaves

alternifolius with alternate leaves

angustifolius narrow-leaved

aquifolius with pointed leaves

argophyllus silver-leaved

argutifolius with sharply toothed leaves

brevifolius with short leaves

capillifolius with hairlike leaves

cardiophyllus with heart-shaped leaves

caudatifolius with tail-like leaves

chrysophyllus with golden leaves

cochlearifolius with spoon-shaped leaves

cordifolius with heart-shaped leaves

crassifolius with thick leaves

dactylifolius with finger-like leaves

dentatus toothed

denticulatus with small teeth

dictyophyllus with leaves showing an obvious network of veins

digitatus hand-shaped; with fingers

dissectus dissected; deeply divided

distichophyllus with leaves in two rows

diversifolius with leaves of differing shapes

filicifolius with fern-like leaves

filifolius thread-leaved

glaucophyllus with glaucous leaves

grandidentatus with large teeth

grandifolius with large leaves

integrifolius with undivided leaves

isophyllus with equal leaves

latifolius broad-leaved

laxifolius loose-leaved

linearifolius with linear leaves

lobularis, lobulatus with small lobes

longifolius long-leaved

macrophyllus with large leaves

megalophyllus with large leaves

microphyllus with small leaves

millefolius, millefoliatus (literally) with a thousand leaves

mucronifolius with pointed leaves

oblongifolius with oblong leaves

obtusifolius with blunt leaves

oppositifolius opposite-leaved

ovalifolius with oval leaves

palmatus palmate

parvifolius with small leaves

pectinatus like a comb, combed

perfoliatus perfoliate (with the leaf surrounding the stem)

petiolaris with a (long) leaf stalk

pinguifolius with fat leaves

pinnatus pinnate

planifolius with flat leaves

platyphyllus, platyphyllos with broad (or flat) leaves

plicatus folded or pleated

podophyllus with stalked leaves

polifolius grey-leaved

porphyrophyllus with purple leaves

repandens, repandus with wavy or turned-up edges

rhombifolius with diamond-shaped leaves

rotundifolius with round leaves

rubrifolius with red leaves

sagittifolius with arrow-shaped leaves

salicifolius with willow-like leaves

serratifolius with serrated leaves

serratus serrated, saw-toothed

sessilifolius with sessile leaves

stenophyllus with narrow leaves

tenuifolius with thin leaves

HELIANTHUS ANNUUS

angustipetalus narrow-petaled
  Hydrangea angustipetalus
angustus narrow
  Gladiolus angustus
anisatus, anisus aniseed-flavored
  Illicium anisatum
  Pimpinella anisum
annularis ring-shaped
annulatus ringed; with rings
annuus annual
  Helianthus annuus (sunflower)
anomalus irregular, abnormal
  Hydrangea anomala subsp. *petiolaris*
anopetalus with upright petals
anserinus pertaining to geese
  Potentilla anserina
antarcticus from Antarctica
  Dicksonia antarctica

anthemoides like *Anthemis*
  Rhodanthe anthemoides
anthemon flower
anthera anther (the pollen-bearing
  part of a flower's stamen)
anthopogon flower beard (hairs or
  bristles)
  Rhododendron anthopogon
anthracinus coal black
-anthus -flowered (e.g. *macranthus*,
  large-flowered)
antillaris from the Antilles (West
  Indies)
antipodeus from the Antipodes
  Geranium × *antipodeum*
antiquus old, ancient, former
apenninus from the Apennines, Italy
  Anemone apennina

ILEX AQUIFOLIUM

apertus open
  Nomocharis aperta
apetalus without petals
  Fuchsia apetala
aphyllus without leaves
apianus of bees
  Salvia apiana
apiculatus with a short pointed
  end
  Luma apiculata
apifer bee-bearing
  Ophrys apifera (bee orchid)
apiifolius with leaves like parsley
  or celery
  Clematis apiifolia

apo- down
apodus without a foot or stalk;
  sessile
  Salix apoda
appendiculatus with small
  appendages
  Francoa appendiculata
applanatus flattened
applicatus joined, attached
appressus see *adpressus*
approximans approaching, near to
  Eucalyptus approximans
apterus without wings
  Euonymus alatus var. *apterus*
aquaticus, aquatilis of water; growing
  by water
  Mentha aquatica
  Ranunculus aquatilis
aqueus watery
aquifolius with pointed leaves
  Ilex aquifolium (holly)
aquilegiifolius with leaves like
  Aquilegia
  Thalictrum aquilegiifolium
aquilinus eagle-like
arabicus Arabian
  Ornithogalum arabicum
arachnoides, arachnoideus like
  a spider or its web
  Sempervivum arachnoideum
aragonensis from Aragon, Spain
arborescens growing to be a tree;
  woody
  Artemisia arborescens

COMMON DESCRIPTIVE TERMS

arboreus treelike, woody
Brugmansia arborea
Ceanothus arboreus
Erica arborea
Lavatera arborea
Linum arboreum
Lupinus arboreus
Pseudopanax arboreus
Rhododendron arboreum

arbusculus like a small tree
   Daphne arbuscula
arbutifolius with leaves like *Arbutus*
   Aronia arbutifolia
arcanus closed, secret
   Phyllostachys arcana
archangelicus of an archangel
   Angelica archangelica
arcticus arctic
   Rubus arcticus
arcuatus bent or curved like a bow
   Ornithogalum arcuatum

COMMON DESCRIPTIVE TERMS

arenarius, arenosus sandy, growing
   on sand
Dianthus arenarius
Jovibarba arenaria
Leymus arenarius
Sisyrinchium arenarium

areolatus marked out into small areas
   Sarracenia × *areolata*

CULTIVAR NAMES
Foreign Expressions
A

ABENDGLUT (*German*)
EVENING GLOW
(*BERGENIA* 'ABENDGLUT')

ALBÂTRE (*French*) ALABASTER
(*PHILADELPHUS* 'ALBÂTRE')

ALLEGRO (*Italian*) CHEERFUL
(*PAPAVER ORIENTALE* 'ALLEGRO')

AMANOGAWA (*Japanese*)
THE MILKY WAY
(*PRUNUS* 'AMANOGAWA')

ANDENKEN AN (…) (*German*)
REMEMBRANCE OF (…)
(*PENSTEMON* 'ANDENKEN AN
FRIEDRICH HAHN')

APFELBLÜTE (*German*)
APPLE BLOSSOM
(*GERANIUM SANGUINEUM*
'APFELBLÜTE')

APRÈS MOI (*French*) AFTER ME
(*HEMEROCALLIS* 'APRÈS MOI')

ARC-EN-CIEL (*French*) RAINBOW
(*NYMPHAEA* 'ARC-EN-CIEL')

ASCHERMITTWOCH (*German*)
ASH WEDNESDAY
(*ROSA* 'ASCHERMITTWOCH')

AUBADE (*French*) DAWN MUSIC
(*CROCUS CHRYSANTHUS* 'AUBADE')

AZURFEE (*German*) AZURE FAIRY
(*ERIGERON* 'AZURFEE')

AZUMA-KAGAMI (*Japanese*)
MIRROR OF THE EAST
(*IRIS ENSATA* 'AZUMA-KAGAMI')

argenteoguttatus silver-spotted
argenteomarginatus silver-edged
argenteovariegatus silver-variegated
   Vinca minor 'Argenteovariegata'

COMMON DESCRIPTIVE TERMS
argenteus silver, **argentatus**
  silvered
Celosia argentea
Cistus × *argenteus*
Ilex aquifolium 'Argentea Marginata'
Plectranthus argentatus
Potentilla argentea
Salvia argentea
Tanacetum argenteum

---

argentinus from Argentina
argillosus rich in clay, full of clay
argophyllus silver-leaved
   Olearia argophylla
argutifolius with sharply toothed
  leaves
   Helleborus argutifolius
argutus sharp
   Spiraea 'Arguta'
argyro- silvery (see below)
argyrophyllus silver-leaved
   Rhododendron argyrophyllum
argyrotrichon silver-haired
   Campanula argyrotricha
aridus dry, withered
   Penstemon aridus
arifolius with leaves like *Arum*
   Asarum arifolium

COMMON DESCRIPTIVE TERMS
aristatus, aristosus awned (like ears
  of corn); bearded
Aloe aristata
Gaillardia aristata
Pinus aristata
Thamnocalamus aristatus

---

arizonicus from Arizona
   Abies lasiocarpa var. *arizonica*
arkansanus from Arkansas
armandii named after Abbé Jean
  Pierre Armand David (1826–
  1900); see also page 65 (*davidii*)
   Clematis armandii
armatus equipped, armored (e.g.
  with thorns)
   Osmanthus armatus
armeniacus, armenus Armenian
   Prunus armeniaca (apricot)
armillaris encircled
aromaticus fragrant, aromatic, spicy
   Clematis × *aromatica*
articulatus jointed; distinct
   Oxalis articulata
arundinaceus like a reed
   Phalaris arundinacea

COMMON DESCRIPTIVE TERMS
arvensis of fields or farmland
Cirsium arvense
Knautia arvensis
Myosotis arvensis
Rosa arvensis

arvoniensis from Caernarvon, Wales

ascendens ascending, rising

asiaticus Asian

   Trachelospermum asiaticum

asperifolius with rough leaves

asperatus roughened

   Arisaema asperatum

asper rough

   Hydrangea aspera

asperrimus very rough

aspleniifolius with leaves like the fern

   Asplenium

   Fagus sylvatica var. *heterophylla*
   'Aspleniifolia'

assurgens standing up, rising

assyriaca from Assyria

   Fritillaria assyriaca

astictus without spots

asturiensis from Asturias, in north-
  western Spain

   Narcissus asturiensis

COMMON DESCRIPTIVE TERMS

ater-, atro- dark, black

atrocyaneus very dark blue:

   Salvia atrocyanea

atropurpureus dark purple:

   Scabiosa atropurpurea 'Ace of Spades'

atrorubens dark red:

   Helleborus atrorubens

atrosanguineus dark blood-red:

   Cosmos atrosanguineus

atroviolaceus dark violet:

   Gladiolus atroviolaceus

---

atlanticus from the Atlas Mountains
  in North Africa

   Cedrus atlantica (Atlas cedar)

atratus dressed in mourning; dark

   Aquilegia atrata

atriplicifolius with leaves like *Atriplex*
  (orache)

   Perovskia atriplicifolia

atro- (see panel, below left)

attenuatus tapering to a point

   Agave attenuata

atticus from Attica or Athens,
  Greece

   Iris attica

GENUS NAMES

A

Abelia named for Dr. Clarke Abel
  (1780–1826), British botanist

Acanthus from Greek *akantha*, thorn

Achillea named for the Greek hero
  Achilles

Agapanthus from Greek *agape*, love,
  and *anthos*, flower

Alstroemeria named for Baron Claus
  Alstroemer (1736–1794)

Ampelopsis from Greek *ampelos*, vine,
  and *opsis*, resemblance

Anemone from Greek *anemos*, wind

Antirrhinum from Greek *anti*, like,
  and *rhis*, a nose or snout

Artemisia named for the Greek
  goddess Artemis

Aubrieta named for Claude
  Aubriet (1668–1743), French
  botanical artist

PRIMULA AURICULA

aucuparius bird-catching
  Sorbus aucuparia
augurius of the augur or soothsayer;
  predicting
augustus venerable, majestic
aulos flute, tube
aurantiacus, aurantius orange-red
  Citrus aurantium (orange tree)
  Pilosella aurantiaca
auratus, aureatus decorated with gold
aureomaculatus gold-spotted
aureomarginatus gold-edged
  Hosta 'Aureomarginata'
aureopictus (literally) gold-painted
aureoreticulatus gold-veined
  Lonicera japonica 'Aureoreticulata'

aureovariegatus gold-variegated
  Buxus sempervirens 'Aureovariegata'

COMMON DESCRIPTIVE TERMS
aureus gold, golden, of gold
  Bidens aurea
  Fritillaria aurea
  Humulus lupulus 'Aureus'
  Juniperus chinensis 'Aurea'
  Origanum vulgare 'Aureum'
  Philadelphus coronarius 'Aureus'
  Phyllostachys aurea
  Sambucus racemosa 'Plumosa Aurea'

---

aureolus golden, gilded
auricomus golden-haired
  Pleioblastus auricomus
auricula ear, ear-shaped appendage
  Primula auricula
auriculatus eared, lobed
  Scrophularia auriculata
auritus eared
  Salix aurita
aurorius of dawn, daybreak, morning
aurosus like gold
australiensis from Australia

COMMON DESCRIPTIVE TERMS
australis southern; from the
  southern hemisphere
  Baptisia australis
  Cordyline australis
  Indigofera australis
  Phragmites australis

---

austriacus from Austria
  Veronica austriaca

COMMON DESCRIPTIVE TERMS
autumnalis of autumn
Colchicum autumnale
Helenium autumnale
Leucojum autumnale
Prunus subhirtella 'Autumnalis'
Scilla autumnalis

---

avellanus from Abella (now called
  Avellino), Campania, Italy (a
  town once noted for its fruit
  and nuts)
  Corylus avellana
avicularis pertaining to small birds
  Solanum aviculare
avium of birds
  Prunus avium (bird cherry; sweet
  cherry)
axillaris axillary; relating to the
  axil
  Pachysandra axillaris
azoricus from the Azores
  Hedera azorica

COMMON DESCRIPTIVE TERMS
azureus azure; deep sky-blue
Anchusa azurea
Muscari azureum
Salvia azurea
Symphytum azureum
Tropaeolum azureum

CULTIVAR NAMES
Colors: Purple

ACER PLATANOIDES 'GOLDSWORTH PURPLE'
AUBRIETA 'GREENCOURT PURPLE'
BUDDLEIA DAVIDII 'NANHO PURPLE'
CLEMATIS 'PURPLE SPIDER'
CLEMATIS HERACLEIFOLIA 'CHINA PURPLE'
CORDYLINE AUSTRALIS 'PURPLE TOWER'
CORYLOPSIS SINENSIS VAR. *SINENSIS* 'SPRING PURPLE'
COTINUS COGGYGRIA 'ROYAL PURPLE'
CROCUS TOMMASINIANUS 'WHITEWELL PURPLE'
ERYTHRONIUM DENS-CANIS 'PURPLE KING'
FAGUS SYLVATICA 'PURPLE FOUNTAIN'
FUCHSIA 'DEEP PURPLE'
GERANIUM PRATENSE 'PURPLE HERON'
HEMEROCALLIS 'PURPLE RAIN'
HEUCHERA MICRANTHA 'PALACE PURPLE'
HOSTA 'PURPLE DWARF'
LAVANDULA ANGUSTIFOLIA 'TWICKEL PURPLE'
LIRIOPE MUSCARI 'ROYAL PURPLE'
LYTHRUM VIRGATUM 'DROPMORE PURPLE'
OCIMUM BASILICUM VAR. *PURPURASCENS* 'PURPLE RUFFLES'
PASSIFLORA 'PURPLE HAZE'
PENSTEMON 'PURPLE BEDDER'
PRUNUS PADUS 'PURPLE QUEEN'
PULMONARIA 'MOURNFUL PURPLE'
SALVIA 'PURPLE MAJESTY'

B

babylonicus Babylonian
  Salix babylonica
baccans berrying
baccatus berry-like; with pulpy fruits
  Taxus baccata
baccifer berry-bearing
bacciflavus with yellow berries
  Ilex aquifolium 'Bacciflava'
bacillaris like a rod or stick
backhouseanus named for an English
  nurseryman and plant collector,
  James Backhouse (1794–1869)
Correa backhouseana
badius reddish brown
baeticus from Andalucia (the Roman
  province of Baetica) in Spain

balcanicus from the Balkans
baldensis from Monte Baldo,
  in northern Italy
baldschuanicus from Baljuan,
  Turkestan
  Fallopia baldschuanica

COMMON DESCRIPTIVE TERMS
balearicus from the Balearic Islands,
  in the Mediterranean Sea
  Arenaria balearica
  Buxus balearica
  Clematis cirrhosa var. *balearica*
  Hypericum balearicum

---

ballardiae named for the English
  gardener and nurserywoman Helen
  Ballard (1908–1995), known
  especially for breeding hellebores
  Helleborus × *ballardiae*

SIR JOSEPH BANKS
(1743–1820)

Wealthy Oxford University graduate and passionate naturalist, Joseph Banks accompanied Captain Cook on his 1768–71 world voyage – an auspicious start to this Englishman's illustrious career in the world of plants. On his return, Banks was appointed Adviser to the Royal Gardens at Kew, presiding over the introduction of numerous new plants and helping to establish Kew's international reputation. He was President of the Royal Society from 1778 until his death. Banks always took a particular interest in the plant life of Australia and it is fitting that he gave his name to an Australasian genus – *Banksia*. Other plants commemorating him include *Astelia banksii* and *Pinus banksiana*, while *Rosa banksiae* is named for his wife.

balsameus balsamic or resinous
  Abies balsamea
balsamifer balsam-bearing
  Populus balsamifera
balteiformis shaped like a belt
balticus from the Baltic Sea region
bambusoides like bamboo
  Phyllostachys bambusoides
banaticus, bannaticus from Banat,
  Romania
  Echinops bannaticus
banksii, banksiae (see panel opposite)
barbadensis from Barbados in the
  West Indies
barba-jovis Jove's beard
  Anthyllis barba-jovis
barbarus foreign; from the Barbary
  Coast of Africa
  Decumaria barbara
barbatus bearded
  Dianthus barbatus (sweet
  William)
barbinervis with hairs on the veins
  Clethra barbinervis
barbulatus with a small beard
  Anemone barbulatus
barystachys with heavy spikes
  Lysimachia barystachys
basilicus princely, royal
  Ocimum basilicum (sweet basil)
battandieri named for Jules Battandier
  (1848–1922), a French botanist
  Cytisus battandieri
bavaricus from Bavaria

CULTIVAR NAMES
Personal Names
B

GALANTHUS 'BARBARA'S DOUBLE'
HOSTA 'BARBARA ANN'
DAHLIA 'BEATRICE'
PELARGONIUM 'BEATRIX'
LEUCANTHEMUM × *SUPERBUM* 'BECKY'
FUCHSIA 'BELINDA JANE'
CLEMATIS 'BELLA'
CAMELLIA SASANQUA 'BEN'
CAMPANULA TRACHELIUM 'BERNICE'
NARCISSUS 'BERYL'
PYRUS COMMUNIS (PEAR) 'BETH'
MAGNOLIA 'BETTY'
FUCHSIA 'BEVERLEY'
FUCHSIA 'BRENDA'
ESCALLONIA LAEVIS 'GOLD BRIAN'
HEMEROCALLIS 'BRIDGET'
RHODODENDRON 'BRIGITTE'
DELPHINIUM 'BRUCE'
HELENIUM 'BRUNO'

---

beesianus named for Bees, a
  nursery and seed supplier in
  Cheshire, UK
  Primula beesiana
belgicus from Belgium or the
  Netherlands
  Lonicera periclymenum 'Belgica'
  (early Dutch honeysuckle)
belladonna beautiful lady (referring
  to the one-time use of deadly
  nightshade as an eye cosmetic)
  Atropa bella-donna

Banksia named for Sir Joseph Banks
  (see page 34)
Baptisia from Greek *bapto*, to dye
Begonia named for Michel Bégon
  (1638–1710), French Canadian
  governor
Bellis from Latin *bellus*, pretty
Bergenia named for Karl August
  von Bergen (1704–1760), German
  professor
Bidens from Latin *bi-*, two, and *dens*,
  tooth
Bougainvillea named for Louis de
  Bougainville (1729–1811), French
  explorer
Brachyscome from Greek *brachys*,
  short, and *kome*, hair
Brunnera named for Samuel Brunner
  (1790–1844), Swiss botanist
Buddleia named for the Rev. Adam
  Buddle (1660–1715), British
  botanist and clergyman

bellidifolius with leaves like *Bellis*
  (daisy)
  Limonium bellidifolium
bellus beautiful
benedictus well spoken of; blessed
  Cnicus benedictus
bengalensis, benghalensis from
  Bengal
benzoin an aromatic gum
  Lindera benzoin
berolinensis from Berlin, Germany
  Populus × *berolinensis*

berthelotii named for a French consul
  and naturalist, Sabin Berthelot
  (1794–1880)
  Lotus berthelotii
bertolonii named for an Italian
  botanist, Antonio Bertoloni
  (1775–1869)
  Aquilegia bertolonii
betaceus like beet
betinus purple like beet
betonicifolius with leaves like *Stachys
  officinalis* (betony)
  Meconopsis betonicifolia
betulifolius with leaves like *Betula*
  (birch)
  Campanula betulifolia
bhutanicus from Bhutan
  Malus bhutanica

COMMON DESCRIPTIVE TERMS
bicolor bicolored
Dietes bicolor
Eucomis bicolor
Galega bicolor
Kniphofia bicolor

bicornis with two horns
  Matthiola bicornis
bicuspidatus with two points
bidentatus with two teeth
biennis biennial
  Oenothera biennis
bifidus divided, split into two parts
  Escallonia bifida

Baby blue-eyes *Nemophila menziesii*
Baby's breath *Gypsophila paniculata*
Bachelor's buttons *Ranunculus aconitifolius*
Balloon flower *Platycodon*
Balsam *Impatiens*
Bamboo *Fargesia, Phyllostachys, Pleioblastus, Pseudosasa* etc.
Banana *Musa*
Barberry *Berberis*
Barberton daisy *Gerbera jamesonii*
Barley *Hordeum*
Barrenwort *Epimedium*
Bay, bay laurel *Laurus nobilis*
Bear's breeches *Acanthus*
Beauty berry *Callicarpa*
Beauty bush *Kolkwitzia amabilis*
Bee balm *Monarda didyma*

BARLEY

Beech *Fagus sylvatica*
Bellflower *Campanula*
Bells of Ireland *Moluccella laevis*
Bergamot *Monarda didyma*
Betony *Stachys officinalis*
Bindweed *Convolvulus*
Birch *Betula*
Bishop weed *Aegopodium podagraria*
Bistort *Persicaria bistorta*
Black gum *Nyssa sylvatica*
Black mulberry *Morus nigra*
Black-eyed Susan *Rudbeckia fulgida; Rudbeckia hirta; Thunbergia alata*

Blackthorn *Prunus spinosa*
Bladder senna *Colutea*
Blanket flower *Gaillardia*
Blazing star *Liatris*
Bleeding heart *Dicentra spectabilis*
Bloodroot *Sanguinaria canadensis*
Bloody cranesbill *Geranium sanguineum*
Blue oat grass *Helictotrichon sempervirens*
Bluebell, English *Hyacinthoides non-scripta*
Bluebell (Australia) *Sollya heterophylla;* (Scotland) *Campanula rotundifolia;* (USA) *Mertensia, Penstemon*
Bluebell, Spanish *Hyacinthoides hispanica*
Blueberry *Vaccinium*
Blueblossom *Ceanothus thyrsiflorus*
Blue-eyed grass *Sisyrinchium graminoides*
Blue-eyed Mary *Omphalodes verna*
Bog myrtle *Myrica gale*
Bogbean *Menyanthes trifoliata*
Boston ivy *Parthenocissus tricuspidata*
Bottlebrush *Callistemon*
Box elder *Acer negundo*
Box, Boxwood *Buxus*
Bramble *Rubus fruticosus*
Bridal wreath *Spiraea* 'Arguta'
Broom *Cytisus; Genista; Spartium*
Buckeye *Aesculus*
Buckthorn *Rhamnus*
Bugle *Ajuga reptans*
Bulrush *Typha*
Busy lizzie *Impatiens*
Butcher's broom *Ruscus aculeatus*
Buttercup *Ranunculus*
Butterfly bush *Buddleia davidii*

CULTIVAR NAMES
Strange but True
B

Iris 'Baboon Bottom'
Pelargonium 'Baby Bird's Egg'
Diascia 'Baby Bums'
Pelargonium 'Baby Snooks'
Chamaecyparis obtusa 'Bambi'
Verbascum 'Banana Custard'
Iris 'Bang'
Luzula sylvatica 'Barcode'
Rhododendron 'Bashful'
Aubrieta 'Belisha Beacon'
Hemerocallis 'Bette Davis Eyes'
Stachys byzantina 'Big Ears'
Fargesia murielae 'Bimbo'
Lupinus 'Bishop's Tipple'
Dianthus Black & White
Minstrels Group
Iris 'Black Tie Affair'
Malus domestica (apple) 'Bloody
Butcher'
Campanula persicifolia 'Blue
Bloomers'
Larix kaempferi 'Blue Rabbit
Weeping'
Pelargonium 'The Boar'
Geranium 'Bob's Blunder'
Iris 'Boo'
Houttuynia cordata 'Boo-Boo'
Fuchsia 'Bow Bells'
Ranunculus ficaria 'Brazen
Hussy'
Phlox paniculata 'Brigadier'
Pelargonium 'Brilliantine'
Lupinus 'Bubblegum'

COMMON DESCRIPTIVE TERMS

biflorus with two flowers
Abelia biflora
Camassia biflora
Crocus biflorus
Fritillaria biflora

bifolius with two leaves
Scilla bifolia
bifurcatus bifurcate; forked
bignonioides like *Bignonia*
Catalpa bignonioides
bilobus, bilobatus with two lobes
Ginkgo biloba
bipinnatus twice pinnate
Cosmos bipinnatus
bisectus divided into two equal parts
biserratus twice toothed (i.e. with
serrated teeth)
bistortus twice twisted
Persicaria bistorta 'Superba'
biternatus twice ternate
bithynicus from Bithynia, a former
region of Asia Minor
Fritillaria bithynica
blandus mild, not bitter; pleasing
Anemone blanda
blepharophyllus with leaves fringed
like eyelashes
Arabis blepharophylla
bodinieri named for a French
missionary and plant collector,
Emile Bodinier (1842–1901)
Callicarpa bodinieri

bodnantensis named for Bodnant
Garden in North Wales, UK
Viburnum × *bodnantense*
bohemicus from the former kingdom
of Bohemia in Eastern Europe
Geranium bohemicum
bolivianus, boliviensis from Bolivia
Fuchsia boliviana
bombycifer with silky hairs
Verbascum bombyciferum
bombycinus of silk
bonariensis from Buenos Aires
Verbena bonariensis
bononiensis from Bologna in Italy
bonus-henricus "good Henry"
Chenopodium bonus-henricus (good
King Henry)
borbonicus Latinized 'Bourbon':
referring to the island of Réunion
in the Indian Ocean (Ile Bourbon)
or the Bourbon kings of France
borealis northern
borisii; borisii-regi named for King
Boris of Bulgaria
Abies borisii-regi
Geum 'Borisii'
borneensis from Borneo
bracchiatus like arms; branched
at right angles
brachy- short-
brachylobus with short lobes
Artemisia brachyloba
brachysiphon with a short tube
Hebe brachysiphon

BIPINNATUS

brachystachyus with a short spike
Kniphofia brachystachya
bracteatus with bracts
Xerochrysum bracteatum
bracteosus with large, showy
or significant bracts
brasiliensis from Brazil
brevifolius with short leaves
Aloe brevifolia

CULTIVAR NAMES
Foreign Expressions
B

BARBAROSSA *(Italian)* RED BEARD
(*BERBERIS* × *CARMINEA* 'BARBAROSSA')

BARBE BLEU *(French)* BLUE BEARD
(*PELARGONIUM* 'BARBE BLEU')

BELLE ETOILE *(French)*
BEAUTIFUL STAR
(*PHILADELPHUS* 'BELLE ETOILE')

BENI-CHIDORI *(Japanese)*
RED THOUSAND BIRDS
(*PRUNUS MUME* 'BENI-CHIDORI')

BENI-SHIDARE *(Japanese)*
WEEPING RED
(*ACER PALMATUM* 'BENI-SHIDARE')

BERCEUSE *(French)* LULLABY
(*NARCISSUS* 'BERCEUSE')

BERGGOLD *(German)*
MOUNTAIN GOLD
(*ALYSSUM MONTANUM* 'BERGGOLD')

BLAUE DONAU *(German)*
BLUE DANUBE
(*CARYOPTERIS* × *CLANDONENSIS* 'BLAUE
DONAU')

BLAUE GLOCKE *(German)*
BLUE BELL
(*PULSATILLA* 'BLAUE GLOCKE')

BLAUES MEER *(German)*
BLUE SEA
(*PULMONARIA ANGUSTIFOLIA* 'BLAUES
MEER')

BLAUFUCHS *(German)* BLUE FOX
(*FESTUCA GLAUCA* 'BLAUFUCHS')

BLAUMEISE *(German)* BLUE TIT
(*HYDRANGEA MACROPHYLLA*
'BLAUMEISE')

BLAUSPIEGEL *(German)*
BLUE MIRROR
(*VERONICA PROSTRATA* 'BLAUSPIEGEL')

BLAUSTRUMPF *(German)*
BLUE STOCKING
(*MONARDA* 'BLAUSTRUMPF')

BLEKITNY ANIOL *(Polish)* BLUE ANGEL
(*CLEMATIS* 'BLEKITNY ANIOL')

BLEU NANTAIS *(French)* NANTES BLUE
(*CHAMAECYPARIS LAWSONIANA* 'BLEU
NANTAIS')

BLÜTENTISCH *(German)*
BLOSSOM TABLE
(*HELENIUM* 'BLÜTENTISCH')

BOULE DE NEIGE *(French)*
SNOWBALL
(*CAMPANULA PERSICIFOLIA* 'BOULE
DE NEIGE')

BRAUTSCHLEIER *(German)*
BRIDAL VEIL
(*ASTILBE* 'BRAUTSCHLEIER')

BRISE D'ANJOU *(French)*
ANJOU BREEZE
(*POLEMONIUM* BRISE D'ANJOU
('BLANJOU'))

BRONZESCHLEIER *(German)*
BRONZE VEIL
(*DESCHAMPSIA CESPITOSA*
'BRONZESCHLEIER')

brevipedunculatus with a short flower-stalk
Ampelopsis brevipedunculata
brevipes with a short foot or stalk
Malus brevipes
brevipetalus with short petals
Hamamelis 'Brevipetala'
brevis short
brewerianus named for the American botanist William Brewer (1828–1910)
Picea breweriana (Brewer's weeping spruce)
britannicus from Great Britain
bryoides like moss
bucarius, bucharicus from Bokhara in Turkestan
Iris bucharica
buchananii named for John Buchanan (1819–1898), a Scottish botanist who worked in New Zealand
Carex buchananii
bucinatus like a curved horn
bufonius relating to toads; growing in damp places
bulbifer bearing bulbs or bulbils
Asplenium bulbiferum
bulbocodium with a woolly bulb
Narcissus bulbocodium
bulbosus bulbous; swollen
bulgaricus from Bulgaria
bullatus blistered, bubbled, studded
Cotoneaster bullatus

bulleyanus named for Arthur Bulley (1861–1942), a wealthy merchant in Liverpool, UK, who sponsored plant hunters and founded Bees' nursery in Cheshire. Bulley's garden became Liverpool Botanic Garden
Primula bulleyana
bungeanus, bungei named for a Russian botanist, Alexander von Bunge (1803–1890)
Euonymus bungeanus

COMMON DESCRIPTIVE TERMS
burkwoodii named for brothers Arthur (1888–1951) and Albert Burkwood, of Park Farm Nursery, Kingston upon Thames, UK
Daphne × *burkwoodii*
Osmanthus × *burkwoodii*
Viburnum × *burkwoodii*

---

burmanicus from Burma
bursa-pastoris shepherd's purse
Capsella bursa-pastoris
buxifolius box-leaved
Berberis buxifolia

COMMON DESCRIPTIVE TERMS
byzantinus from Istanbul, Turkey (formerly Byzantium)
Colchicum byzantinum
Galanthus plicatus subsp. *byzantinus*
Gladiolus communis subsp. *byzantinus*
Stachys byzantina

C

cachemirianus, cachemiricus from Kashmir (see also *cashmerianus*)
  Aralia cachemirica
  Lavatera cachemiriana
cadens falling
cadmicus metallic

COMMON DESCRIPTIVE TERMS
caeruleus deep sky blue
Allium caeruleum
Catananche caerulea
Molinia caerulea
Passiflora caerulea
Polemonium caeruleum

---

caesius light grayish blue
caespitosus, cespitosus clump-forming
  Deschampsia cespitosa
  Salvia caespitosa
caffer from South Africa
  Geranium caffrum
cairicus from Cairo
calabricus from Calabria in southern Italy
  Putoria calabrica
calamifolius with reedlike leaves
calamus reedlike
  Acorus calamus
calathinus cup-shaped; like a basket

calcaratus spurred
  Origanum calcaratum
calcareus of limestone; chalky white
  Polygala calcarea
calceiformis, calceolatus shaped like a little shoe or slipper
calcicola growing on limy soil
  Narcissus calcicola
calendulinus orange like *Calendula* (pot marigold)
calidus warm, hot

COMMON DESCRIPTIVE TERMS
californicus from California
Aesculus californica
Brodiaea californica
Carpenteria californica
Erythronium californicum
Eschscholzia californica
Fremontodendron californicum
Sisyrinchium californicum
Zauschneria californica

---

calli-, calo- beautiful (see below)
callianthus with beautiful flowers
  Gladiolus callianthus
callicarpus with beautiful fruit
callimorphus beautifully shaped
callosus with a hard skin
  Saxifraga callosa
calthifolius with leaves like *Caltha* (marsh marigold)
  Geum calthifolium
calvus bald, hairless

CULTIVAR NAMES
Famous Gardens of the UK—Past and Present

PITTOSPORUM TENUIFOLIUM 'ABBOTSBURY GOLD'

POTENTILLA FRUTICOSA 'ABBOTSWOOD'

ORIGANUM VULGARE 'ACORN BANK'

HEMEROCALLIS 'APPLE COURT RUBY'

VIOLA 'BARNSDALE GEM'

LAVATERA × *CLEMENTII* 'BARNSLEY'

CARPENTERIA CALIFORNICA 'BODNANT'

HOSTA 'BRESSINGHAM BLUE'

ASTRANTIA 'BUCKLAND'

MAGNOLIA 'CAERHAYS BELLE'

PRUNUS LAUROCERASUS 'CASTLEWELLAN'

HELIOTROPIUM ARBORESCENS 'CHATSWORTH'

OLEA EUROPAEA 'CHELSEA PHYSIC GARDEN'

SALVIA PATENS 'CHILCOMBE'

EUPHORBIA GRIFFITHII 'DIXTER'

RHODODENDRON 'EXBURY NAOMI'

ERICA × *DARLEYENSIS* 'FURZEY'

SOLANUM CRISPUM 'GLASNEVIN'

CLEMATIS 'GRAVETYE BEAUTY'

ANEMONE HUPEHENSIS 'HADSPEN ABUNDANCE'

CONVALLARIA MAJALIS 'HARDWICK HALL'

CLEMATIS HARLOW CARR ('EVIPO004')

LAMIUM MACULATUM 'HATFIELD'

PENSTEMON 'HERGEST CROFT'

LAVANDULA ANGUSTIFOLIA 'HIDCOTE'

HELIANTHEMUM 'HIGHDOWN APRICOT'

SKIMMIA JAPONICA 'HIGHGROVE REDBUD'

VERBASCUM 'HYDE HALL SUNRISE'

PRIMULA 'INVEREWE'

CISTUS × *DANSEREAUI* 'JENKYN PLACE'

ABUTILON × *SUNTENSE* 'JERMYNS'

SKIMMIA × *CONFUSA* 'KEW GREEN'

ROSA FILIPES 'KIFTSGATE'

CAREX ELATA 'KNIGHTSHAYES'

ARTEMISIA ABSINTHIUM 'LAMBROOK SILVER'

MAGNOLIA SPRENGERI VAR. *DIVA* 'LANHYDROCK'

BUDDLEIA 'LOCHINCH'

LAVANDULA ANGUSTIFOLIA 'MUNSTEAD'

PENSTEMON 'MYDDELTON GEM'

EUCRYPHIA × *NYMANSENSIS* 'NYMANSAY'

FUCHSIA MAGELLANICA VAR. *MOLINAE* 'SHARPITOR'

GERANIUM × *MAGNIFICUM* 'ROSEMOOR'

CHAENOMELES × *SUPERBA* 'ROWALLANE'

NYSSA SYLVATICA 'SHEFFIELD PARK'

PULMONARIA 'SISSINGHURST WHITE'

GERANIUM 'SPINNERS'

SALVIA × *JAMENSIS* 'TREBAH'

WATSONIA 'TRESCO DWARF PINK'

CEANOTHUS ARBOREUS 'TREWITHEN BLUE'

BETULA UTILIS 'WAKEHURST PLACE'

CISTUS × *CRISPATUS* 'WARLEY ROSE'

NARCISSUS 'WATERPERRY'

PINUS SYLVESTRIS 'WESTONBIRT'

HELIANTHEMUM 'WISLEY PRIMROSE'

LILIUM CANDIDUM

calycinus with a prominent or lasting
   calyx
   Halimium calycinum
calystegioides like *Calystegia* (e.g.
   bindweed)
cambessedesii named for a French
   botanist, Jacques Cambessedes
   (1799–1863)
   Paeonia cambessedesii
cambricus Welsh, from Wales, UK
   Meconopsis cambrica (Welsh
   poppy)
camellifolius with leaves like *Camellia*
   Ilex × *altaclerensis* 'Camellifolia'
campaniflorus with bell-shaped
   flowers
   Clematis campaniflora

COMMON DESCRIPTIVE TERMS
campanulatus bell-shaped
   Agapanthus campanulatus
   Enkianthus campanulatus
   Penstemon campanulatus
   Persicaria campanulatus
   Rhododendron campanulatum

campestris of plains, flat land
   or fields
   Acer campestre
camphoratus like camphor
   Nepeta camphorata
camporum of plains
campylo- curved, bent
camtschatcensis, camtschaticus from
   Kamchatka, Siberia
   Lysichiton camtschatcensis
   Filipendula camtschatica

COMMON DESCRIPTIVE TERMS
canadensis from Canada or the
   north-eastern USA
   Amelanchier canadensis
   Cercis canadensis
   Cornus canadensis
   Populus × *canadensis*
   Sanguinaria canadensis
   Sanguisorba canadensis
   Tsuga canadensis

canaliculatus with a channel, like
   a pipe
   Narcissus canaliculatus

COMMON DESCRIPTIVE TERMS

canariensis from the Canary Islands
Genista canariensis
Hedera canariensis
Lavandula canariensis
Phoenix canariensis
Pinus canariensis
Salvia canariensis

canarinus canary yellow
candicans becoming white
  Galtonia candicans
candidissimus very white
  Arisaema candidissimum
candidulus rather white
  Berberis candidula
candidus pure white
  Lilium candidum (Madonna lily)
canescens becoming grayish white
  Populus × *canescens*
caninus relating to dogs (used to
  denote something inferior or
  coarse)
  Rosa canina

COMMON DESCRIPTIVE TERMS

cannabinus like hemp
Althaea cannabina
Datisca cannabina
Eupatorium cannabinum
Hibiscus cannabinus

cantabricus from Cantabria in Spain
  Daboecia cantabrica

CULTIVAR NAMES
Strange but True
C

IRIS SIBIRICA 'CAESAR'S BROTHER'
SEMPERVIVUM 'CAFÉ'
CALLUNA VULGARIS 'CALIFORNIA
MIDGE'
GERANIUM PHAEUM 'CALLIGRAPHER'
HEUCHERA 'CAN-CAN'
PRIMULA 'CAPTAIN BLOOD'
HOSTA 'CAPTAIN KIRK'
RANUNCULUS REPENS 'CAT'S EYES'
MALUS DOMESTICA (APPLE)
'CATSHEAD'
CIRCAEA LUTETIANA 'CAVEAT EMPTOR'
PHLOX DIVARICATA SUBSP. *LAPHAMII*
'CHATTAHOOCHEE'
SAXIFRAGA 'CHEAP CONFECTIONS'
IRIS 'CHICKEN LITTLE'
NARCISSUS 'CHIT CHAT'
MENTHA 'CHOCOLATE PEPPERMINT'
PAPAVER ORIENTALE 'CHOIR BOY'
IRIS 'CHUBBY CHEEKS'
PHLOX PANICULATA 'CINDERELLA'
PANICUM VIRGATUM 'CLOUD NINE'
SEDUM CAUTICOLA 'COCA-COLA'
SEMPERVIVUM 'COBWEB CAPERS'
FUCHSIA 'COME DANCING'
PRIMULA AURICULA 'CONSERVATIVE'
PHLOX DOUGLASII 'CRACKERJACK'
PITTOSPORUM 'CRINKLES'
FUCHSIA 'CRINKLEY BOTTOM'
PELARGONIUM 'CROCODILE'
JUNCUS DECIPIENS 'CURLY-WURLY'
CROCOSMIA × *CROCOSMIIFLORA*
'CUSTARD CREAM'

cantabrigiensis relating to
Cambridge, England
Rosa 'Cantabrigiensis'

CULTIVAR NAMES
Colors: Yellow

CAMELLIA × WILLIAMSII 'JURY'S YELLOW'

CORNUS SERICEA 'BUDD'S YELLOW'

CROCOSMIA MASONIORUM 'ROWALLANE YELLOW'

DAHLIA 'YELLOW HAMMER'

EREMURUS 'YELLOW GIANT'

ERICA CARNEA 'WESTWOOD YELLOW'

GENISTA PILOSA 'YELLOW SPREADER'

HEMEROCALLIS 'YELLOW LOLLIPOP'

HOSTA 'YELLOW RIVER'

IRIS SIBIRICA 'DREAMING YELLOW'

KNIPHOFIA 'SUNNINGDALE YELLOW'

MAGNOLIA × BROOKLYNENSIS 'YELLOW BIRD'

NARCISSUS 'YELLOW CHEERFULNESS'

OENOTHERA FRUTICOSA 'YELLOW RIVER'

PENSTEMON PINIFOLIUS 'MERSEA YELLOW'

PHILADELPHUS 'YELLOW CAB'

PHORMIUM 'YELLOW WAVE'

PHYGELIUS AEQUALIS 'YELLOW TRUMPET'

PITTOSPORUM TENUIFOLIUM 'MELLOW YELLOW'

POTENTILLA FRUTICOSA 'YELLOW BIRD'

PRIMULA 'LISMORE YELLOW'

RHODODENDRON 'YELLOW HAMMER'

---

canterburiensis from the Canterbury
Plains of New Zealand
Hebe canterburiensis
cantoniensis from Guangzhou
(Canton), China
Disporum cantoniense
capensis from the Cape (of Good
Hope), meaning South Africa
Phygelius capensis
caperatus wrinkled
capillaris hairlike, slender
Artemisia capillaris
capillifolius with hairlike leaves
Eupatorium capillifolium
capillipes slender-footed
Acer capillipes
capillus-veneris Venus' hair
Adiantum capillus-veneris

COMMON DESCRIPTIVE TERMS
capitatus with a solid head or tip
Cornus capitata
Persicaria capitata
Picea abies 'Capitata'
Primula capitata

---

cappadocicus from Cappadocia,
Turkey
Omphalodes cappadocica
caprea a nanny goat; relating to goats
Salix caprea (goat willow)
capreolatus with tendrils or
supports
Bignonia capreolata

Angelica *Angelica archangelica*
Apple mint *Mentha suaveolens*
Basil, sweet *Ocimum basilicum*
Bay *Laurus nobilis*
Borage *Borago officinalis*
Caraway thyme *Thymus herba-barona*
Chamomile, Roman *Chamaemelum nobile*
Chervil *Anthriscus cerefolium*
Chives *Allium schoenoprasum*
Cilantro or Coriander *Coriandrum sativum*
Corsican mint *Mentha requienii*
Costmary (Alecost) *Tanacetum balsamita*

CHIVES

Dill *Anethum graveolens*
Eau de Cologne mint *Mentha × piperita* f. *citrata*
Fennel *Foeniculum vulgare*
Feverfew *Tanacetum parthenium*
Garden myrrh *Myrrhis odorata*
Garden sorrel *Rumex acetosa*
Garlic chives *Allium tuberosum*
Ginger mint *Mentha × gracilis*
Hyssop *Hyssopus officinalis*
Lavender *Lavandula*
Lemon balm *Melissa officinalis*
Lemon grass *Cymbopogon citratus*
Lemon thyme *Thymus × citriodorus*
Lemon verbena *Aloysia triphylla*
Lovage *Levisticum officinale*
Marjoram *Origanum*
Mint *Mentha*
Oregano *Origanum vulgare*
Parsley *Petroselinum crispum*
Pennyroyal *Mentha pulegium*
Peppermint *Mentha × piperita*
Pineapple mint *Mentha suaveolens*
Poet's laurel *Laurus nobilis*
Rosemary *Rosmarinus officinalis*
Rue *Ruta graveolens*
Sage *Salvia officinalis*
Salad burnet *Sanguisorba minor*
Southernwood *Artemisia abrotanum*
Spearmint *Mentha spicata*
Summer savory *Satureja hortensis*
Sweet cicely *Myrrhis odorata*
Sweet marjoram *Origanum majorana*
Tansy *Tanacetum vulgare*
Tarragon *Artemisia dracunculus*
Thyme *Thymus vulgaris*
Winter savory *Satureja montana*

caprifolius with goatlike leaves
 Lonicera caprifolium
capsicinus red like *Capsicum* (pepper)
capsularis like a capsule
capucinus red like *Tropaeolum*
 (nasturtium)
carbonaceus black like charcoal

cardia-, cardio- heart-
cardiacus relating to the heart
 Leonurus cardiaca
cardinalis cardinal red
 Lobelia cardinalis
cardiophyllus with heart-shaped
 leaves
 Codonopsis cardiophylla
cardunculus like a little thistle
 Cynara cardunculus
carens absent or lacking
caricus from Caria, in Asia Minor
 Ficus carica
carinatus with a keel or shell
 Allium carinatum
cariosus decayed
carlesii named for the British
 plant-collector William Carles
 (1867–1900)
 Viburnum carlesii
carmesinus crimson
carmineus carmine
 Metrosideros carminea

COMMON DESCRIPTIVE TERMS
carneus flesh-colored
Erica carnea
Gladiolus carneus
Lychnis chalcedonica 'Carnea'
Polemonium carneum

---

carniolicus from Carniola, an area
 of the former Yugoslavia
 Primula carniolica

carnosulus slightly fleshy
  Hebe carnosula
carnosus fleshy, succulent
  Hoya carnosa
carolinianus from North or South
  Carolina
  Anemone caroliniana
carophyllus with fleshy leaves
  Dianthus carophyllus
carpaticus from the Carpathian
  Mountains, Eastern Europe
  Campanula carpatica
carpicus relating to fruits
carpinifolius with leaves like *Carpinus*
  (hornbeam)
  Acer carpinifolium
-carpus -fruit, -fruited
  Physocarpus
carthusianus, carthusianorum relating
  to Carthusian monks
  Dianthus carthusianorum
  Dryopteris carthusiana
carvifolius with leaves like *Carum*
  carvi (caraway)
  Erodium carvifolium
caryo- nut

COMMON DESCRIPTIVE TERMS
cashmerianus from Kashmir
Campanula cashmeriana
Corydalis cashmeriana
Cupressus cashmeriana
Phlomis cashmeriana
Polemonium cashmerianum

CULTIVAR NAMES
British Towns and Cities

FUCHSIA 'COUNTESS OF ABERDEEN'
PITTOSPORUM 'ARUNDEL GREEN'
MALUS DOMESTICA (APPLE) 'BEAUTY
  OF BATH'
FUCHSIA 'BRIGHTON BELLE'
PASSIFLORA 'STAR OF BRISTOL'
CLEMATIS 'BURFORD WHITE'
MONARDA 'CAMBRIDGE SCARLET'
DIANTHUS 'CONWY STAR'
ERICA × VEITCHII 'EXETER'
MAGNOLIA GRANDIFLORA 'EXMOUTH'
CLEMATIS 'ELEANOR OF GUILDFORD'
DIANTHUS 'HEREFORD BUTTER
  MARKET'
GERANIUM SANGUINEUM 'INVERNESS'
DIANTHUS 'IPSWICH PINK'
SALIX CAPREA 'KILMARNOCK'
AGAPANTHUS 'KINGSTON BLUE'
FUCHSIA 'CITY OF LEICESTER'
CLEMATIS 'LINCOLN STAR'
DAHLIA 'BISHOP OF LLANDAFF'
RANUNCULUS FICARIA 'NEWTON
  ABBOT'
AGAPANTHUS CAMPANULATUS
  'OXFORD BLUE'
CALLUNA VULGARIS 'RADNOR'
ROSA 'SOUTHAMPTON'
HEMEROCALLIS 'STAFFORD'
CYTISUS × PRAECOX 'WARMINSTER'
LONICERA PERICLYMENUM
  'WINCHESTER'
CLEMATIS 'BELLE OF WOKING'
CARYOPTERIS × CLANDONENSIS
  'WORCESTER GOLD'

cassideus shaped like a helmet

cassus empty, hollow, devoid of

castaneifolius with leaves like
  Castanea (chestnut)
  Quercus castaneifolia

castaneus chestnut-colored

castellanus relating to castles

catalpifolius with leaves like
  Catalpa
  Acer longipes subsp. *catalpifolium*

catarius of cats
  Nepeta cataria

catarractae of waterfalls
  Parahebe catarractae

catenatus like a chain

catharticus purgative, purifying
  Rhamnus cathartica

cathayanus from China
  Cardiocrinum cathayanum

catilliformis shaped like a saucer

COMMON DESCRIPTIVE TERMS
caucasicus from the Caucasus
Arabis alpina subsp. *caucasica*
Artemisia caucasica
Corydalis caucasica
Fritillaria caucasica
Veronica caucasica

---

caudatifolius with tail-like leaves
  Acer caudatifolium

caudatus with a tail
  Amaranthus caudatus

caudiformis shaped like a tail

COMMON DESCRIPTIVE TERMS
caulescens with a stem
Agapanthus caulescens
Asarum caulescens
Kniphofia caulescens
Mandragora caulescens

---

caulinus of or on the stem

-caulis -stemmed

cavernosus full of cavities or hollows

cavus hollow
  Corydalis cava

celatus concealed

cellulosus cellular

celsus high

cembra Italian name for Arolla pine
  Pinus cembra

centi-, *centum* hundred- (sometimes
  used to mean "too many to count
  easily," as in centipede)
  Rosa × *centifolia*

cephallenicus, *cephalonicus* from the
  Greek island of Cephallonia
  Abies cephalonica
  Campanula garganica subsp.
  cephallenica

-cephalus head

ceraceus waxy

cerasifer cherry-bearing
  Prunus cerasifera (cherry plum)

cerasinus cherry red

cerastioides Like *Cerastium* (snow-in-
  summer; mouse-ear)
  Gypsophila cerastioides

Cabbage palm *Cordyline*
Calico bush *Kalmia*
California buckeye *Aesculus californica*
Californian lilac *Ceanothus*
Californian poppy *Eschscholzia*
Californian tree poppy *Romneya*
Camomile *Chamaemelum nobile*
Canary creeper *Tropaeolum peregrinum*
Candytuft *Iberis*
Canterbury bells *Campanula medium*
Cape figwort *Phygelius capensis*
Caper spurge *Euphorbia lathyris*
Cardinal flower *Lobelia cardinalis*
Cardoon *Cynara cardunculus*
Carnation *Dianthus*
Castor oil plant *Ricinus*
Catmint, catnip *Nepeta*
Cedar of Lebanon *Cedrus libani*
Celandine, greater *Chelidonium majus*
Celandine, lesser *Ranunculus ficaria*
Chatham Island forget-me-not
  Myosotidium hortensia
Cheddar pink *Dianthus
  gratianopolitanus*
Cherry *Prunus*

LESSER CELANDINE

Cherry laurel *Prunus laurocerasus*
Cherry plum *Prunus cerasifera*
Cherry-pie *Heliotropium arborescens*
Chestnut, horse *Aesculus hippocastanum*
Chestnut, sweet *Castanea sativa*
Chilean glory flower *Eccremocarpus
  scaber*
Chimney bellflower *Campanula
  pyramidalis*
China aster *Callistephus*
Chinese lanterns *Physalis alkekengi*
Chocolate vine *Akebia quinata*
Chokeberry *Aronia*
Christmas box *Sarcococca*
Christmas rose *Helleborus niger*
Chusan palm *Trachycarpus fortunei*
Cider gum *Eucalyptus gunnii*
Cinquefoil *Potentilla*
Clary *Salvia viridis* var. *comata*
Cockspur thorn *Crataegus crus-galli*
Coleus *Solenostemon*
Columbine *Aquilegia*
Comfrey *Symphytum*
Coneflower *Echinacea; Rudbeckia*
Coral bells, Coral flower *Heuchera*
Coral-bark maple *Acer palmatum*
  'Sango-kaku'
Corkscrew hazel *Corylus avellana*
  'Contorta'
Cornelian cherry *Cornus mas*
Cornflower *Centaurea cyanus*
Cowslip *Primula veris*
Cranesbill *Geranium*
Crown imperial *Fritillaria imperialis*
Cuckoo flower *Cardamine pratensis*
Curry plant *Helichrysum italicum*
Cypress *Cupressus*
Cypress spurge *Euphorbia cyparissias*

ceratocarpus with horned fruits
Euphorbia ceratocarpa
cercidifolius with leaves like *Cercis*
Disanthus cercidifolius
cerealis related to farming
cerefolius with waxy leaves
Anthriscus cerefolium (chervil)

COMMON DESCRIPTIVE TERMS
cernuus drooping, downturned
Allium cernuum
Lilium cernuum
Primula cernua
Pulsatilla cernua

---

cervinus fawn-colored
Mentha cervina
cespitosus (see *caespitosus*)
cevennensis from the Cevennes
in southern France
Pulmonaria longifolia subsp.
cevennensis
chaetocarpus with very hairy fruits
Lonicera chaetocarpa
chaixii named for Dominique Chaix
(1730–1799), a French botanist
Verbascum chaixii
chalcedonicus from Chalcedon,
a former region of Asia Minor
Lychnis chalcedonica
chamae- low-growing, on the ground
chamaecyparissus like *Chamaecyparis*,
false cypress
Santolina chamaecyparissus

chamaemelifolius with leaves like
  Chamaemelum (camomile)
  Artemisia chamaemelifolia
chasmanthus with wide-open flowers
chathamicus from the Chatham
  Islands in the South Pacific
  Astelia chathamica
cheilanthus with lipped flowers
chilensis from Chile
  Puya chilensis
chiloensis from Chiloé, an island
  off the west coast of Chile
  Fragaria chiloensis
chilus -lipped

COMMON DESCRIPTIVE TERMS

chinensis Chinese (see also *sinensis*)
Abelia chinensis
Astilbe chinensis
Betula chinensis
Cornus kousa var. *chinensis*
Corylus chinensis
Enkianthus chinensis
Juniperus chinensis
Schisandra chinensis

---

chionanthus with snow-white flowers
  Primula chionantha
chionophilus snow-loving
  Ornithogalum chionophilum
chiton covering
  Rhodochiton
chloranthus with green flowers
  Lathyrus chloranthus

CILIATUS

chlorinus yellow-green
chloro- green
chloropetalus with green petals
  Trillium chloropetalum
chrom-, -chromus, -chrous relating
  to color; colored
  Euphorbia polychroma
chrys- gold
chrysanthus with golden flowers
  Crocus chrysanthus
chrysocomus with golden hairs
  Achillea chrysocoma
chrysographes marked with gold
  Iris chrysographes
chrysolepis with golden scales
chrysophyllus with golden leaves
  Phlomis chrysophylla

COMMON DESCRIPTIVE TERMS
ciliaris, ciliatus, ciliosus fringed
  with hairs (like an eyelid)
Bergenia ciliata
Chrysocoma ciliata
Erica ciliaris
Lysimachia ciliata
Melica ciliata
Mertensia ciliata

GENUS NAMES
C

Callicarpa from Greek *kalli-*, beautiful, and *karpos*, fruit

Callistephus from Greek *kalli-*, beautiful, and *stephos*, crown

Calluna from Greek *kalluno*, to clean (heather was used to make brooms)

Camellia named for Georg Kamel (1661–1706), a pharmacist and botanical author working in the Philippines

Campanula from Latin *campana*, bell

Caryopteris from Greek *karyon*, nut, and *pteron*, wing

Chimonanthus from Greek *cheimon*, winter, and *anthos*, flower

Chionodoxa from Greek *chion*, snow, and *doxa*, glory

Chrysanthemum from Greek *chrysos*, gold, and *anthos*, flower

Claytonia named for John Clayton (1686–1773), American botanist

Colchicum from Colchis, a region of the Caucasus

Convolvulus from Latin *convolvo*, to twine round

Coreopsis from Greek *koris*, a bug or tick, and *opsis*, resemblance

Coronilla from Latin *corona*, crown

Corylopsis from Greek *korylos*, hazel, and *opsis*, resemblance

Cosmos in Greek, beautiful

Crocus from Greek *krokos*, saffron

Cryptomeria from Greek *krypto*, to conceal, and *meris*, a part

Cyclamen from Greek *kyklos*, a circle

Cynoglossum from Greek *kyon*, dog, and *glossa*, tongue

cilicicus from Cilicica, a region of Asia Minor
  Cyclamen cilicicum

cineraria ash-colored
  Senecio cineraria

cinereus like ashes, ash-gray
  Geranium cinereum

cinnamomeus cinnamon-brown
  Osmunda cinnamomea

circinatus coiled, circular
  Acer circinatum

cirratus, cirrhosus with tendrils
  Arthropodium cirratum
  Clematis cirrhosa

cirrhifolius with tendril-like leaves
  Polygonatum cirrhifolium

cissifolium with leaves like *Cissus,* a vine-like climber
  Acer cissifolium

citratus like *Citrus*
  Cymbopogon citratus

COMMON DESCRIPTIVE TERMS

citrinus lemon-yellow
Callistemon citrinus
Coronilla valentina subsp. *glauca* 'Citrina'
Erythronium citrinum
Hemerocallis citrina
Iris foetidissima var. *citrina*
Kniphofia citrina

---

citriodorus lemon-scented
  Thymus × *citriodorus*

itroides like *Citrus*

lad-, -cladus branch, shoot

landestinus hidden

Panicum clandestinum

landonensis named for Clandon
Park, Surrey, UK

Caryopteris × clandonensis

larkei named for C.B. Clarke
(1832–1906), superintendent
of Calcutta Botanic Gardens

Geranium clarkei

lathratus like a lattice or trellis

lausus closed

Hosta clausa var. normalis

lavatus, claviformis club-shaped

lavellatus like a small club

lematideus like *Clematis*

Codonopsis clematidea

lethroides like *Clethra* (sweet pepper
bush)

Lysimachia clethroides

livorum of slopes

lusianus, clusii named for a Flemish
botanist, Carolus Clusius (1526–
1609)

Gentiana clusii

Tulipa clusiana

lypeolatus rather like a *clipeus*, a
small circular shield used by the
Romans

Achillea clypeolata

oactus felted

oarctatus pressed closely together

obaltinus cobalt blue

COMMON DESCRIPTIVE TERMS

coccineus deep red

Hedychium coccineum

Hibiscus coccineus

Pyracantha coccinea

Salvia coccinea

Schizostylis coccinea

CULTIVAR NAMES
Foreign Expressions
C, D

CALIENTE (*Spanish*) HOT
(*IRIS* 'CALIENTE')

CHITOSEYAMA (*Japanese*)
1,000-YEAR-OLD MOUNTAIN
(*ACER PALMATUM*
'CHITOSEYAMA')

CLAIR DE LUNE (*French*)
MOONLIGHT
(*PAEONIA* 'CLAIR DE LUNE')

DIAMANT (*German*)
DIAMOND
(*ASTILBE* 'DIAMANT')

DU MAÎTRE D'ECOLE (*French*)
OF THE SCHOOLMASTER
(*ROSA* 'DU MAÎTRE D'ECOLE')

DUNKELPRACHT (*German*)
DARK BEAUTY
(*HELENIUM* 'DUNKELPRACHT')

DUNKELSTE ALLER (*German*)
DARKEST OF ALL
(*ERIGERON* 'DUNKELSTE ALLER')

DÜSTERLOHE (*German*)
DARK FLAME
(*PHLOX PANICULATA* 'DÜSTERLOHE')

cochlearifolius with spoon-shaped
leaves
Campanula cochlearifolia
cochleatus shaped like a snail-shell,
in a spiral
Cotoneaster cochleatus
cockburnianus named for the
Cockburn family, living in China
Rubus cockburnianus
-codon bell
Platycodon
coelestinus sky blue
Eupatorium coelestinum
coeruleus blue
Puya coerulea
cognatus related
Lychnis cognata
cognitus known, understood
-cola -dweller (e.g. *monticola*,
mountain-dweller)
colchicus from Colchis, a region
of Georgia in the Caucasus
Hedera colchica
collapsus collapsed
collinus of hills
Geranium collinum
colombinus like a dove
coloratus colored
Pseudowintera colorata
colubrinus like a snake
columbianus from British Columbia
or the Columbia River, north-
western North America
Lilium columbianum

columnaris columnar
Acer platanoides 'Columnaris'
comans hairy; leafy
Carex comans
comatus tufted
Salvia viridis var. *comata*
commiscens intermingling
commixtus mixed together
Sorbus commixta

Common descriptive terms
communis general, universal
Ferula communis
Gladiolus communis subsp. *byzantinus*
Juniperus communis
Myrtus communis
Pyrus communis
Ricinus communis

Myrtus communis

WHAT'S IN A NAME?

BOTANISTS AND NATURALISTS

banksii Sir Joseph Banks (1743–1820)

battandieri Jules Battandier (1848–1922)

brewerianus William Brewer (1828–1910)

buchananii John Buchanan (1819–1898)

bungeanus, bungei Alexander von Bunge (1803–1890)

clusianus, clusii Carolus Clusius (1526–1609)

coulteri Thomas Coulter (1793–1843)

dammeri Carl Dammer (1860–1920)

darwinii Charles Darwin (1809–1882)

delavayi, delavayanus Jean Marie Delavay (1834–1895)

fontanesianus, fontanesii René Desfontaines (1750–1833)

grayi Asa Gray (1810–1888)

gunnii Ronald Gunn (1808–1881)

hookeri Sir William Hooker (1785–1865) or son Sir Joseph (1817–1911)

jacquemontii, jacquemontianus Victor Jacquemont (1801–1832)

juddii William Judd (1888–1946)

lamarckii Chevalier Jean-Baptiste de Monet Lamarck (1744-1829)

langsdorffii Georg Langsdorf (1774–1852)

lavalleei Pierre Lavalle (1836–1884)

linnaeoides Carl Linnaeus (1707–1778)

ludlowii Frank Ludlow (1885–1972)

maackii Richard Maack (1825–1886)

makinoi Tomitaro Makino (1863–1957)

maximowiczianus, maximowiczii Karl Maximowicz (1827–1891)

menziesii Archibald Menzies (1754–1842)

mlokosewitschii Ludwik Mlokosiewicz (1831–1909)

nuttallii Thomas Nuttall (1786–1859)

perralderianus Henri de la Perraudière (1831–1861)

sargentii, sargentianus Charles Sprague Sargent (1841–1927)

schillingii Tony Schilling

selloanus Friedrich Sello or Sellow (1789–1831)

sibthorpianus, sibthorpii Humphrey Sibthorp (1713–1797) or his son John (1758–1796)

sieboldianus, sieboldii Philipp von Siebold (1796–1866)

spooneri Herman Spooner (1878–1976)

stewartii Laurence Stewart (1877–1934)

thunbergii Carl Thunberg (1743–1828)

tommasinianus Muzio de' Tommasini (1794–1879)

---

commutatus changing; close to another species

   Papaver commutatum (ladybird poppy)

comosus hairy, tufted

   Muscari comosum

COMMON DESCRIPTIVE TERMS

compactus compact, dense

Abies concolor 'Compacta'

Brachyglottis compacta

Deutzia compacta

Viburnum opulus 'Compactum'

complexus complex; encircled

complicatus complex

   Rosa 'Complicata'

compositus compound

   Erigeron compositus

compressus flattened

   Juniperus communis 'Compressa'

concatenatus linked together

   Cardamine concatenata

concholobus with lobes like sea-shells

   Primula concholoba

concinnatum, concinnus well
   arranged, neat

   Arum concinnatum

   Arisaema concinnum

concolor the same color all over; of
   the same color

   Abies concolor

condensatus condensed, closely
   packed

   Phlox condensata

conditus preserved, stored

confertus crowded

   Penstemon confertus

conflatus united, fused together

conformis of the same shape

COMMON DESCRIPTIVE TERMS

confusus uncertain; easily mistaken;
   mingled

Iris confusa

Mahonia confusa

Sarcococca confusa

Skimmia × *confusa*

---

congestiflorus with closely packed
   flowers

   Lysimachia congestiflora

congestus congested, closely packed
   together

   Cotoneaster congestus

conglomeratus conglomerate,
   clustered

   Hedera helix 'Conglomerata'

congolanus Congolese

conicus cone-shaped

   Carex conica

conifer cone-bearing

   Manglieta conifera

conjugatus joined in twos

conjunctus joined

conoideus like a cone

consanguineus related

   Arisaema consanguineum

consimilis similar in every way,
   completely alike

conspicuus conspicuous

   Cotoneaster conspicuus

constantinopolitanus from Istanbul
   (formerly Constantinople), Turkey

   Ranunculus constantinopolitanus

contaminatus contaminated,
   impure

   Lachenalia contaminata

contiguus adjoining

continentalis continental

   Aralia continentalis

contortus twisted, contorted

   Corylus avellana 'Contorta'

controversus turned against, lying opposite; disputed
 Cornus controversa
convexus convex
 Ilex crenata 'Convexa'
convolutus rolled up lengthways
 Sisyrinchium convolutum
convolvulaceus like *Convolvulus* (bindweed etc.)
 Codonopsis convolvulacea
cookianum named for the English navigator Captain James Cook (1728–1779)
 Phormium cookianum
corallinus coral-colored
 Berberidopsis corallina
coralloides like coral
 Ozothamnus coralloides

COMMON DESCRIPTIVE TERMS

cordatus, cordiformis heart-shaped

Alnus cordata

Aralia cordata

Carya cordiformis

Houttuynia cordata

Macleaya cordata

Pontederia cordata

cordifolius with heart-shaped leaves

Aster cordifolius

Bergenia cordifolia

Crambe cordifolia

Eucryphia cordifolia

Globularia cordifolia

---

coreanus from Korea
 Carpinus coreana
coriaceus, coriarius leathery
 Holboellia coriacea
corifolius with leathery leaves
corniculatus with little horns
 Glaucium corniculatum
corniger horned
 Euphorbia cornigera
-cornis -horned
cornubiensis from Cornwall, UK
 Polypodium interjectum 'Cornubiense'

CULTIVAR NAMES
Fictional Characters

PRIMULA AURICULA 'BILBO BAGGINS'

CLEMATIS 'DANIEL DERONDA'

LIGULARIA DENTATA 'DESDEMONA'

DAHLIA 'LITTLE DORRIT'

MALUS DOMESTICA (APPLE) 'FALSTAFF'

PRIMULA AURICULA 'ELI JENKINS'

ROSA 'LONG JOHN SILVER'

CLEMATIS 'LITTLE NELL'

CLEMATIS 'NIOBE'

PIERIS JAPONICA 'SCARLETT O'HARA'

PELARGONIUM 'SANCHO PANZA'

PAPAVER ORIENTALE 'PETER PAN'

× *PHYLLIOPSIS HILLIERI* 'PINOCCHIO'

HOSTA 'POOH BEAR'

PHLOX PANICULATA 'PROSPERO'

TULIPA 'RED RIDING HOOD'

NARCISSUS 'RIP VAN WINKLE'

PELARGONIUM 'JUST WILLIAM'

cornutus horned
   Viola cornuta

<small>COMMON DESCRIPTIVE TERMS</small>
coronarius used for wreaths
   or garlands
Anemone coronaria
Hedychium coronarium
Lychnis coronaria
Malus coronaria
Philadelphus coronarius

---

corrugatus corrugated, furrowed

<small>COMMON DESCRIPTIVE TERMS</small>
corsicus from the island of Corsica
Acinos corsicus
Cistus creticus subsp. *corsicus*
Colchicum corsicum
Crocus corsicus
Erodium corsicum

---

corymbiflorus with flowers arranged
   in a corymb
   Deutzia setchuenensis var.
   corymbiflora
corymbosus corymbose; with corymbs
   Vaccinium corymbosum
costatus ribbed
   Betula costata
cosyrensis from Pantellaria (formerly
   Cosyra), a small island between
   Sicily and North Africa
   Limonium cosyrense

CULTIVAR NAMES
Countries of the World

JUNIPERUS HORIZONTALIS 'ANDORRA
   COMPACT'
DAHLIA 'ARABIAN NIGHT'
CANNA 'AUSTRALIA'
NERINE 'KING OF THE BELGIANS'
RHODODENDRON 'BRAZIL'
GERANIUM MACRORRHIZUM 'BULGARIA'
CLEMATIS 'BURMA STAR'
HEMEROCALLIS 'CANADIAN BORDER
   PATROL'
MISCANTHUS SINENSIS 'CHINA'
FUCHSIA 'ROSE OF DENMARK'
BRUGMANSIA VERSICOLOR 'ECUADOR
   PINK'
PELARGONIUM 'LA FRANCE'
ASTILBE 'DEUTSCHLAND'
PHLOX PANICULATA 'MISS HOLLAND'
CLEMATIS 'STAR OF INDIA'
NARCISSUS 'EMPRESS OF IRELAND'
CANNA 'ITALIA'
ARGYRANTHEMUM 'JAMAICA
   PRIMROSE'
HEMEROCALLIS 'MOROCCO RED'
HEBE ODORA 'NEW ZEALAND GOLD'
CLEMATIS 'POLISH SPIRIT'
EUPHORBIA CHARACIAS 'PORTUGUESE
   VELVET'
PENSTEMON 'RUSSIAN RIVER'
HEMEROCALLIS 'SCOTLAND'
PELARGONIUM 'SPANISH ANGEL'
NARCISSUS 'TIBET'
FUCHSIA 'TURKISH DELIGHT'
PENSTEMON 'WELSH DAWN'
PRIMULA AURICULA 'ZAMBIA'

coulteri named for Thomas Coulter (1793–1843), an Irish botanist and plant collector
  Romneya coulteri
coum from the Greek island of Kos
  Cyclamen coum

CRENATUS

COMMON DESCRIPTIVE TERMS
crassifolius with thick leaves
Bergenia crassifolia
Fritillaria crassifolia
Gladiolus crassifolius
Ilex aquifolium 'Crassifolia'
Pittosporum crassifolium
Pseudopanax crassifolius

---

crassus thick
creber pressed closely together
crenatus with rounded teeth
  Ilex crenata
crenulatus with small rounded teeth
  Eucalyptus crenulata
crescens growing
cretaceus chalky white

COMMON DESCRIPTIVE TERMS
creticus from Crete
Campanula cretica
Cistus creticus
Cyclamen creticum
Eryngium creticum

---

crinitus covered with long hairs
  Carex crinita

crispulus curly-haired
  Hosta crispula

COMMON DESCRIPTIVE TERMS
crispus, crispatus curled
Asplenium scolopendrium Crispum Group
Buddleia crispa
Cistus × *crispatus* 'Warley Rose'
Ilex aquifolium 'Crispa'
Mentha spicata var. *crispa*
Petroselinum crispum (parsley)
Solanum crispum
Teucrium scorodonia 'Crispum Marginatum'

---

crista-galli a cockerel's comb
  Erythrina crista-galli
cristatellus with a small crest
  Carex cristatella
cristatus crested
  Iris cristata
crithmoides like *Crithmum* (rock samphire)
  Inula crithmoides

WHAT'S IN A NAME?

GARDENS AND GARDENERS

bodnantensis Bodnant Garden in North Wales, UK

clandonensis Clandon Park, Surrey, UK

elwesii Henry John Elwes (1846–1922), British plantsman

ericsmithii Eric Smith (1917–1986), plantsman and gardener at Hadspen, Somerset, UK

fletcheri Harold Fletcher (1907–1978), Director of RHS Garden Wisley and Keeper of the Royal Botanic Garden Edinburgh, UK

kewensis the Royal Botanic Gardens at Kew, London

lyonii John Lyon (1765–1814), Scottish gardener and botanist

nymansensis Nymans Garden, West Sussex, UK

poscharskyanus Gustav Poscharsky (1832–1914), German gardener

robinsonianus William Robinson (1839–1935), Irish-born gardener, designer and influential plantsman (see page 173)

sternianus, sternii Sir Frederick Stern (1884–1967), plantsman, author and creator of a remarkable garden at Highdown near Worthing, Sussex, UK

tradescantii John Tradescant (1570–1638) and his son (1608–1662) of the same name, English travelers, plantsmen and royal gardeners

warleyensis, willmottianum Ellen Willmott (1858–1934), plantswoman and creator of an extravagant garden at Warley Place, Essex, UK

croaticus from Croatia
   Helleborus croaticus

crocatus, croceus saffron yellow
   Iris crocea
   Tritonia crocata

cruciatus, cruciformis cross-shaped
   Gentiana cruciata

cruentus bloody
   Dianthus cruentus

crus-galli a cockerel's spur
   Crataegus crus-galli

cucullarius like a hood
   Dicentra cucullaria

cucullatus hooded
   Pelargonium cucullatum

cultorum of cultivated land
   Aubrieta × *cultorum*

cuneatus, cuneiformis cuneate (wedge-shaped)
   Prostanthera cuneata

cuneifolius with wedge-shaped leaves
   Saxifraga cuneifolia

cupanianus named for an Italian monk, Francesco Cupani (1657–1711)
   Anthemis punctata subsp. *cupaniana*

cupressoides like *Cupressus* (cypress)
   Hebe cupressoides

cupreus coppery
   Helianthemum cupreum

curassavicus from Curaçao in the Caribbean
   Asclepias curassavica

curviflorus with curved flowers

urvistylus with a curved style
  Polygonatum curvistylum
urvulus slightly curved
  Eragrostis curvula
uspidatus cuspidate; with a sharp
  point
  Taxus cuspidata
yaneus, cyanus dark blue
  Centaurea cyanus (cornflower)
yathiformis cup-shaped
yclamineus like *Cyclamen*
  Narcissus cyclamineus
ycloglossus with tongues arranged
  in a circle
  Iris cycloglossa
yclophyllus with leaves in a circle
  Helleborus cyclophyllus

COMMON DESCRIPTIVE TERMS

ylindricus, cylindraceus cylindrical
  Anemone cylindrica
  Heuchera cylindrica 'Greenfinch'
  Imperata cylindrica 'Rubra'
  Magnolia cylindrica
  Plectranthus cylindraceus

---

ymosus with cymes
yparissias like cypress
  Euphorbia cyparissias
yprius from Cyprus
  Cistus × *cyprius*
yrenaicus from Cyrenaica, a region
  of Libya
  Arum cyrenaicum

CULTIVAR NAMES
Islands of the World

HEMEROCALLIS 'BALI HAI'

FUCHSIA 'BERMUDA'

FUCHSIA 'BORA BORA'

NERIUM OLEANDER 'ISLE OF CAPRI'

HEMEROCALLIS 'CHRISTMAS ISLAND'

RHODODENDRON 'CRETE'

FUCHSIA 'FALKLANDS'

RHODODENDRON CALOSTROTUM 'GIGHA'

CANNA 'GRAN CANARIA'

CLEMATIS 'GUERNSEY CREAM'

IRIS ENSATA 'HOKKAIDO'

HOSTA 'IONA'

MAGNOLIA 'JERSEY BELLE'

ROSMARINUS OFFICINALIS 'MAJORCA PINK'

FUCHSIA 'ISLE OF MULL'

FUCHSIA 'LINDISFARNE'

ROSA 'MANX QUEEN'

GERANIUM 'ORKNEY PINK'

MUSA BASJOO 'SAKHALIN'

MALUS DOMESTICA (APPLE) 'SCILLY PEARL'

IRIS 'STATEN ISLAND'

NARCISSUS 'TAHITI'

PLUMBAGO AURICULATA 'TOBAGO BLUE'

FUCHSIA 'TRESCO'

FRITILLARIA AFFINIS 'VANCOUVER ISLAND'

GERANIUM × CANTABRIGIENSE 'WESTRAY'

CEANOTHUS 'PERSHORE ZANZIBAR'

D

dactyl- finger- (see below)
dactylifer finger-bearing
  Phoenix dactylifera

COMMON DESCRIPTIVE TERMS
dahuricus, dauricus from Dauria
  (Siberia/Mongolia)
Actaea dahurica
Betula dahurica
Gentiana dahurica
Lilium dauricum

---

dalmaticus from Dalmatia
  Geranium dalmaticum
damascenus from Damascus in Syria
  Nigella damascena
dammeri named for a German
  botanist, Carl Dammer (1860–
  1920)
  Cotoneaster dammeri
daphnoides like *Daphne*
  Salix daphnoides
darwinii named after Charles
  Darwin (1809–1882), the British
  naturalist, traveler and author
  of *Origin of Species*
  Berberis darwinii

WHAT'S IN A NAME?

SEASONS, WEATHER AND TIMING

aestivalis, aestivus of summer
aizoon ever-living
algidus cold
annuus annual
aurorius of dawn, daybreak, morning
autumnalis autumnal, of autumn
biennis biennial
calidus warm, hot
chion- snow
chionophilus snow-loving
diurnus diurnal, flowering by day
ephemerus ephemeral, short-lived
flos-cuculi flowering when the cuckoo
  sings
fugax fleeting, transitory, ephemeral
glacialis from glaciers or cold places
hyemalis of winter
longaevus long-lived
majalis of May, flowering in May

matronalis named for *Matronalia*,
  a Roman festival on 1 March
meridionalis (flowering at) midday,
  noon
nivalis, niveus snowy, snow-like
noctiflorus night-flowering
nyctagineus night-flowering
perennis perennial
praecox precocious, developing early
semperflorens always flowering
sempervirens evergreen
senescens growing old
serotinus late
solaris sun-loving
tardiflorus late-flowering
tardivus, tardus late
transitorius passing, transitory
trimestris of three months
veris, vernalis, vernus vernal, of spring

dasy- shaggy, hairy
dasycladus with hairy branches
dasyphyllus with hairy leaves
  Sedum dasyphyllum
dauricus see *dahuricus*

COMMON DESCRIPTIVE TERMS

davidii, davidianum named for
  the French missionary and plant
  collector Abbé Jean Pierre Armand
  David (1826–1900)
Acer davidii
Buddleia davidii
Chrysosplenium davidianum
Epimedium davidii
Photinia davidiana
Sophora davidii
Viburnum davidii

---

dealbatus whitened, powdery white
  Acacia dealbata
deca- ten- (see below)
decapetalus with ten petals
  Helianthus decapetalus
decaphyllus with ten leaves or
  leaflets
deciduus deciduous
  Larix decidua
decipiens deceiving (e.g. where one
  plant is easy to mistake for
  another)
  Corydalis decipiens
declivis sloping downward
decolor discolored, faded

COMMON DESCRIPTIVE TERMS

decoratus, decorus decorative
Hosta decorata
Iris decora
Osmanthus decorus
Phyllostachys decora
Sorbus decora
Thalictrum decorum

---

decorticans, decorticatus with peeling
  bark; stripped of bark
decrescens becoming less or narrower
decumanus very large

decumbens decumbent; prostrate
but with upright tips
Cistus dansereaui 'Decumbens'
Correa decumbens
Cytisus decumbens
Hebe decumbens

decurrens, decursivus decurrent,
running down the stem
Calocedrus decurrens
decurvatus, decurvus decurved
decussatus decussate
Melaleuca decussata
deflexus bent downward
Enkianthus deflexus

WHAT'S IN A NAME?

COLOR: BLACK
anthracinus coal black, bluish black
ater pure black
atratus clothed in black for
mourning; dark
carbonaceus black like charcoal
coracinus, corvinus crow black,
shiny black
denigratus blackened
ebenaceus, ebenus black like ebony
mela-, melano- pure black
nigellus blackish
niger black
nigrescens, nigricans blackish,
blackening
nigritus dressed in black
piceus brownish black, pitch black
pullus dusky, gayish black

---

deformis misshapen
dehiscens dehiscent
delapsus fallen away

---

delavayi, delavayanus named for
the French botanist and missionary
Jean Marie Delavay (1834–1895)
Asarum delavayi
Incarvillea delavayi
Iris delavayi
Ligustrum delavayanum
Magnolia delavayi
Osmanthus delavayi
Paeonia delavayi
Philadelphus delavayi
Podophyllum delavayi

---

delicatus delicate
deliciosus delicious
Actinidia deliciosa (kiwi fruit)
delphicus from Delphi, in Greece
deltoides triangular (like the Greek
letter delta)
Dianthus deltoides
demissus hanging, drooping
dendro- tree-
dendroideus like a tree
dens-canis dog's tooth
Erythronium dens-canis
densiflorus densely flowered
Hedychium densiflorum
densus, densatus dense, compact
Tanacetum densum

COMMON DESCRIPTIVE TERMS

dentatus toothed
Dodecatheon dentatum
Hedera colchica 'Dentata'
Lavandula dentata
Ligularia dentata
Quercus dentata

DENTATUS

denticulatus with small teeth
Primula denticulata
denudatus stripped (e.g. of leaves)
Magnolia denudata
depauperatus impoverished, dwarfed
Carex depauperata
dependens hanging down
deplanatus leveled
depressus flattened
Juniperus communis 'Depressa Aurea'
diabolicus like a devil
Acer diabolicum
dianthifolius with leaves like *Dianthus*
Commelina dianthifolia
dicentrifolius with leaves like *Dicentra*
Codonopsis dicentrifolia
dichotomus dividing repeatedly in two
Eryngium dichotomum
dictyophyllus with leaves showing an obvious network of veins
Berberis dictyophylla
didymus paired, two-lobed
Monarda didyma
difformis unusual in form
Vinca difformis

Daffodil *Narcissus*
Daisy *Bellis perennis*
Dame's violet *Hesperis matronalis*
Dandelion *Taraxacum*
Date palm *Phoenix dactylifera*
Dawn redwood *Metasequoia glyptostroboides*
Daylily *Hemerocallis*
Deadly nightshade *Atropa bella-donna*
Deadnettle *Lamium*
Deodar *Cedrus deodara*
Desert candle *Eremurus*

ELECAMPANE

Devil's walking stick *Aralia spinosa*
Dittany *Dictamnus albus*
Dock *Rumex*
Dog rose *Rosa canina*
Dog violet *Viola riviniana*
Dog's tooth violet *Erythronium dens-canis*
Dogwood *Cornus*
Douglas fir *Pseudotsuga menziesii*
Dove tree *Davidia involucrata*
Downy birch *Betula pubescens*
Dragon arum *Dracunculus vulgaris*
Dropwort *Filipendula vulgaris*
Durmast oak *Quercus petraea*
Dutchman's breeches *Dicentra spectabilis*
Dutchman's pipe *Aristolochia*
Dyer's greenweed *Genista tinctoria*
Eastern hemlock *Tsuga canadensis*
Eastern red cedar *Juniperus virginiana*
Eglantine *Rosa rubiginosa*
Egyptian bean *Lablab purpureus*
Elder *Sambucus*
Elecampane *Inula helenium*
Elephant's ears *Bergenia*
Elm *Ulmus*
English oak *Quercus robur*
European larch *Larix decidua*
Evening primrose *Oenothera*
Evergreen oak *Quercus ilex*
Everlasting pea *Lathyrus grandiflorus; Lathyrus latifolius*

diffractus broken in pieces
diffusus spreading
  Lithodora diffusa
digitatus hand-shaped; with fingers
  Carex digitata

digitiformis finger-shaped
digynus with two styles or carpels
  Sarcococca hookeriana var. *digyna*
dilatatus spread out, expanded
  Dryopteris dilatata

dilutus diluted, weak

diminutus small, diminished

dimorphus existing in two forms

COMMON DESCRIPTIVE TERMS

dioicus dioecious (i.e. with male and female reproductive organs on separate plants)
   Aruncus dioicus
   Carex dioica
   Gymnocladus dioica
   Silene dioica (red campion)

---

dioscoridis like *Dioscoria* (yam), named for the 1st-century AD Greek physician Dioscorides
   Arum dioscoridis

diosmifolius, diosmatifolius with leaves like *Diosma*
   Hebe diosmifolia

diphyllus two-leaved
   Cardamine diphylla

diplo- double-

dipsaceus, dipsacoides like *Dipsacus* (teasel)
   Carex dipsacea

dipterocarpus with two-winged fruit

dipterus two-winged

directus straight

discedens dividing

disciformis disc-shaped

discolor of different colors
   Aquilegia discolor

CULTIVAR NAMES
Colors: Green

CAMELLIA JAPONICA 'FOREST GREEN'

CONVALLARIA MAJALIS 'GREEN TAPESTRY'

ERYNGIUM YUCCIFOLIUM 'GREEN SWORD'

EUONYMUS JAPONICUS 'GREEN SPIDER'

HEBE 'GREENSLEEVES'

HEDERA HELIX 'GREEN RIPPLE'

HELLEBORUS FOETIDUS 'GREEN GIANT'

HEMEROCALLIS FULVA 'GREEN KWANSO'

HEMEROCALLIS 'GREEN FLUTTER'

HEUCHERA CYLINDRICA 'GREENFINCH'

HYDRANGEA PANICULATA 'GREENSPIRE'

IRIS 'GREEN SPOT'

JOVIBARBA HEUFFELII 'GREENSTONE'

JUNIPERUS CHINENSIS 'ROBUST GREEN'

KNIPHOFIA 'GREEN JADE'

MALUS DOMESTICA (APPLE) 'GREENSLEEVES'

NICOTIANA LANGSDORFFII 'LIME GREEN'

PACHYSANDRA TERMINALIS 'GREEN CARPET'

PITTOSPORUM EUGENIOIDES 'GREEN ELF'

PRIMULA AURICULA 'GREEN ISLE'

RANUNCULUS FICARIA 'GREEN PETAL'

SEDUM 'GREEN EXPECTATIONS'

SEMPERVIVUM 'GREEN APPLE'

ZANTEDESCHIA AETHIOPICA 'GREEN GODDESS'

Born in Scone, Scotland, David Douglas became a gardener and, by 1820, was working at the Glasgow Botanic Garden. Recruited by the Horticultural Society as a plant collector, in 1824 he left for the west coast of North America, sailing round Cape Horn and via the Galapagos Islands up to the Columbia River in Oregon. Over the next 10 years he took many plants back to Britain, including penstemons, camassias and *Eschscholzia californica*, but he is best known for the conifers he introduced as seeds, including the Douglas fir, Monterey pine and Sitka spruce. Plants named for him include *Iris douglasiana*, *Limnanthes douglasii* and *Phlox douglasii*. Douglas died in Hawaii, aged only 35, killed by a bull in a terrible accident.

**DAVID DOUGLAS
(1798–1834)**

---

discretus separate

disjunctus separate
  Salvia disjuncta

dispersus, displicatus scattered

disruptus broken off

dissectus dissected; deeply divided
  Acer palmatum var. *dissectum*

dissimilis dissimilar

dissitus spaced out

dissolutus dissolved

distachyus with two spikes
  Ephedra distachya

distichophyllus with leaves in two rows
  Eustachys distichophylla

distichus in two rows
  Abeliophyllum distichum

distylus with two styles
  Acer distylum

diurnus diurnal, flowering by day

COMMON DESCRIPTIVE TERMS
divaricatus spreading, straggling
Aster divaricatus
Cotoneaster divaricatus
Phlox divaricata
Plagianthus divaricatus

---

divergens diverging

diversifolius with differing leaves
  Clematis × *diversifolia*

diversiformis of different forms

diversus opposite, distinct, turned in different directions

divisus divided

divulgatus widespread

divulsus torn apart

dodeca- 12- (e.g. *Dodecatheon*)

dodecandrus with 12 stamens

dolabratus shaped like a pickaxe

dolicho- long- (see below)

dolichopetalus with long petals

dolichostachyus with a long spike

   Carex dolichostachya

dolomiticus from the Dolomites in northern Italy

   Campanula dolomitica

domestica domesticated

   Malus domestica (apple)

   Nandina domestica

donax named after a kind of reed

   Arundo donax

douglasii, douglasianus (see panel opposite)

dracocephalus with a head like a dragon

   Fargesia dracocephala

dracunculus little dragon

   Artemisia dracunculus (tarragon)

drakensbergensis from the Drakensberg range in South Africa

   Scabiosa drakensbergensis

drummondii named for the Scottish plant-collecting brothers James (1786–1863) and Thomas Drummond (1793–1835)

   Phlox drummondii

COMMON DESCRIPTIVE TERMS

dulcis sweet, pleasant

Euphorbia dulcis

Hovenia dulcis

Lippia dulcis

Phyllostachys dulcis

Prunus dulcis (almond)

dumetorum of thickets and hedgerows

   Helleborus dumetorum

dumosus bushy

   Holodiscus dumosus

durandii named for the French nursery Durand Frères

   Clematis × *durandii*

dysentericus for the treatment of dysentery

   Pulicaria dysenterica

GENUS NAMES
D, E

Dahlia named for Dr. Anders Dahl (1751–1789), Swedish botanist

Davidia named for Abbé Jean Pierre Armand David (see page 65)

Dicentra from Greek *di-*, two, and *kentron*, spur

Dicksonia named for James Dickson (1738–1822), British nurseryman and botanist

Dierama in Greek, a funnel

Digitalis from Latin *digitus*, finger

Dodecatheon from Greek *dodeka*, 12, and *theos*, god

Echinacea, Echinops from Greek *echinos*, a hedgehog

Epilobium from Greek *epi*, on, and *lobos*, pod

Equisetum from Latin *equus*, horse, and *seta*, bristle

Erodium from Greek *erodios*, heron

Erythronium from Greek *erythros*, red

Eucomis from Greek *eu*, good, and *kome*, hair

E

ebenaceus, ebenus black like ebony
ebracteatus without bracts
eburneus ivory white
  Eryngium eburneum
echinatus prickly, spiny
echiniformis shaped like a hedgehog
  or sea-urchin (*echinus*)
  Picea glauca 'Echiniformis'

CULTIVAR NAMES
Personal Names
E

CORNUS 'EDDIE'S WHITE WONDER'
CARDAMINE PRATENSIS 'EDITH'
CYRTANTHUS 'EDWINA'
PELARGONIUM 'EILEEN'
CLEMATIS 'ELEANOR'
FUCHSIA 'ELFRIDA'
POTENTILLA FRUTICOSA 'ELIZABETH'
ESCALLONIA LAEVIS 'GOLD ELLEN'
FUCHSIA 'ELSA'
GERANIUM SANGUINEUM 'ELSBETH'
MONARDA 'ELSIE'S LAVENDER'
GLADIOLUS 'ELVIRA'
IRIS 'BROADLEIGH EMILY'
DIASCIA 'EMMA'
ASTER ERICOIDES 'ESTHER'
PRIMULA 'EUGÉNIE'
ANTHEMIS TINCTORIA 'EVA'
PENSTEMON 'EVELYN'

---

echinocarpus with prickly fruit
echinocephalus with a prickly head
  Ptilostemon echinocephalus
ecorticatus (see also *excorticatus*)
  without bark
edgeworthii named for Michael
  Edgeworth (1812–1881), a British
  amateur botanist and plant collector
  Rhododendron edgeworthii

COMMON DESCRIPTIVE TERMS
edulis edible
Passiflora edulis
Canna edulis
Carpobrotus edulis
Phyllostachys edulis

---

effusus spreading, straggly
  Milium effusum
elaeagnifolius with leaves like
  Elaeagnus
  Pyrus elaeagnifolia
elasticus elastic
  Ficus elastica

COMMON DESCRIPTIVE TERMS
elatus tall; **elatior, elatius** taller
Aralia elata
Arrhenatherum elatius
Aspidistra elatior
Carex elata
Persicaria elata
Primula elatior
Rehmannia elata

WHAT'S IN A NAME?

PLANT LOOK-ALIKES

abietinus like *Abies* (fir)
acanthifolius with leaves like *Acanthus*
agavoides like *Agave*
alnifolius with leaves like *Alnus* (alder)
althaeoides like *Althaea* (hollyhock)
alyssoides like *Alyssum*
amaranthoides like *Amaranthus*
amygdaloides almond-like
anemoneflorus anemone-flowered
aquilegiifolius with leaves like *Aquilegia*
arundinaceus like a reed
bambusoides like bamboo
betulifolius with leaves like *Betula* (birch)
bryoides like moss
buxifolius box-leaved
calamus reedlike
cardunculus like a little thistle
clematideus like *Clematis*
cupressoides like *Cupressus* (cypress)
cyclamineus like *Cyclamen*
daphnoides like *Daphne*
dendroideus like a tree
dianthifolius with leaves like *Dianthus*
elaeagnifolius with leaves like *Elaeagnus*
ericoides like *Erica* (heath)
festucoides resembling *Festuca* (fescue)
ficifolius with leaves like *Ficus* (fig)
fuchsioides like *Fuchsia*
gentianoides like *Gentiana* (gentian)
gramineus like grass
graminifolius with grass-like leaves
ilicifolius with leaves like *Ilex* (holly)
iridiflorus with flowers like *Iris*
jasminoides like *Jasminum* (jasmine)
juncifolius with rushlike leaves
ligustrinus like *Ligustrum* (privet)
liliago lily-like

linifolius with leaves like *Linum* (flax)
malviflorus with flowers like *Malva* (mallow)
muscosus mossy, like moss
ocymoides like *Ocimum* (basil)
oleoides like *Olea* (olive)
opulifolius with maple-like leaves
orchidiflorus with flowers like orchid
pandanifolius with leaves like *Pandanus* (screw pine)
persicifolius with leaves like *Prunus persica* (peach tree)
persimilis very similar (e.g. to another species)
phlogopappus with seeds like *Phlox*
pinifolius with leaves like pine
platanoides like *Platanus*
plumbaginoides like *Plumbago*
prunifolia with leaves like *Prunus*
pseud-, pseudo- false (e.g. *pseudoplatanus*: "false" *Platanus* or plane)
quercifolius with leaves like *Quercus* (oak)
ranunculoides like *Ranunculus*
rhamnoides like *Rhamnus* (buckthorn)
salicifolius with leaves like *Salix* (willow)
salviifolius with leaves like *Salvia*
scilloides like *Scilla*
taxifolius with leaves like *Taxus* (yew)
typhoides like *Typha* (bulrush)
ulmarius like *Ulmus* (elm)
urticifolius with leaves like *Urtica* (nettle)
uvarius like grapes
viburnoides like *Viburnum*
vitifolius with leaves like *Vitis* (vine)

COMMON DESCRIPTIVE TERMS
elegans elegant; *elegantissimus* very
elegant
Buxus sempervirens 'Elegantissima'
Clarkia elegans
Cornus alba 'Elegantissima'
Desmodium elegans
Echeveria elegans
Liatris elegans

elegantulus rather elegant
Acer elegantulum
eleuther- free, not joined
ellipsoidalis ellipsoid
Quercus ellipsoidalis
ellipticus elliptic
Garrya elliptica

elongatus elongated
Melianthus elongatus
elwesii named after the English
naturalist and arboriculturist Henry
John Elwes (1846–1922)
Galanthus elwesii
emeticus emetic, causing vomiting
eminens projecting
emodensis, emodi from the Himalayas
Paeonia emodi
empetriformis shaped like *Empetrium*
(crowberry)
Phyllodoce empetriformis
endressii named for Philip Endress
(1806–1831), a German
plant collector,
Geranium endressii
engelmannii named for George
Engelmann (1809–1884) a
German botanist and doctor living
and working in the USA
Picea engelmannii
enneaphyllus with nine leaflets
or leaves
Oxalis enneaphylla

COMMON DESCRIPTIVE TERMS
ensatus, ensiformis sword-shaped;
ensifolius sword-leaved
Aristea ensifolia
Inula ensifolia
Iris ensata
Juncus ensifolius
Kniphofia ensifolia

ephemerus ephemeral, short-lived
  Lysimachia ephemerum
epi- on, on top of
epilithicus (growing) on stones
epigaeus growing near the ground
equinus, equestris relating to horses

COMMON DESCRIPTIVE TERMS
erectus erect, upright
Hedera helix 'Erecta'
Potentilla erecta
Tagetes erecta
Trillium erectum

---

erianthus with woolly flowers
  Geranium erianthum
ericifolius with leaves like *Erica*
  (heath)
  Melaleuca ericifolia
ericoides like *Erica* (heath)
  Aster ericoides
ericsmithii named for Eric Smith
  (1917–1986), plantsman and
  gardener at Hadspen, Somerset, UK
  Helleborus × *ericsmithii*
erinaceus like a hedgehog
  Dianthus erinaceus
eri-, erio- woolly- (see below)
eriocarpus with woolly fruits
  Potentilla eriocarpa
eriophyllus with woolly leaves
eriostemon with woolly stamens
erromenus vigorous, healthy
  Hosta undulata var. *erromena*

erubescens reddening, blushing
  Arisaema erubescens
erythro- red- (see below)
erythrocarpus with red fruits
  Lindera erythrocarpa

CULTIVAR NAMES
Foreign Expressions
E

ECLAIREUR (*French*)
SCOUT
(*PHLOX PANICULATA* 'ECLAIREUR')

ELFENAUGE (*German*)
ELF'S EYE
(*OMPHALODES VERNA* 'ELFENAUGE')

ELMFEUER (*German*)
ST ELMO'S FIRE
(*LOBELIA FULGENS* 'ELMFEUER')

ENZIANDOM (*German*)
GENTIAN DOME
(*HYDRANGEA MACROPHYLLA*
'ENZIANDOM')

ERDBLUT (*German*)
EARTH BLOOD
(*SEDUM SPURIUM* 'ERDBLUT')

ERSTE ZUNEIGUNG (*German*)
FIRST LOVE
(*PAPAVER ORIENTALE* 'ERSTE
ZUNEIGUNG')

ESCARBOUCLE (*French*)
CARBUNCLE
(*NYMPHAEA* 'ESCARBOUCLE')

ETOILE (*French*)
STAR
(*CLEMATIS* 'ETOILE ROSE',
CLEMATIS 'ETOILE VIOLETTE')

TEXTURE

acanth-, acantho- spiny, thorny
aculeatus prickly
adamantinus hard, steely
alutaceus leathery
amylaceus starchy
asper rough
asperatus roughened
asperrimus very rough
bombycifer with silky hairs
bullatus blistered, bubbled, studded
callosus with a hard skin
calvus bald, hairless
caperatus wrinkled
ceraceus waxy
cerefolius with waxy leaves
coactus felted
comatus, comosus tufted
coriaceus, coriarius leathery
corrugatus corrugated, furrowed
costatus ribbed
crinitus covered with long hairs
echinatus prickly, spiny
erio- woolly
eriocarpus with woolly fruits
farinosus mealy, covered with farina
fibrosus fibrous
flaccidus flaccid, soft
floccosus floccose, woolly
foveatus, foveolatus pitted
furfuraceus scurfy, covered with bran-like scales or powder
glaber glabrous (hairless, smooth)
glabellus rather smooth
glutinosus glutinous, sticky
gossypinus cottony
hirsutus hairy
hispidus bristly
laevigatus smooth
laevis soft
lanatus, laniger woolly
lanuginosus woolly
lisso- smooth
malacoides soft, supple
membranaceus like skin or membrane
mollis soft
mucosus slimy
muricatus rough with sharp points
nervosus fibrous, sinewy; with conspicuous veins
pilosus with long soft hairs, shaggy
plumarius, plumosus feathery
polytrichus with many hairs
pubens, pubescens, pubiger downy
pulverulentus dusty, powdery
pustulatus blistered or pimply
resinifer, resinosus resinous
rhytidophyllus with wrinkled leaves
rigens, rigidus stiff
rugosus, ruginosus, rugulosus wrinkled
scaber, scabrosus rough, gritty
sericeus silky
setaceus, setosus, setiferus bristly
spinosus, spinifer thorny
spinulifer with little spines
squamatus, squamosus scaly
squarrosus rough, scurfy; with protruding scales
stimulosus with stings or prickles
strigosus bristly
strobilaceus scaly like a pine-cone
subhirtellus rather hairy
tomentosus tomentose, woolly
velutinus velvety
verrucosus, verruculosus warty
villosus softly hairy
viscosus sticky, viscous

erythropodus with a red stem
  Alchemilla erythropoda
erythrosorus with red sori
  Dryopteris erythrosora
erythrostictus with red spots
  Sedum erythrostictum
esculentus edible
  Colocasia esculenta
esthonicus from Estonia
  Milium effusum var. *esthonicum*
estriatus not striped
etruscus from Tuscany, Italy
  Lonicera etrusca
eu- well, good (see below)
eudoxus of good repute
eucharis pleasing, agreeable
eugenioides like *Eugenia,* named for
  Prince Eugene of Savoy
  Pittosporum eugenioides

COMMON DESCRIPTIVE TERMS

europaeus European
Asarum europaeum
Euonymus europaeus
Olea europaea
Tilia × *europaea*
Trollius europaeus

---

evenosus not conspicuously veined
  Hebe evenosa
evolutus unfolded
exaltatus raised high, tall
  Nephrolepis exaltata
exasperatus roughened

COMMON DESCRIPTIVE TERMS

excelsus lofty, high, tall; ***excelsior***
  higher
Doronicum × *excelsum*
Fraxinus excelsior
Ligustrum lucidum 'Excelsum
  Superbum'
Lobelia excelsa
Rhapis excelsa

---

excorticatus, ecorticatus without bark
  Fuchsia excorticata
exiguus small, weak
  Salix exigua
exiliflorus with small or slender
  flowers
  Liriope exiliflora
eximius distinguished, extraordinary
  Daphne cneorum 'Eximia'
exoniensis from Exeter, UK, (usually
  from the nursery of Veitch & Sons,
  see page 204)
  Passiflora × *exoniensis*
exoticus foreign
expansus spread out, expanded
  Juniperus chinensis 'Expansa
  Variegata'
exstipulatus exstipulate
  Passiflora exstipulatum
eystettensis named for the garden
  of Prince Bishop Conrad von
  Gemmingen at Eichstätt in
  Germany
  Narcissus 'Eystettensis'

F

fabiformis bean-shaped

facetus choice, fine
  Rhododendron facetum

faeroensis from the Faeroe Islands, in the north Atlantic
  Alchemilla faeroensis

fagifolius with leaves like *Fagus* (beech)

falcatus falcate, curved like a sickle
  Polygonatum falcatum

fargesii named for the French missionary and plant hunter in China, Paul Farges (1844–1912)
  Abies fargesii

CULTIVAR NAMES
Personal Names
F

Rosa 'Felicia'

Jasminum officinale Fiona Sunrise ('Frojas')

Fragaria × *ananassa* (strawberry) 'Florence'

Erodium 'Fran's Delight'

Campanula persicifolia 'Frances'

Primula 'Francisca'

Pinus nigra 'Frank'

Clematis 'Frankie'

Fuchsia 'Fred's First'

Clematis 'Freda'

Rhododendron 'Freya'

---

farinaceus starchy
  Salvia farinacea

farinosus mealy, covered with farina
  Primula farinosa

farreri (see panel opposite)

fasciatus banded, striped

fasciculatus clustered, in bundles
  Primula fasciculata

fasciculiflorus with flowers in clusters
  Clematis fasciculiflora

Common descriptive terms

fastigiatus fastigiate; with an upright habit
  Gypsophila fastigiata
  Ilex crenata 'Fastigiata'
  Liriodendron tulipifera 'Fastigiatum'
  Malva alcea var. *fastigiata*
  Taxus baccata 'Fastigiata'

---

fastuosus proud, haughty
  Semiarundinaria fastuosa

faveolatus; favosus finely honeycombed

febrifugus driving out fever
  Dichroa febrifuga

fecundus fruitful; fertile

fenestralis with windowlike openings

fennicus Finnish

ferax fruit-bearing, fruitful, fertile

ferdinandi named for King Ferdinand of Bulgaria (1861–1948)
  Agave ferdinandi-regis
  Arabis ferdinandi-coburgi

ferens carrying, bearing

ferox fierce (generally used of very
   spiny plants)
   Ilex aquifolium 'Ferox Argentea'
   Pseudopanax ferox

ferreus iron gray; hard like iron

ferrugineus; ferruginosus rusty; light
   reddish brown
   Digitalis ferruginea

fertilis producing many seeds, fruitful

ferulaceus; ferulifolius like *Ferula*
   (giant fennel)

ferus wild

festalis, festivus festive, bright
   Hymenocallis × *festalis*

festucoides resembling *Festuca* (fescue)

fibrillosus fibrillose

fibrosus fibrous
   Dicksonia fibrosa

ficifolius with leaves like *Ficus carica*
   (fig)

figlinus terra-cotta

figuratus formed, shaped

filamentosus, filarius with filaments
   or threads
   Yucca filamentosa

fili- thread (see below)

filicaulis with a threadlike stem

filici- fern- (*filix*; see below)

filicifolius with fernlike leaves
   Acacia filicifolia

filicoides fernlike

filiculoides like a small fern
   Azolla filiculoides

REGINALD FARRER (1880–1920)

The young Reginald Farrer took
a particular interest in the flora of
his native Yorkshire, in the UK,
and went on to explore the plant
life of the Alps, Japan and China,
becoming an outstanding plant
collector and author. On his travels
in the Far East he collected many
species that are now garden favorites,
such as *Buddleia alternifolia*, as
well as new species of primula and
rhododendron. He wrote extensively
about his travels, and about alpines:
his two-volume book *The English
Rock Garden* is a classic work on the
subject. Poor health always made
the danger and discomfort of a
plant hunter's life especially difficult
for Farrer, and he died aged only
40 on a trip to Burma, where he
is buried. Plants named after him
include *Viburnum farreri*, as well as
Gentiana farreri, which he found in
north-west China, and the alpine
Geranium farreri.

filifer thread-bearing
Washingtonia filifera
filifolius thread-leaved
filiformis threadlike
Juncus filiformis 'Spiralis'
filipendulinus like *Filipendula* (meadowsweet)
Achillea filipendulina
filipendulus hanging by a thread
filipes with a threadlike foot or stalk
Rosa filipes
filix fern
Athyrium filix-femina (lady fern)

fimbriatus fimbriate, fringed
Dianthus 'Fimbriatus'
firmus strong, firm
fissifolius with split leaves
fissilis, fissus split, cleft
fissuratus fissured
fistulosus fistular; hollow like a pipe, but closed at the ends
Monarda fistulosa
flabellatus, flabelliformis fan-shaped
Crataegus flabellata
flaccidus flaccid, soft
Yucca flaccida
flagellaris whiplike
Saxifraga flagellaris
flagellifer whip-bearing
Carex flagellifera
flagelliformis shaped like a whip
flammeus; flammeolus flame-colored
flammula small flame
Clematis flammula

COMMON DESCRIPTIVE TERMS
flavus pure yellow; **flavens** yellow; **flavescens, flavicans, flavidus** yellowish
Chionochloa flavicans
Crocus flavus subsp. *flavus*
Disporum flavens
Glaucium flavum
Ilex aquifolium 'Flavescens'
Linum flavum
Pyracantha rogersiana 'Flava'
Rhododendron flavidum

flavissimus very yellow

flavovirens yellowish green

fletcheri named for Harold Fletcher (1907–1978), British botanist, Director of RHS Garden Wisley, Surrey, and Keeper of Royal Botanic Garden Edinburgh, UK
  Chamaecyparis lawsoniana 'Fletcheri'

flexibilis; flexilis flexible, pliant
  Pinus flexilis

flexipes with a flexible stem or foot
  Trillium flexipes

COMMON DESCRIPTIVE TERMS

flexuosus zigzag
Corydalis flexuosa
Deschampsia flexuosa
Helenium flexuosum
Phyllostachys flexuosa

---

floccosus floccose, woolly
  Cotoneaster floccosus

floralis floral, relating to the flower

florentinus from Florence, Italy
  Cistus × *florentinus*

COMMON DESCRIPTIVE TERMS

flore pleno with double flowers
Clematis florida var. *flore-pleno*
Galanthus nivalis f. *pleniflorus* 'Flore Pleno'
Genista tinctoria 'Flore Pleno'
Ranunculus ficaria flore-pleno

WHAT'S IN A NAME?

COLOR CLUES:
GENERAL COLOR TERMS

ater, atro- dark, blackish

bicolor bicolored

concolor the same color all over; of the same color

discolor of different colors

floridus bright

fucatus painted, colored

fulgens, fulgidus shining, brightly colored

fuscopictus dark-colored

fuscotinctus dark-tinged

fuscus dark

impolitus matt

iridescens iridescent

laetus bright

lucidus shining, clear, transparent

margaritaceus pearly

mutabilis changing, changeable (e.g. in colour)

nitens, nitidus shining

obscurus obscure, indistinct, dark

opacus shady, dark, opaque

pallescens rather pale, becoming pale

pallidus pale

pallidulus rather pale

phaeus dusky

pictus (literally) painted; vividly colored

polychromus many-colored

pullus dark in color

purus pure

refulgens shining

splendens brilliant

squalidus dirty

tricolor three-colored

vernicosus varnished

versicolor in various colors

Fairy moss *Azolla filiculoides*
False acacia *Robinia pseudoacacia*
False cypress *Chamaecyparis*
False indigo *Baptisia australis*
Fawn lily *Erythronium revolutum*
Feather grass *Stipa*
Fennel *Foeniculum vulgare*
Fern-leaved beech *Fagus sylvatica* var.
  heterophylla 'Aspleniifolia'
Fescue *Festuca*
Feverfew *Tanacetum parthenium*
Field maple *Acer campestre*
Fig *Ficus carica*
Figwort *Scrophularia*
Fir *Abies*
Firethorn *Pyracantha*
Fireweed *Chamerion angustifolium*
Fishbone cotoneaster *Cotoneaster
  horizontalis*
Flag *Iris*
Flame of the forest *Pieris*; *Butea
  monosperma*

Flannel bush *Fremontodendron
  californicum*
Flax *Linum*
Fleabane *Erigeron*
Flowering currant *Ribes sanguineum*
Flowering rush *Butomus umbellatus*
Foam flower *Tiarella cordifolia*
Foam of May *Spiraea* 'Arguta'
Forget-me-not *Myosotis*
Fountain grass *Pennisetum alopecuroides*
Four o'clock flower *Mirabilis jalapa*
Foxglove *Digitalis*
Foxglove tree *Paulownia tomentosa*
Foxtail lily *Eremurus*
French lavender *Lavandula stoechas*
French marigold *Tagetes patula*
Fringe tree *Chionanthus*
Fritillary *Fritillaria*
(Fruits, see page 169)
Fuji cherry *Prunus incisa*
Fumitory, Fumeroot *Corydalis*
Furze *Ulex*

FEVERFEW

floribundus profusely flowering
   Rhododendron floribundum
floridanus from Florida
   Illicium floridanum
floridulus rather free-flowering
   Miscanthus floridulus

COMMON DESCRIPTIVE TERMS

floridus flowering abundantly
Clematis florida
Cornus florida
Primula florida
Weigela florida

florifer bearing flowers, flowering
florindae named by the British plant
   hunter Frank Kingdon Ward (see
   page 210) for his first wife Florinda
   Primula florindae
-florus -flowered (e.g. *parviflorus*,
   small-flowered)
flos flower
flos-cuculi flower of the cuckoo
   Lychnis flos-cuculi (ragged robin)
flos-jovis flower of Jove
   Lychnis flos-jovis
fluminalis, flumineus of rivers
fluminensis from Rio de Janeiro
   Tradescantia fluminensis
fluviatilis of rivers
   Equisetum fluviatile
foemineus female
foeniculaceum resembling *Foeniculum*
   (fennel)

GENUS NAMES
F

Festuca in Latin, a stalk or straw
Forsythia named for William
   Forsyth (1737–1804), Scottish
   horticulturist
Fothergilla named for Dr. John
   Fothergill (1712–1780), English
   doctor and expert on American
   plants
Fritillaria from Latin *fritillus*,
   a dice-box
Fuchsia named for Leonhart Fuchs
   (1501–1566), German professor
   and herbalist

foetidissimus very evil-smelling
   Iris foetidissima
foetidus stinking, evil-smelling
   Helleborus foetidus
foliaceus leafy, leaf-like
foliatus leaf-bearing
foliosissimus very leafy
   Polemonium foliosissimum
foliosus leafy, many-leaved
   Kniphofia foliosa
-folius -leaved (e.g. *grandifolius*,
   large-leaved)
follicularis follicle-like
fontanesianus, fontanesii named for
   the French botanist and author
   René Desfontaines (1750–1833)
   Leucothoe fontanesiana
fontanus; fontinalis growing in or
   near springs

foratus pierced with holes
forficatus shaped like scissors
formicarius attractive to ants; of ants
formis -shaped (e.g. *cruciformis*)

COMMON DESCRIPTIVE TERMS

COMMON DESCRIPTIVE TERMS
formosanus from Taiwan (Formosa)
Lilium formosanum
Liquidambar formosana
Ophiopogon formosanus
Pleione formosana
Tricyrtis formosana

formosissimus very beautiful
formosus finely formed, handsome, beautiful
   Leycesteria formosa
fornicalis, fornicatus arched
forrestii (see panel below)
fortis strong, vigorous

COMMON DESCRIPTIVE TERMS
fortunei named for the Scottish plant collector Robert Fortune (1812–1880)
Euonymus fortunei
Eupatorium fortunei
Hosta fortunei
Lysimachia fortunei
Mahonia fortunei
Paulownia fortunei
Rhododendron fortunei
Trachycarpus fortunei

foveatus pitted
foveolatus rather pitted
fractiflexus zigzag
fractus broken
fragarioides like *Fragaria* (strawberry)
fragilis fragile
   Salix fragilis

GEORGE FORREST
(1873–1932)

Born in Falkirk, Scotland, George Forrest traveled to Australia as a young man, returning to work in the Botanic Garden in Edinburgh. This proved to be good grounding for his later career: his first trip, to China in 1904, was followed by six more expeditions. A courageous and prolific plant collector, he braved many dangers in order to send back carefully classified specimens and seeds of thousands of plants, aided by teams of Chinese villagers. Rhododendrons, including *Rhododendron forrestii*, were his specialty, but other discoveries included the very special *Gentiana sino-ornata*. Perhaps the most familiar of the plants named for Forrest is *Pieris formosa* var. *forrestii*; others include *Primula forrestii, Iris forrestii* and *Hypericum forrestii*.

fragrans fragrant
   Petasites fragrans
fragrantissimus very fragrant
   Lonicera fragrantissima
frangulus brittle
   Rhamnus frangula
fraseri named for the London
   nurseryman and plant collector
   John Fraser (1750–1811)
   Photinia × *fraseri*
fraxinifolius with leaves like
   Fraxinus (ash)
   Pterocarya fraxinifolia

frigidus cold; growing in cold places
   Cotoneaster frigidus
frikartii named for Carl Frikart
   (1879–1964), a Swiss nurseryman
   Aster × *frikartii*
frondosus leafy, leaf-like, leaf-bearing
   Primula frondosa
fructifer, frugifer fruit-bearing
fructu albo with white fruits
   Iris foetidissima 'Fructu Albo'
fructu luteo with yellow fruits
   Ilex aquifolium 'Pyramidalis
   Fructu Luteo'

CULTIVAR NAMES
Colors: Blue

BUDDLEIA DAVIDII 'EMPIRE BLUE'

CAMPANULA COCHLEARIFOLIA 'BAVARIA BLUE'

CARYOPTERIS × CLANDONENSIS 'HEAVENLY BLUE'

CEANOTHUS 'BLUE MOUND'

CHAMAECYPARIS LAWSONIANA 'PEMBURY BLUE'

CORYDALIS FLEXUOSA 'BLUE PANDA'

CROCUS CHRYSANTHUS 'BLUE PEARL'

DELPHINIUM 'BLUE DAWN'

ECHINOPS BANNATICUS 'TAPLOW BLUE'

ERYNGIUM ALPINUM 'BLUE STAR'

FESTUCA GLAUCA 'ELIJAH BLUE'

GENTIANA 'BLUE SILK'

GERANIUM 'JOHNSON'S BLUE'

HOSTA 'BLUE ANGEL'

HYACINTHUS ORIENTALIS 'DELFT BLUE'

HYDRANGEA SERRATA 'BLUEBIRD'

IPOMOEA TRICOLOR 'HEAVENLY BLUE'

IRIS 'BLUE DENIM'

JUNIPERUS HORIZONTALIS 'BLUE CHIP'

LAVANDULA ANGUSTIFOLIA 'LODDON BLUE'

PEROVSKIA 'BLUE SPIRE'

PRUNUS DOMESTICA (PLUM) 'BLUE TIT'

RHODODENDRON 'BLUE DANUBE'

RUTA GRAVEOLENS 'JACKMAN'S BLUE'

SALVIA PATENS 'CAMBRIDGE BLUE'

VERONICA PEDUNCULARIS 'GEORGIA BLUE'

VIOLA 'BELMONT BLUE'

COMMON DESCRIPTIVE TERMS
fruticosus, frutescens, fruticans
shrubby

Argyranthemum frutescens

Jasminum fruticans

Oenothera fruticosa

Penstemon fruticosus

Phlomis fruticosa

Potentilla fruticosa

Teucrium fruticans

---

fruticulosus shrubby and small
Matthiola fruticulosa

fucatus painted, colored

fuchsii named after the German physician Leonhart Fuchs (1501–1566), a German professor and herbalist
Dactylorhiza fuchsii

fuchsioides like *Fuchsia*
Begonia fuchsioides

fuegianus from Tierra del Fuego, Chile/Argentina

fugax fleeting, transitory, ephemeral
Moraea fugax

COMMON DESCRIPTIVE TERMS
fulgens, fulgidus shining, brightly colored

Fuchsia fulgens

Lobelia fulgens

Pelargonium fulgidum

Rudbeckia fulgida

Salvia fulgens

fuligineus; fuliginosus dark brown, sooty

fullonum of fullers
  Dipsacus fullonum (teasel)

fulmineus like lightning

COMMON DESCRIPTIVE TERMS
fulvus, fulvellus, fulvescens, fulvidus
  tawny yellow, yellowish brown
Digitalis × *fulva*
Hemerocallis fulva
Rhododendron fulvum

---

fumariifolius with leaves like *Fumaria* (fumitory)
  Corydalis fumariifolia

fumeus, fumidus, fumosus smoky, gray-brown

funalis rope-like

funebris funereal; of cemeteries

fungiformis mushroom-shaped

funicularis, funiculatus rope-like

funiculosus arranged in ropes or bundles

furcatus forked; with two long lobes

furfuraceus scurfy, covered with bran-like scales or powder

fuscopictus dark-colored
  Disporopsis fuscopicta

fuscoruber dark red
  Corylus avellana 'Fuscorubra'

fuscotinctus dark-tinged
  Crocus chrysanthus var. *fuscotinctus*

fuscus dark; blackish brown

DIPSACUS FULLONUM

fusiformis fusiform, shaped like a spindle, thicker in the middle than at the ends

WHAT'S IN A NAME?

COUNTRIES OF EUROPE

anglicus England
austriacus Austria
belgicus Belgium or the Netherlands
bulgaricus Bulgaria
cambricus Wales
croaticus Croatia
gallicus France
germanicus Germany
graecus Greece
hispanicus Spain
italicus Italy
lusitanicus Portugal
scoticus Scotland
suecicus Sweden

G

gaditanus from Cadiz in Spain
Narcissus gaditanus

gala- milk-
Galactites; Galanthus

galeatus with a helmet or helmet-like covering
Arisaema galeatum

gallicus Gallic, from France
Rosa gallica

galpinii named for Ernest Galpin (1858–1941), a South African banker and plant collector
Kniphofia galpinii

gardenii named for Dr. Alexander Garden (1730–1791)
Fothergilla gardenii

geminiflorus with twin flowers
Polygonatum geminiflorum

gemmifer bearing buds
Primula gemmifera

gemmosus jeweled
Crataegus gemmosa

CULTIVAR NAMES
Colors: Gold

AUCUBA JAPONICA 'GOLDEN KING'

BERBERIS THUNBERGII BONANZA GOLD ('BOGOZAM')

CALLUNA VULGARIS 'GOLD HAZE'

CAREX OSHIMENSIS 'EVERGOLD'

CHAMAECYPARIS LAWSONIANA 'ELLWOOD'S GOLD'

COTINUS GOLDEN SPIRIT ('ANCOT')

CYTISUS × PRAECOX 'ALLGOLD'

ELAEAGNUS × EBBINGEI 'COASTAL GOLD'

ERICA ARBOREA 'ALBERT'S GOLD'

EUONYMUS FORTUNEI 'EMERALD 'N' GOLD'

EUPHORBIA CHARACIAS SUBSP. WULFENII 'LAMBROOK GOLD'

FORSYTHIA 'GOLDEN TIMES'

HEDERA HELIX 'GOLDCHILD'

HEMEROCALLIS 'GOLDEN CHIMES'

HOSTA 'GOLD STANDARD'

ILEX × ALTACLERENSIS 'GOLDEN KING'

ILEX CRENATA 'GOLDEN GEM'

JUNIPERUS × PFITZERIANA 'OLD GOLD'

LIGULARIA 'GREGYNOG GOLD'

LUMA APICULATA 'GLANLEAM GOLD'

MALUS DOMESTICA (APPLE) 'JONAGOLD'

MALUS × ZUMI 'GOLDEN HORNET'

MELISSA OFFICINALIS 'ALL GOLD'

NARCISSUS 'GOLDFINGER'

ORIGANUM VULGARE 'GOLD TIP'

PHYSOCARPUS OPULIFOLIUS 'DART'S GOLD'

PITTOSPORUM TENUIFOLIUM 'WARNHAM GOLD'

PYRACANTHA 'GOLDEN CHARMER'

RHODODENDRON 'GOLDEN TORCH'

RUBUS COCKBURNIANUS 'GOLDENVALE'

SAMBUCUS RACEMOSA 'SUTHERLAND GOLD'

generosus noble, eminent
   Populus × *generosa* 'Beaupré'
gentianoides like *Gentiana* (gentian)
   Veronica gentianoides
georgianus from Georgia (USA)
   Quercus georgiana
georgicus from Georgia (Caucasus)
   Pulsatilla georgica
geraniifolius with leaves like
   Geranium
   Androsace geraniifolia
germanicus from Germany
   Iris germanica
gibbosus hunchbacked; swollen
   on one side
   Patrinia gibbosa
gibraltaricus from Gibraltar
   Iberis gibraltarica

COMMON DESCRIPTIVE TERMS

giganteus giant, gigantic, very large
Allium giganteum
Cardiocrinum giganteum
Eryngium giganteum
Miscanthus × *giganteus*
Sequoiadendron giganteum
Stipa gigantea

---

gigas giant
   Angelica gigas
giraldianus, giraldii named for
   Giuseppe Giraldi (1848–1901), an
   Italian missionary and plant hunter
   Callicarpa bodinieri subsp. *giraldii*

CULTIVAR NAMES
Personal Names
G

CLEMATIS 'GABRIELLE'
OSTEOSPERMUM 'GEMMA'
CLEMATIS 'GEORG'
IRIS 'GEORGE'
ROSA GERALDINE ('PEAHAZE')
IRIS 'GORDON'
COTINUS 'GRACE'
ERICA × *WATSONII* 'GWEN'
DAHLIA 'GWYNETH'

---

glabellus rather glabrous
   Epilobium glabellum
glaber glabrous (hairless, smooth)
   Penstemon glaber
glabratus almost glabrous
   Hoheria glabrata

GENUS NAMES
G

Galanthus from Greek *gala*, milk,
   and *anthos*, flower
Gaura from Greek *gauros*, superb
Gazania named for Theodore of
   Gaza (1398–1478), translator of the
   botanical writings of Theophrastus
Geranium from Greek *geranos*, crane
Gladiolus in Latin, a small sword
Glyceria from Greek *glykys*, sweet
Gunnera named for Johan Gunnerus,
   Norwegian botanist and bishop
Gypsophila from Latin *gypsos,* chalk
   or gypsum, and *philos,* loving

glabrescens becoming glabrous
 Corylopsis glabrescens
glacialis from glaciers or cold places
 Artemisia glacialis

Common descriptive terms
glandulosus glandular
Arctostaphylos glandulosa
Calamintha nepeta subsp. *glandulosa*
Erodium glandulosum
Prunus glandulosa

---

glaucescens rather glaucous, becoming glaucous
 Primula glaucescens
glaucophyllus with glaucous leaves
 Hebe glaucophylla

Common descriptive terms
glaucus glaucous
Canna glauca
Carex glauca
Coronilla valentina subsp. *glauca*
Erigeron glaucus
Euphorbia glauca
Festuca glauca
Phyllostachys glauca
Picea glauca
Pinus pumila 'Glauca'
Rosa glauca

---

globiferus bearing globe-shaped clusters
 Androsace globifera
globispica with globose spikes
 Betula globispica

Common descriptive terms
globosus globular, spherical
Acer platanoides 'Globosum'
Buddleia globosa
Magnolia globosa
Picea pungens 'Globosa'

---

globulifer bearing small globe-shaped clusters

Galingale *Cyperus*

Gardener's garters *Phalaris arundinacea* var. *picta*

Gas plant *Dictamnus albus*

Gayfeather *Liatris spicata*

Gean *Prunus avium*

Gentian *Gentiana*

Geranium (tender) *Pelargonium*

Germander *Teucrium*

Germander speedwell *Veronica chamaedrys*

Giant fennel *Ferula communis*

Giant hogweed *Heracleum mantegazzianum*

Gillyflower *Matthiola*

Ginger, Ginger lily *Hedychium; Zingiber*

Glasswort *Salicornia europaea*

Globe amaranth *Gomphrena globosa*

Globe flower *Trollius*

Globe thistle *Echinops ritro*

Glory bush *Tibouchina*

Glory flower *Clerodendrum bungei; Eccremocarpus scaber*

Glory of the snow *Chionodoxa*

Goat willow *Salix caprea*

Goat's beard *Aruncus dioicus*

Goat's rue *Galega*

Golden oak of Cyprus *Quercus alnifolia*

Golden oats *Stipa gigantea*

Golden rain *Laburnum*

Golden rain tree *Koelreuteria paniculata*

Golden rod *Solidago*

Goldilocks *Ranunculus auricomus*

Gorse *Ulex*

Granny's bonnets *Aquilegia vulgaris*

Grape hyacinth *Muscari*

Grape vine *Vitis vinifera*

GLOBE FLOWER

Grass of Parnassus *Parnassia palustris*

Gray alder *Alnus incana*

Gray birch *Betula populifolia*

Gray poplar *Populus canescens*

Great mullein *Verbascum thapsus*

Great white cherry *Prunus* 'Taihaku'

Gromwell *Lithospermum officinale; Buglossoides*

Ground elder *Aegopodium podagraria*

Ground ivy *Glechoma hederacea*

Groundsel *Senecio vulgaris*

Guelder rose *Viburnum opulus*

Gum tree *Eucalyptus*

globulus like a little ball
   Eucalyptus globulus
glomeratus clustered in a head
   Campanula glomerata
gloriosus glorious
   Yucca gloriosa
glutinosus glutinous, sticky
   Eucryphia glutinosa
glycyrrhiza liquorice
   Polypodium glycyrrhiza

CAMPANULA GLOMERATA

gmelinii named for a German
   naturalist, Johann Gmelin (1709–
   1755)
   Artemisia gmelinii
gossypinus like cotton
   Gerbera gossypina
gracilifolius with slender leaves
   Clematis gracilifolia
gracilipes with a slender stalk
   Primula gracilipes

COMMON DESCRIPTIVE TERMS
gracilis slender
Deutzia gracilis
Fuchsia magellanica var. *gracilis*
Galanthus gracilis
Geranium gracile
Mentha × *gracilis* (ginger mint)

---

gracillimus very slender
   Miscanthus sinensis 'Gracillimus'
graecus Greek
   Cyclamen graecum
gramineus like grass
   Iris graminea
graminifolius with grass-like leaves
   Polygonatum graminifolium
granatus with many seeds
   Punica granatum (pomegranate)
grandiceps with a large head
   Dryopteris filix-mas 'Grandiceps
   Wills'
grandidentatus with large teeth
   Fagus sylvatica 'Grandidentata'

CULTIVAR NAMES
Foreign Expressions
G

GARTENSONNE (*German*)
GARDEN SUN
(*HELENIUM* 'GARTENSONNE')

GELBE MANTEL (*German*)
YELLOW CLOAK
(*IRIS* 'GELBE MANTEL')

GERBE D'OR (*French*)
GOLD SPRAY
(*CROCOSMIA* 'GERBE D'OR')

GEWITTERWOLKE (*German*)
THUNDERCLOUD
(*MISCANTHUS SINENSIS*
'GEWITTERWOLKE')

GLOCKENTURM (*German*)
BELL TOWER
(*BERGENIA* 'GLOCKENTURM')

GLOIRE DE ... (*French*)
GLORY OF ...
(*CEANOTHUS* × *DELILEANUS* 'GLOIRE
DE VERSAILLES'; *HEDERA CANARIENSIS*
'GLOIRE DE MARENGO')

GLUT (*German*)
GLOW
(*ASTILBE* 'GLUT')

GOLDBUKETT (*Swedish*)
GOLDEN BOUQUET
(*RHODODENDRON* 'GOLDBUKETT')

GOLDENE JUGEND (*German*)
GOLDEN YOUTH
(*HELENIUM* 'GOLDENE JUGEND')

GOLDFUCHS (*German*)
GOLD FOX
(*HELENIUM* 'GOLDFUCHS')

GOLDGEFIEDER (*German*)
GOLD PLUME
(*HELIOPSIS HELIANTHOIDES* VAR.
SCABRA 'GOLDGEFIEDER')

GOLDKLUMPEN (*German*)
GOLDEN CLOGS
(*POTENTILLA AUREA* 'GOLDKLUMPEN')

GOLDKRONE (*German*)
GOLDEN CROWN
(*RHODODENDRON* 'GOLDKRONE')

GOLDQUELLE (*German*)
GOLD FOUNTAIN
(*RUDBECKIA LACINIATA* 'GOLDQUELLE')

GOLDRAUSCH (*German*)
GOLD RUSH
(*HELENIUM* 'GOLDRAUSCH')

GOLDSTURM (*German*)
GOLD STORM
(*RUDBECKIA FULGIDA* VAR. *SULLIVANTII*
'GOLDSTURM')

GOLDTAU (*German*) GOLD DEW
(*DESCHAMPSIA CESPITOSA* 'GOLDTAU')

GOSHIKI (*Japanese*)
FIVE-COLORED
(*OSMANTHUS HETEROPHYLLUS*
'GOSHIKI')

GRAUE WITWE (*German*)
GRAY WIDOW
(*PAPAVER ORIENTALE* 'GRAUE WITWE')

GROSSE FONTÄNE (*German*)
BIG FOUNTAIN
(*MISCANTHUS SINENSIS* 'GROSSE
FONTÄNE')

COMMON DESCRIPTIVE TERMS
grandiflorus large-flowered
Abelia × *grandiflora*
Clematis montana 'Grandiflora'
Digitalis grandiflora
Erythronium grandiflorum
Hydrangea anomala 'Grandiflora'
Magnolia grandiflora
Tellima grandiflora
Trillium grandiflorum

grandifolius with large leaves
  Achillea grandifolia
grandis big

gratianopolitanus from Grenoble
  in France
  Dianthus gratianopolitanus
  (Cheddar pink)

COMMON DESCRIPTIVE TERMS
graveolens strongly scented
Anethum graveolens (dill)
Apium graveolens
Pelargonium graveolens
Ruta graveolens (rue)

grayi named for the American
  botanist Asa Gray (1810–1888)
  Carex grayi
gregarius gregarious
  Nematanthus gregarius
griffithii named for William Griffith
  (1810–1845), a British botanist
  Euphorbia griffithii
griseus gray
  Acer griseum
groenlandicus from Greenland
  Ledum groenlandicum
grossularioides like gooseberry
  Pelargonium grossularioides
gruinus like a crane
  Erodium gruinum
gunnii named for Ronald Gunn
  (1808–1881), a South African-
  born Tasmanian botanist
  Eucalyptus gunnii
guttatus spotted
  Helleborus orientalis subsp. *guttatus*

CULTIVAR NAMES
Say it with Flowers

Galanthus nivalis 'April Fool'

Iris sibirica 'Baby Sister'

Narcissus 'Best of Luck'

Rosa Best Wishes ('Chessnut')

Hosta 'Big Daddy'

Malva sylvestris 'Brave Heart'

Rosa Congratulations ('Korlift')

Hemerocallis 'Cool It'

Rosa Crazy for You ('Wekroalt')

Dianthus 'Dad's Favourite'

Iris ensata 'Darling'

Rhododendron 'Dear Grandad'

Rosa 'Dearest'

Paeonia lactiflora 'Do Tell'

Fuchsia 'Forget-me-Not'

Alstroemeria 'Friendship'

Trifolium repens 'Good Luck'

Rheum × *hybridum* (rhubarb) 'Grandad's Favourite'

Dianthus 'Gran's Favourite'

Pelargonium 'Greetings'

Liquidambar styraciflua 'Happidaze'

Rosa Happy Retirement ('Tantoras')

Tulipa 'Heart's Delight'

Hosta 'Hope'

Lilium 'Journey's End'

Rosa Keep in Touch ('Hardrama')

Fuchsia 'Keepsake'

Rosa Keepsake ('Kormalda')

Iris 'Let's Elope'

Rosa Love Knot ('Chewglorious')

Primula auricula 'Lovebird'

Rosa Loving Memory ('Korgund')

Rosa Marry Me ('Dicwonder')

Lavatera × *clementii* Memories ('Stelav')

Malus domestica (apple) 'Mother'

Paeonia lactiflora 'Mother's Choice'

Dahlia 'My Valentine'

Dahlia 'New Baby'

Hosta 'Remember Me'

Fuchsia 'Remembrance'

Rhododendron 'Second Honeymoon'

Lilium 'Silly Girl'

Fuchsia 'Sister Sister'

Pelargonium 'Something Special'

Pelargonium 'Souvenir'

Rosa Special Child ('Tanaripsa')

Nepeta subsessilis 'Sweet Dreams'

Tulipa 'Sweetheart'

Rosa Thank You ('Chesdeep')

Fuchsia 'Three Cheers'

Rosa Top Marks ('Fryministar')

Rosa Warm Wishes ('Fryxotic')

Iris sibirica 'Welcome Return'

Rosa 'Well Done'

Camellia japonica 'Yours Truly'

See also Anniversaries (page 183); Birthdays (page 150); Christmas (page 98); Special Occasions; (page 107); Weddings (page 188).

H

haageanus named for a German seedsman, J. Haage (1826–1878)
Lychnis haageana

haastii named for Sir Johann von Haast (1824–1887), a German plant collector in New Zealand
Olearia × *haastii*

habrotrichus with soft hairs

hadriaticus from the Adriatic

haem- blood red (see below)

haemanthus with blood-red flowers

haematocalyx with a blood-red calyx
Dianthus haematocalyx

haematocarpus with blood-red fruits

haematodes blood red
Rhododendron haematodes

hakusanensis from Mount Haku in Japan
Sanguisorba hakusanensis

halo- salt

halophilus salt-loving

hamatus, hamosus hooked, barbed

hamulosus with small hooks

haplo- single (see below)

haplocalyx with a single calyx
Mentha haplocalyx

haplocaulis with a single stem

haplostichus with a single row

harpophyllus with sickle-shaped leaves

hastatus with a spear; spear-shaped
Verbena hastata

hastifolius with spear-shaped leaves
Scutellaria hastifolia

hebe- downy (see below)

hebecarpus with downy fruit

hebepetalus with downy petals
Indigofera hebepetala

hebephyllus with downy leaves

hebetatus made dull or blunt

hederaceus like *Hedera* (ivy)
Glechoma hederacea

hederifolius with leaves like *Hedera*
Cyclamen hederifolium

heldreichii named for a German botanist, Theodor von Heldreich (1822–1902)
Pinus heldreichii

heleo-, helo- marsh-

helianthoides like *Helianthus*
Heliopsis helianthoides

helicus coiled

heli-, helio- sun-

heliolepis with glittering scales

helix in a spiral; twining
Hedera helix

hellenicus Greek

helodes of marshes

COMMON DESCRIPTIVE TERMS

helveticus Swiss
Erysimum helveticum
Onosma helvetica
Salix helvetica

---

helvolus pale yellow
  Nymphaea 'Pygmaea Helvola'
helvus light bay in color
hemi- half-
hemisphaericus hemispherical
hemitrichotus hairy on one side only
hemsleyanus, hemsleyi named for
  William Hemsley (1843–1924), a
  botanist at Kew Gardens, London
  Aconitum hemsleyanum
  Sorbus hemsleyi

COMMON DESCRIPTIVE TERMS

henryanus, henryi named for the
  Irish botanist and plant collector
  Augustine Henry (1857–1930)
  Acer henryi
  Emmenopterys henryi
  Hepatica henryi
  Lilium henryi
  Lonicera henryi
  Parthenocissus henryana
  Rubus henryi
  Tilia henryana

hepta- seven- (see below)
heptalobus with seven lobes
  Acer palmatum var. *heptalobum*
heptaphyllus with seven leaves or
  leaflets
  Cardamine heptaphyllus
heracleifolius with leaves like
  hogweed (*Heracleum*)
  Clematis heracleifolia

CULTIVAR NAMES
Public Figures

Narcissus 'King Alfred'

Leucanthemum × superbum 'Barbara Bush'

Clematis 'Prince Charles'

Fuchsia 'Winston Churchill'

Clematis 'Princess Diana'

Colchicum 'Disraeli'

Iris 'Duke of Edinburgh'

Clematis 'King Edward VII'

Canna 'General Eisenhower'

Rosa 'The Queen Elizabeth'

Penstemon 'King George V'

Clematis 'W.E. Gladstone'

Clematis 'Jan Pawel' (Pope John Paul)

Clematis 'Lady Bird Johnson'

Paeonia lactiflora 'Lord Kitchener'

Magnolia 'Princess Margaret'

Heliotropium arborescens 'Princess Marina'

Primula 'Napoleon'

Rosa 'Cardinal de Richelieu'

Paeonia lactiflora 'President Franklin D. Roosevelt'

Primula auricula 'Anwar Sadat'

Rosa Queen Mother ('Korquemu')

Lobelia 'Queen Victoria'

Heliotropium arborescens 'The Speaker'

Clematis 'Princess of Wales'

Juniperus horizontalis 'Prince of Wales'

Sempervivum 'Duke of Windsor'

herbaceus herbaceous, not woody; grass-green

hercegovinus from Hercegovina
Helleborus multifidus subsp. *hercegovinus*

hesperus of the west; of evening

heter-, hetero- diverse, various

heteracanthus with differing spines

heteranthus with diverse flowers (i.e. different kinds – such as sterile and fertile – on one plant)
Indigofera heterantha

heterocarpus with differing fruits

heterodontus with differing teeth
Rhodiola heterodonta

heterodoxus differing from others in its genus
Penstemon heterodoxus

heterolepis with differing scales

heteromorphus with differing forms

SIR HAROLD HILLIER (1905–1985)

The grandson of Edwin Hillier, who founded Hillier Nurseries in 1864, Sir Harold took over the business in 1944. An eminent plantsman, he created a world-class arboretum at his home, Jermyns House, Ampfield, Hampshire, UK, and later in life traveled widely to study plants in the wild. Many plant names have Hillier associations. As well as the obvious ones (*Robinia* × *slavinii* 'Hillieri', *Viburnum* × *hillieri, Thuja plicata* 'Hillieri' etc.), *wintonensis* (from Winchester) usually indicates a Hillier plant (e.g. × *Halimiocistus wintonensis*). Several plants have the cultivar name 'Jermyns' (e.g. *Abutilon* × *suntense* 'Jermyns').

heterophyllus with diverse leaves (i.e. different forms on one plant)

Cirsium heterophyllum

Fagus sylvatica var. *heterophylla*

Osmanthus heterophyllus

Penstemon heterophyllus

hexa- six- (see below)

hexagonus six-angled

hexandrus with six stamens

Podophyllum hexandrum

hibernicus Irish

Hedera hibernica

hibernus of winter; Irish

hiemalis of winter, winter-flowering

hieraciifolius like *Hieracium* (hawkweed)

hillieri (see panel opposite)

COMMON DESCRIPTIVE TERMS

himalaicus, himalayensis from the Himalayas

Aster himalaicus

Eremurus himalaicus

Geranium himalayense

Incarvillea himalayensis

himanto- strap-shaped

hinnuleus fawn in color

hippocastanus horse chestnut

Aesculus hippocastanum

hippocrepis like a horseshoe

hircinus like a goat; smelling goaty

CULTIVAR NAMES
Strange but True
H

ALLIUM VINEALE 'HAIR'

PELARGONIUM 'HAPPY THOUGHT'

MALUS DOMESTICA (APPLE) 'HARRY MASTER'S JERSEY'

POLEMONIUM BOREALE 'HEAVENLY HABIT'

PANICUM VIRGATUM 'HEAVY METAL'

RANUNCULUS ACRIS 'HEDGEHOG'

IRIS 'HELLO DARKNESS'

RHODODENDRON ABERCONWAYI 'HIS LORDSHIP'

FUCHSIA 'HOBO'

GERANIUM PRATENSE 'HOCUS POCUS'

PHLOX STOLONIFERA 'HOME FIRES'

IRIS 'HONKY TONK BLUES'

RHODODENDRON 'HOPPY'

ORIGANUM 'HOT AND SPICY'

CAMPANULA PUNCTATA 'HOT LIPS'

HEMEROCALLIS 'HOUDINI'

EUPHORBIA CHARACIAS SUBSP. *CHARACIAS* 'HUMPTY DUMPTY'

PINUS MUGO 'HUMPY'

PELARGONIUM 'HURDY-GURDY'

COMMON DESCRIPTIVE TERMS

hirsutus, hirtus hairy

Kniphofia hirsuta

Lotus hirsutus

Penstemon hirsutus

Polygonatum hirtum

Primula hirsuta

Rudbeckia hirta

CULTIVAR NAMES
Foreign Expressions
H

HEIDEBRAUT (*German*)
HEATHLAND BRIDE
(*MOLINIA CAERULEA* SUBSP. *CAERULEA* 'HEIDEBRAUT')

HERBSTFEUER (*German*)
AUTUMN FIRE
(*COTONEASTER SALICIFOLIUS* 'HERBSTFEUER')

HERBSTFREUDE (*German*)
AUTUMN JOY
(*SEDUM* 'HERBSTFREUDE')

HERBSTSCHNEE (*German*)
AUTUMN SNOW
(*ASTER NOVAE-ANGLIAE* 'HERBSTSCHNEE')

HERBSTSONNE (*German*)
AUTUMN SUN
(*RUDBECKIA LACINIATA* 'HERBSTSONNE')

HERBSTZAUBER (*German*)
AUTUMN MAGIC
(*PENNISETUM ALOPECUROIDES* 'HERBSTZAUBER')

HIGASAYAMA (*Japanese*)
PARASOL MOUNTAIN
(*ACER PALMATUM* 'HIGASAYAMA')

HIMMELBLAU (*German*)
SKY BLUE
(*PINUS STROBUS* 'HIMMELBLAU')

hispanicus Spanish
Angelica hispanica
Genista hispanica
Hyacinthoides hispanica
Platanus × *hispanica*
Quercus × *hispanica*
Sedum hispanicum

hispidus bristly
Carex hispida
Drosanthemum hispidum
Elymus hispidus
Heuchera hispida
Pterostyrax hispida
Robinia hispida

hollandicus from Holland
   Allium hollandicum
holo- entirely, completely, wholly
   (see below)
holocarpus with entire (i.e.
   undivided) fruits
holochrysus completely golden
   Phyllostachys bambusoides
   'Holochrysa'
hololeucus completely white
holophyllus with entire (i.e.
   undivided) leaves
   Abies holophylla
homo- like; of the same kind
   (see below)
homocarpus with fruit of only
   one kind

hirtellus rather hairy
hirtiflorus with hairy flowers
hirtipes with a hairy foot or stalk
   Rhododendron hirtipes

homolepis with uniform scales
  Abies homolepis
homomallus, homotropus all turned in the same direction
hondoensis from Hondo, Japan
hookeri, hookerianus (see panel above)
horizontalis horizontal, spreading horizontally
  Cotoneaster horizontalis
hormophorus with a necklace
horricomis bristly, shaggy
horridulus standing up, projecting
  Meconopsis horridula
horridus standing on end; prickly
  Eryngium horridum
hortensis of gardens, raised in a garden
  Atriplex hortensis
hortorum of gardens
hortulanorum of gardeners

hugonis named after Father Hugh (1851–1928), an Irish missionary who spent many years in China
  Rosa xanthina f. *hugonis*
humectus moist, damp
humifusus spread on the ground
  Sedum humifusum

COMMON DESCRIPTIVE TERMS
humilis dwarf, low-growing
Chamaerops humilis
Jasminum humile
Penstemon humilis
Phyllostachys humilis
Pleioblastus humilis
Polygonatum humile

---

humulifolius with leaves like *Humulus* (hop)
hungaricus Hungarian
  Acanthus hungaricus

Hackberry *Celtis*

Hair grass *Deschampsia*

Handkerchief tree *Davidia involucrata*

Hard fern *Blechnum spicant*

Hardheads *Centaurea nigra*

Hardy plumbago *Ceratostigma*

Hare's tail *Lagurus ovatus*

Harebell *Campanula rotundifolia*

Harry Lauder's walking stick *Corylus avellana* 'Contorta'

Hart's tongue fern *Asplenium scolopendrium*

Hattie's pincushion *Astrantia*

Hawksbeard *Crepis*

Hawkweed *Hieracium; Pilosella*

Hawthorn *Crataegus*

Hazel *Corylus avellana*

Heartsease *Viola tricolor*

Heath *Erica; Daboecia*

Heather *Calluna*

Hedgehog holly *Ilex aquifolium* 'Ferox'

Heliotrope *Heliotropium arborescens*

Hellebore *Helleborus*

Hemlock *Tsuga; Conium maculatum*

Hemp agrimony *Eupatorium cannabinum*

Hen-and-chickens houseleek *Jovibarba sobolifera*

Herb Robert *Geranium robertianum*

(Herbs, see page 47)

Hiba *Thujopsis dolabrata*

Hickory *Carya*

Highclere holly *Ilex × altaclerensis*

Himalayan birch *Betula utilis*

Himalayan blue poppy *Meconopsis betonicifolia*

Himalayan pine *Pinus wallichiana*

Hinoki cypress *Chamaecyparis obtusa*

Hogweed *Heracleum sphondylium*

Holly *Ilex*

Hollyhock *Alcea rosea*

Holm oak *Quercus ilex*

Honesty *Lunaria annua*

Honey bush *Melianthus major*

Honey locust *Gleditsia triacanthos*

Honeysuckle *Lonicera*

Hop *Humulus lupulus*

Hop hornbeam *Ostrya carpinifolia*

Hornbeam *Carpinus betulus*

Horned-poppy *Glaucium*

Horse chestnut *Aesculus hippocastanum*

Horsetail *Equisetum*

Hot water plant *Achimenes*

Hottentot fig *Carpobrotus edulis*

Hound's tongue *Cynoglossum*

Houseleek *Sempervivum*

Huckleberry *Gaylussacia*

HOLLYHOCK

hupehensis from Hubei province
   in China
Anemone hupehensis
Malus hupehensis
Sorbus hupehensis

hyacinthinus deep purplish-blue, like
   Hyacinthus
hyacinthoides like *Hyacinthus*
hyalinus colorless, transparent
hybernus Irish
   Euphorbia hyberna

COMMON DESCRIPTIVE TERMS

hybridus hybrid; of mixed parentage
Anemone × *hybrida*
Arctotis × *hybrida*
Cistus × *hybridus*
Helleborus × *hybridus*
Polygonatum × *hybridum*
Rheum × *hybridum* (rhubarb)

hydrangeoides like *Hydrangea*
hydro- water-
hydrophilus water-loving
hyemalis of winter
   Eranthis hyemalis
hygro- damp
hylaeus of woods
hymen- membrane
hymenodes like a membrane
hymenorrhizus with membranous
   roots

GENUS NAMES
H

Hakonechloa named for Mount
   Hakone, in Japan
Hebe named for the Greek goddess
   of youth
Hedychium from Greek *hedys*, sweet,
   and *chion*, snow
Helianthus from Greek *helios,* sun,
   and *anthos*, flower
Hemerocallis from Greek *hemera*, day,
   and *kallos*, beauty
Hepatica from Greek *hepar*, liver
Hesperis from Greek *hespera*, evening
Heuchera named for Johann von
   Heucher (1677–1747), a German
   professor
Hosta named for Nicolaus Host
   (1761–1834), Austrian doctor

hymenosepalus with membranous
   sepals
hyper- beyond, above
hyperboreus from the far north
hypericoides like *Hypericum*
hypnoides like moss
hypo- beneath (see below)
hypogaeus growing underground
hypoglaucus glaucous beneath
hypoleucus white beneath
hyrcanus from Hyrcania, an old
   region near the Caspian Sea
hyssopifolius with leaves like the herb
   Hyssopus officinalis (hyssop)
hystrix porcupine; spiny
   Picea abies 'Hystrix'

I

ibericus from the Iberian peninsula
  Geranium ibericum
icterinus jaundice-yellow
  Salvia officinalis 'Icterina'
idahoensis from Idaho
  Sisyrinchium idahoense

CULTIVAR NAMES
Personal Names
H, I

Clematis viticella 'Hanna'
Hamamelis × intermedia 'Harry'
Lavandula 'Hazel'
Geranium cinereum 'Heather'
Achillea 'Heidi'
Primula auricula 'Helen'
Eremurus 'Helena'
Hibiscus syriacus 'Helene'
Itea virginica 'Henry's Garnet'
Vaccinium corymbosum 'Herbert'
Prunus domestica (plum) 'Herman'
Fuchsia 'Holly's Beauty'
Sedum telephium 'Hester'
Iris 'Ida'
Pelargonium 'Dark Red Irene'
Campanula carpatica 'Isabel'
Erica carnea 'Isabell'
Rosa Isabella ('Poulisab')
Geranium 'Ivan'

---

ida-maia named for Ida May Burke, a 19th-century plant hunter in California
igneus fiery red
  Cuphea ignea
ikariae from the Greek island, Ikaria
  Galanthus ikariae
ilicifolius with leaves like *Ilex* (holly)
  Itea ilicifolia
illinoinensis from Illinois
  Carya illinoinensis (pecan)
illustris brilliant, clear, lit up
  Amsonia illustris
illyricus from Illyria (the Adriatic coast of Croatia and Dalmatia)
  Gladiolus illyricus
imbricatus overlapping regularly, like tiles
  Fabiana imbricata
impeditus hindered, obstructed
  Rhododendron impeditum

COMMON DESCRIPTIVE TERMS
imperialis imperial, showy
Alnus glutinosa 'Imperialis'
Dahlia imperialis
Fritillaria imperialis

---

implexus entangled, interwoven
  Lonicera implexa
impressus impressed, sunken
  Ceanothus impressus
inapertus closed
  Agapanthus inapertus

SHAPE

acerosus needle-shaped
acetabulosus cup-shaped, concave
acicularis like a pin or needle
aciformis needle-shaped
acuminatus tapering to a point
alveolatus hollowed out, channeled
annularis ring-shaped
apiculatus with a short pointed end
applanatus flattened
arcuatus bent or curved like a bow
attenuatus tapering to a point
bucinatus like a curved horn
calathinus cup-shaped; like a basket
calceiformis, calceolatus shaped like a
  little shoe or slipper
campanulatus bell-shaped
canaliculatus with a channel, like a pipe
cassideus shaped like a helmet
catilliformis shaped like a saucer
caudiformis shaped like a tail
clathratus like a lattice or trellis
clavatus, claviformis club-shaped
conicus cone-shaped
convolutus rolled up lengthways
cordatus, cordiformis heart-shaped
corniculatus with little horns
cornutus horned
cristatus crested
cruciatus, cruciformis cross-shaped
cucullatus hooded
curvulus slightly curved
cuspidatus with a sharp point
cyathiformis cup-shaped
cylindricus, cylindraceus cylindrical
deltoides triangular
depressus flattened
ellipticus elliptic
ensatus, ensiformis sword-shaped

falcatus falcate, curved like a sickle
flabellatus fan-shaped
flexuosus, fractiflexus zigzag
fornicatus arched
fungiformis mushroom-shaped
fusiformis shaped like a spindle
gibbosus hunchbacked
lanceolatus lanceolate, spear-shaped
lunulatus like a crescent moon
mucronatus pointed
nidiformis nest-shaped
nummularius like a coin
obconicus like an inverted cone
orbiculatus, orbicularis disc-shaped
ovalis oval, broadly elliptic
ovatus ovate, egg-shaped
peltatus like a *pelta*, a small, half-moon-
  shaped shield
planus flat
platy- broad, flat
poculiformis cup-shaped
prismaticus prism-shaped
pulvinaris, pulvinatus like a cushion
pungens ending in a hard sharp point
pyramidalis pyramid-shaped
reniformis kidney-shaped
rhombeus, rhombicus, rhombiformis
  rhomboidal, diamond-shaped
rotatus shaped like a wheel
saccatus like a bag; with sacs
sagittalis, sagittatus arrow-shaped
sphaerocephalus with globose heads
spicatus spicate, bearing a spike
stellatus stellate, star-shaped
strepto- twisted
tabularis, tabuliformis flat like a board
uncinatus hooked, with a hooked end
undulatus, undatus wavy

WHAT'S IN A NAME?

COLOR: BROWN

badius reddish brown
brunneus dark, dull brown
castaneus chestnut
cervinus fawn
cinnamomeus cinnamon brown
cupreus coppery
ferrugineus; ferruginosus rusty; light reddish brown
fuligineus; fuliginosus dark brown, sooty
fuscus dark; blackish brown
glandulaceus tawny brown
hepaticus liver-colored
luridus dirty brown
testaceus terra-cotta-colored
umbrinus umber

COMMON DESCRIPTIVE TERMS

incanus gray, hoary
Alnus incana
Crepis incana
Geranium incanum
Marrubium incanum
Matthiola incana
Scutellaria incana

---

incarnatus flesh-colored
Passiflora incarnata
incisus deeply cut
Prunus incisa
incompletus incomplete
Paris incompleta
incomptus unadorned
Pennisetum incomptum

incurvus curved inwards
Campanula incurva

COMMON DESCRIPTIVE TERMS

indicus Indian (often used more generally to mean from the Far East)
Aesculus indica
Canna indica
Duchesnea indica
Ipomoea indica
Plumbago indica

---

indivisus undivided
Cordyline indivisa
inermis unarmed (i.e. without prickles)
Bromus inermis 'Skinner's Gold'
inflatus inflated, blown up, swollen
Cistus inflatus
inflexus bent inwards
Juncus inflexus
innominatus unnamed
Iris innominata
inodorus scentless
Hypericum × *inodorum*

INCISUS

INTEGER

insignis distinguished
  Rhododendron insigne
insititius grafted
insuetus unusual
insularis of islands, insular
  Fraxinus insularis var. *henryana*
intaminatus undefiled, pure
  Cyclamen intaminatum
integer entire, undivided
  Salix integra
integerrimus completely entire
  Diascia integerrima

CULTIVAR NAMES
Special Occasions

FUCHSIA 'BICENTENNIAL'
FUCHSIA 'BRITISH JUBILEE'
IRIS 'CARNIVAL TIME'
FUCHSIA 'CELEBRATION'
HOSTA 'CELEBRATION'
CEANOTHUS 'CENTENNIAL'
HEMEROCALLIS 'CHILDREN'S FESTIVAL'
IRIS SIBIRICA 'CORONATION ANTHEM'
RHODODENDRON 'CORONATION DAY'
ACHILLEA 'CORONATION GOLD'
DIANTHUS 'CORONATION RUBY'
ROSA 'DIAMOND JUBILEE'
FUCHSIA 'EASTER BONNET'
NARCISSUS 'EASTER BONNET'
PRIMULA 'EASTER BONNET'
LIQUIDAMBAR STYRACIFLUA 'FESTIVAL'
ERYSIMUM 'GOLDEN JUBILEE'
CAMELLIA JAPONICA 'GRAND PRIX'
HELIANTHEMUM 'JUBILEE'

ROSA 'JUBILEE CELEBRATION'
GERANIUM SANGUINEUM 'JUBILEE PINK'
RHODODENDRON 'MARDI GRAS'
RHODODENDRON 'MAY DAY'
FUCHSIA 'MILLENNIUM'
RHODODENDRON 'MOTHER'S DAY'
PHYSOSTEGIA VIRGINIANA 'OLYMPIC GOLD'
PAPAVER ORIENTALE 'ROYAL WEDDING'
NARCISSUS 'SAINT PATRICK'S DAY'
ROSA 'SCOTTISH CELEBRATION'
OZOTHAMNUS ROSMARINIFOLIUS 'SILVER JUBILEE'
ROSA 'SILVER JUBILEE'
CLEMATIS 'SPECIAL OCCASION'
RHODODENDRON 'WASHINGTON STATE CENTENNIAL'
GYPSOPHILA FASTIGIATA 'WHITE FESTIVAL'

integrifolius with undivided leaves
Calceolaria integrifolia
Clematis integrifolia
Cotoneaster integrifolius
Hydrangea integrifolia
Meconopsis integrifolia

interjectus placed between,
  intermediate
  Polypodium interjectum

GENUS NAMES
I, J, K

Impatiens in Latin, impatient
Incarvillea named for Pierre
  d'Incarville (1706–1757), French
  missionary and botanist
Iris Roman goddess of the rainbow
Jovibarba from medieval Latin
  meaning beard of Jupiter
Kalmia named for Pehr Kalm (1715–
  1779), a Finn who traveled in North
  America and studied with Linnaeus
Kerria named for William Kerr
  (d. 1814), Scottish horticulturist at
  Kew Gardens, London, and plant
  collector in China
Knautia named for Christoph Knaut
  (1638–1694), German botanist
Kniphofia named for Johann Kniphof
  (1704–1763), German professor
  and botanical author
Kolkwitzia named for Richard
  Kolkwitz (1873–1956), German
  botanist

intermedius intermediate (in form,
  color etc.; usually applied to a
  hybrid that is intermediate between
  its parents)
Eucryphia × *intermedia*
Forsythia × *intermedia*
Hamamelis × *intermedia*
Lavandula × *intermedia*

interruptus scattered, not continuous
  Salvia interrupta
intricatus tangled
  Clematis intricata

involucratus having an involucre
  (a circle of bracts around the
  flowers)
Astrantia major subsp. *involucrata*
Cyperus involucratus
Davidia involucrata
Fritillaria involucrata
Hydrangea involucrata
Lonicera involucrata
Salvia involucrata

iridescens iridescent
  Phyllostachys iridescens
iridiflorus with flowers like *Iris*
  Canna iridiflora
irroratus sprinkled with dew; finely
  spotted
  Salix irrorata

CULTIVAR NAMES
Foreign Expressions
I, J, K

INDIANERSOMMER (*German*)
INDIAN SUMMER
(*HELENIUM* 'INDIANERSOMMER')

JULIGLUT (*German*) JULY GLOW
(*PHLOX PANICULATA* 'JULIGLUT')

KAGIRI-NISHIKI (*Japanese*)
GLORIOUS COLOR
(*ACER PALMATUM* 'KAGIRI-NISHIKI')

KIKU-SHIDARE-ZAKURA (*Japanese*)
CHRYSANTHEMUM WEEPING CHERRY
(*PRUNUS* 'KIKU-SHIDARE-ZAKURA')

KISSEN (*German*) CUSHION
(*PINUS MUGO* 'KISSEN')

KLEINE LIEBLING (*German*)
LITTLE DARLING
(*PELARGONIUM* 'KLEINE LIEBLING')

KLEINE SILBERSPINNE (*German*)
LITTLE SILVER SPIDER
(*MISCANTHUS SINENSIS* 'KLEINE
SILBERSPINNE')

KLEINE TÄNZERIN (*German*)
LITTLE DANCER
(*PAPAVER ORIENTALE* 'KLEINE
TÄNZERIN')

KLEINER FUCHS (*German*)
LITTLE FOX
(*HELENIUM* 'KLEINER FUCHS')

KOJO-NO-MAI (*Japanese*)
DANCE IN THE ANCIENT CASTLE
(*PRUNUS INCISA* 'KOJO-NO-MAI')

KÖNIGIN (*German*) QUEEN
(E.G. *ECHINACEA PURPUREA*
'AUGUSTKÖNIGIN')

KÖNIGSKIND (*German*) KING'S CHILD
(*CLEMATIS* 'KÖNIGSKIND')

KONINGIN (*Dutch*) QUEEN
(*TRITELEIA LAXA* 'KONINGIN FABIOLA')

KRASAVITSA MOSKVY (*Russian*)
BEAUTY OF MOSCOW
(*SYRINGA VULGARIS* 'KRASAVITSA
MOSKVY')

KUMO-NO-OBI (*Japanese*)
BEAR'S BELT
(*IRIS ENSATA* 'KUMO-NO-OBI')

KUPFERTEPPICH (*German*)
COPPER CARPET
(*ACAENA MICROPHYLLA*
'KUPFERTEPPICH')

---

isabellinus tawny yellow
 Eremurus × *isabellinus*
isophyllus with equal leaves
 Campanula isophylla
italicus (see panel, right)
itinerans travelling
ixioides like *Ixia*

COMMON DESCRIPTIVE TERMS
italicus Italian
Arum italicum
Gladiolus italicus
Helichrysum italicum
Phlomis italica
Populus nigra 'Italica'

J

jackmanii named for George Jackman (1801–1869) and his son George (1837–1887), pioneering British clematis breeders at their nursery in Woking, Surrey, UK
Clematis 'Jackmanii'

COMMON DESCRIPTIVE TERMS
jacquemontii, jacquemontianus named for the French naturalist Victor Jacquemont (1801–1832)
Arisaema jacquemontii
Betula utilis var. *jacquemontii*
Euphorbia jacquemontii
Parrotiopsis jacquemontiana

CULTIVAR NAMES
World of Sport

NARCISSUS 'ARKLE'
LUPINUS ARBOREUS 'ASTON VILLA'
PRIMULA AURICULA 'DAVID BECKHAM'
FUCHSIA 'SIR MATT BUSBY'
ROSA 'BOBBY CHARLTON'
FUCHSIA 'KENNY DALGLISH'
PRIMULA AURICULA 'GAZZA'
ROSA 'JIMMY GREAVES'
DAHLIA 'SIR ALF RAMSEY'
PRIMULA AURICULA 'RED RUM'
CROCUS CHRYSANTHUS 'ARD SCHENK'
FUCHSIA 'TORVILL AND DEAN'

---

jalapa from Jalapa in Mexico
Mirabilis jalapa

COMMON DESCRIPTIVE TERMS
japonicus Japanese
Acer japonicum
Aucuba japonica
Camellia japonica
Chaenomeles japonica
Cryptomeria japonica
Euonymus japonicus
Fatsia japonica
Kerria japonica
Pieris japonica
Primula japonica
Skimmia japonica
Spiraea japonica

---

jasminoides like *Jasminum* (jasmine)
Trachelospermum jasminoides
javanicus from Java
Oenanthe javanica
jeffreyi named for the Scottish plant collector John Jeffrey (1826–1854)
Pinus jeffreyi
jonquilla like *Juncus* (rush)
Narcissus jonquilla
jouinianus named for Emile Jouin, nursery manager at Simon-Louis Frères in Metz, France, where the plant was raised
Clematis × *jouiniana*
jubatus with a mane or crest
Hordeum jubatum

CULTIVAR NAMES
Personal Names
J

Agapanthus 'Jack's Blue'

Verbascum 'Jackie'

Erysimum 'Jacob's Jacket'

Diascia 'Jacqueline's Joy'

Clematis 'Jacqui'

Hedera helix 'Jake'

Plectranthus fruticosus 'James'

Magnolia 'Jane'

Hosta 'Janet'

Fuchsia 'Janice Ann'

Erica carnea 'Jean'

Erythronium 'Jeannine'

Schizostylis coccinea 'Jennifer'

Narcissus 'Jenny'

Fuchsia 'Jess'

Crocosmia × *crocosmiiflora* 'Jessie'

Papaver orientale 'Big Jim'

Iris 'Broadleigh Joan'

Erythronium 'Joanna'

Eremurus 'Joanne'

Rosa 'Jocelyn'

Dianthus 'Little Jock'

Clematis × *cartmannii* 'Joe'

Primula auricula 'Joel'

Primula 'Johanna'

Iris 'John'

Primula 'Jo-Jo'

Clematis Josephine ('Evijohill')

Geranium 'Joy'

Iris 'Joyce'

Magnolia 'Judy'

Rosa 'Julia's Rose'

Viola 'Julian'

Geranium nodosum 'Julie's Velvet'

Rosa Sweet Juliet ('Ausleap')

Cotoneaster × *suecicus* 'Juliette'

Fuchsia 'Justin's Pride'

---

jucundus pleasant, delightful
  Osteospermum jucundum

juddii named for William Judd
  (1888–1946), propagator at the
  Arnold Arboretum, Massachusetts
  Viburnum × *juddii*

junceus like *Juncus* (rush)
  Spartium junceum

juncifolius with rushlike leaves

juniperifolius with leaves like
  Juniperus (juniper)
  Armeria juniperifolia

juniperinus like juniper
  Grevillea juniperina

Camellia japonica

K

kaempferi named for a German traveler and botanical author, Engelbert Kaempfer (1651–1716)
Larix kaempferi

kaki persimmon (Japanese)
Diospyros kaki

kalmiiflorus with flowers like *Kalmia*
Deutzia kalmiiflora

CULTIVAR NAMES
Personal Names
K

HELIANTHEMUM 'KAREN'S SILVER'
PAPAVER ORIENTALE 'KARINE'
PHLOX PANICULATA 'KATARINA'
GERANIUM 'KATE'
LAVANDULA ANGUSTIFOLIA 'MISS KATHERINE'
ROSA 'KATHLEEN'
CAMPANULA CARPATICA 'KATHY'
CAMELLIA JAPONICA 'KATIE'
FUCHSIA 'KATRINA'
DAHLIA 'KEITH'S CHOICE'
CAMELLIA JAPONICA 'KENNY'
CALLUNA VULGARIS 'KERSTIN'
IRIS 'KEVIN'S THEME'
ECHINACEA 'KIM'S KNEE HIGH'
CAMELLIA JAPONICA 'KIMBERLEY'
LIQUIDAMBAR STYRACIFLUA 'KIRSTEN'
NARCISSUS 'KITTY'
ASTER 'KYLIE'

---

kamtschaticus from Kamchatka
Sedum kamtschaticum

kansuensis from Gansu province in north-western China
Malus kansuensis

karataviensis, karatavicus from the Karatau Mountains of Kazakhstan
Allium karataviense
Thymus karatavicus

karvinskianus named for Wilhelm Karwinsky von Karwin, a 19th-century German explorer
Erigeron karvinskianus

kashmirianus, kashmiriensis from Kashmir
Iris kashmiriana

kaufmannianus named for General von Kaufmann, a governor in Kazakhstan
Tulipa kaufmanniana

kermesinus carmine, purplish red
Clematis 'Kermesina'

kerneri, kernerianus named for Johann von Kerner (1755–1830), a German botanist; or for Anton Kerner von Marilaun (1831–1898), an Austrian botanist and author

---

COMMON DESCRIPTIVE TERMS
kewensis named for the Royal Botanic Gardens at Kew, London
Buddleia colvilei 'Kewensis'
Cytisus × *kewensis*
Sorbus × *kewensis*

GLOBE ARTICHOKE

Artichoke, globe *Cynara scolymus* Scolymus Group

Artichoke, Jerusalem (sunchoke, girasole) *Helianthus tuberosus*

Asparagus *Asparagus officinalis*

Aubergine *Solanum melongena*

Beans, lima *Phaseolus limensis*

Beans, scarlet runner *Phaseolus coccineus*

Beans, snap *Phaseolus vulgaris*

Beet *Beta vulgaris*

Bell pepper *Capsicum annuum*

Broccoli *Brassica oleracea* Italica Group

Brussels sprouts *Brassica oleracea* Gemmifera Group

Cabbage *Brassica oleracea* Capitata Group

Carrot *Daucus carota* subsp. *sativa*

Cauliflower *Brassica oleracea* Botrytis Group

Celeriac *Apium graveolens* var. *rapaceum*

Celery *Apium graveolens* var. *dulce*

Chicory *Cichorium intybus*

Chili (cayenne) pepper *Capsicum annuum*

Collard greens *Brassica oleracea* Acephala Group

Corn *Zea mays*

Cucumber *Cucumis sativus*

Eggplant Solanum melongena

Endive *Cichorium endivia*

Fennel, Florence (finnochio) *Foeniculum vulgare* var. *azoricum*

Garlic *Allium sativum*

Japanese bunching onion *Allium fistulosum*

Kohlrabi *Brassica oleracea* Gongylodes Group

Leek *Allium ampeloprasum* var. *porrum*

Lettuce *Lactuca sativa*

Okra *Abelmoschus esculentus*

Onion *Allium cepa*

Parsnip *Pastinacea sativa*

Peas *Pisum sativum*

Potato *Solanum tuberosum*

Radish *Raphanus sativus*

Rutabaga *Brassica napus* Napobrassica Group

Salsify (oyster plant) *Tragopogon porrifolium*

Shallot *Allium cepa* Aggregatum Group

Spinach *Spinacia oleracea*

Squash *Cucurbita pepo; Cucurbita maxima; Cucurbita moschata*

Sweet potato *Ipomoea batatas* .

Swiss chard *Beta vulgaris* subsp. *cicla*

Tomato *Lycopersicon esculentum*

Turnip *Brassica rapa* Rapifera Group

Watercress *Nasturtium officinalis*

Yam *Dioscorea batatus*

Zucchini *Cucurbita pepo*

Ice plant *Sedum spectabile*
Iceland poppy *Papaver nudicaule*
Incense cedar *Calocedrus decurrens*
Indian bean *Lablab purpureus*
Indian bean tree *Catalpa bignonoides*
Indian horse chestnut *Aesculus indica*
Indian paint-brush *Castilleja*
Indian shot *Canna*
Irish yew *Taxus baccata* 'Fastigiata'
Ironbark *Eucalyptus*
Ironwood *Ostrya virginiana*
Italian alder *Alnus cordata*
Italian cypress *Cupressus sempervirens*
Ivy *Hedera*
Jack-go-to-bed-at-noon *Tragopogon pratensis*
Jacob's ladder *Polemonium caeruleum*
Jacob's rod *Asphodeline lutea*
Jade plant *Crassula ovata*
Japanese anemone *Anemone* × *hybrida*; *Anemone hupehensis*
Japanese angelica tree *Aralia elata*
Japanese cedar *Cryptomeria japonica*
Japanese cherries *Prunus* (many named forms)
Japanese crab *Malus floribunda*
Japanese maples *Acer palmatum*
Japanese quince, Japonica *Chaenomeles*
Japanese snowbell *Styrax japonica*
Japanese strawberry tree *Cornus kousa*
Jasmine, Jessamine *Jasminum*
Jerusalem sage *Phlomis fruticosa*
Joe Pye weed *Eupatorium purpureum*
Jonquil *Narcissus jonquilla*
Joshua tree *Yucca brevifolia*
Judas tree *Cercis siliquastrum*
June berry *Amelanchier*
Juniper *Juniperus*

Kaffir lily *Schizostylis*
Kansas gayfeather *Liatris*
Kashmir cypress *Cupressus cashmeriana*
Katsura tree *Cercidiphyllum japonicum*
Keaki *Zelkova serrata*
Kentucky coffee tree *Gymnocladus dioica*
Kerosene bush *Ozothamnus ledifolius*
Kilmarnock willow *Salix caprea* 'Kilmarnock'
Kingcup *Caltha palustris*
Knapweed *Centaurea*
Knotweed *Persicaria*
Korean fir *Abies koreana*
Kowhai *Sophora microphylla*
Kumquat *Fortunella*

KINGCUP

kishtvariensis named for a valley
in Kashmir
Geranium kishtvariense
kitaibelii named for a Hungarian
botanist, Paul Kitaibel (1757–
1817)
Cardamine kitaibelii
kiusianus from Kyushu, Japan
Veronica kiusiana
koehneanus named for Bernhard
Koehne (1848–1918), a German
botanist
Sorbus koehneana
kokanicus from Khokand, Turkestan
Morina kokanica
komarovii named for Vladimir
Komarov (1869–1945), a Russian
botanist and explorer in Siberia
and Korea
Syringa komarovii

COMMON DESCRIPTIVE TERMS
koreanus, koraiensis from Korea
Abies koreana
Clematis koreana
Geranium koraiense
Geranium koreanum
Thuja koraiensis

---

kotschyanus, kotschyi named for
Theodore Kotschy (1813–1866),
an Austrian botanist and plant
collector
Erysimum kotschyanum kouytchensis

from Guizhou province
in China
Hypericum kouytchense
kurdicus from Kurdistan
Tulipa kurdica

L

laceratus lacerated, torn
  Asplenium scolopendrium Laceratum
  Group

COMMON DESCRIPTIVE TERMS
laciniatus, laciniosus cut into
  narrow divisions, jagged
  Alnus glutinosa 'Laciniata'
  Betula pendula 'Laciniata'
  Sambucus nigra f. *laciniata*
  Rudbeckia laciniata

---

lacteus milky
  Cotoneaster lacteus
lactiflorus with milky-colored flowers
  Campanula lactiflora
lacustris of lakes
  Iris lacustris
ladakhianus from Ladakh in
  northern India
  Clematis ladakhiana

LACINIATUS

ladanifer bearing a medicinal resin
  called ladanum
  Cistus ladanifer
laetiflorus with bright flowers
  Helianthus × *laetiflorus*
laetus bright
  Pseudopanax laetus

COMMON DESCRIPTIVE TERMS
laevigatus smooth
Crataegus laevigata
Crocus laevigatus
Hosta laevigata
Origanum laevigatum

---

laevis soft
Amelanchier laevis
Aster laevis
Escallonia laevis
Moluccella laevis

---

lagocephalus with a head like a hare
  Artemisia lagocephalus
lamarckii named for the French
  naturalist Chevalier Jean-Baptiste
  de Monet Lamarck (1744–1829)
  Amelanchier lamarckii

COMMON DESCRIPTIVE TERMS
lanatus woolly
Digitalis lanata
Lavandula lanata
Phlomis lanata
Salix lanata

---

lancasteri named for the eminent
British plantsman, broadcaster,
lecturer and botanical author
Roy Lancaster
Hypericum lancasteri

COMMON DESCRIPTIVE TERMS

lanceolatus lanceolate, spear-shaped
Azara lanceolata
Codonopsis lanceolata
Coreopsis lanceolata
Drimys lanceolata
Hoya lanceolata
Ornithogalum lanceolatum
Plantago lanceolata

---

lancifolius lance-leaved
    Hosta lancifolia
langsdorffii named for Georg
    Langsdorf (1774–1852), a German
    physician and botanist
    Nicotiana langsdorffii
laniger woolly
    Leptospermum lanigerum
lanuginosus woolly
    Androsace lanuginosa
lappa a bur
    Arctium lappa
laricifolius with leaves like larch
    Minuartia laricifolia
lasiandrus with woolly stamens
    Oxalis lasiandrus
lasianthus with woolly flowers
    Halimium lasianthum

CULTIVAR NAMES
Foreign Expressions
L

LA SÉDUISANTE (*French*)
TEMPTRESS
(*HEBE* 'LA SÉDUISANTE')

LACHSKÖNIGIN (*German*)
SALMON QUEEN
(*ASTILBE* 'LACHSKÖNIGIN')

LACHSSCHÖNHEIT (*German*)
SALMON BEAUTY
(*ACHILLEA* 'LACHSSCHÖNHEIT')

LANDHOCHZEIT (*German*)
COUNTRY WEDDING
(*PHLOX PANICULATA*
'LANDHOCHZEIT')

LANG TIDLIG ... (*Danish*)
EARLY LONG ...
(*CORYLUS* 'LANG TIDLIG
ZELLER')

LAVENDELWOLKE (*German*)
LAVENDER CLOUD
(*PHLOX PANICULATA*
'LAVENDELWOLKE')

LE PHARE (*French*) LIGHTHOUSE
(*PENSTEMON* 'LE PHARE')

LEUCHTFEUER (*German*)
FIRELIGHT
(*PAPAVER ORIENTALE* 'LEUCHTFEUER')

LEUCHTFUNK (*German*) (USUALLY
TRANSLATED AS) FLASHING LIGHT
(*DIANTHUS DELTOIDES*
'LEUCHTFUNK')

LEUCHTKÄFER (*German*)
FIREFLY (*HEUCHERA*
'LEUCHTKÄFER')

CULTIVAR NAMES
Personal Names
L

CLEMATIS 'LAURA'

PAPAVER ORIENTALE 'LAUREN'S LILAC'

GALANTHUS 'LAVINIA'

FUCHSIA 'LENA'

HIBISCUS SYRIACUS 'LENNY'

LONICERA SEMPERVIRENS 'LEO'

FUCHSIA 'LEONORA'

CAMPANULA PORTENSCHLAGIANA 'LIESELOTTE'

GAULTHERIA MUCRONATA 'LILIAN'

RHODODENDRON 'LINDA'

PRIMULA AURICULA 'LISA'S SMILE'

FUCHSIA 'LIZ'

FUCHSIA LIZA ('GOETZLIZA')

PHLOX PANICULATA 'LIZZY'

RHODODENDRON 'LORNA'

LAVANDULA ANGUSTIFOLIA LITTLE LOTTIE ('CLARMO')

HOSTA 'LOUISA'

HEBE 'LOUISE'

CLEMATIS 'LUCIE'

PELARGONIUM 'LUCILLA'

ALSTROEMERIA 'LUCINDA'

PELARGONIUM 'LUCY'

PENSTEMON 'LYNETTE'

COMMON DESCRIPTIVE TERMS
lasiocarpus with woolly fruits

Abies lasiocarpa

Campanula lasiocarpa

Musa lasiocarpa

Populus lasiocarpa

---

lateriflorus with flowers at the side
  Aster lateriflorus
lateritius brick red
  Malvastrum lateritium

COMMON DESCRIPTIVE TERMS
latifolius broad-leaved

Campanula latifolia

Kalmia latifolia

Lavandula latifolia

Lathyrus latifolius

Limonium latifolium

Muscari latifolium

Phillyrea latifolia

---

latilobus with wide lobes
  Campanula latiloba
latisepalus with broad sepals
  Epimedium latisepalum
laureola a laurel crown or garland
  Daphne laureola
laurifolius with leaves like *Laurus* (bay)
  Cistus laurifolius
laurocerasus cherry laurel – from *laurus* (laurel) and *cerasus* (cherry)
  Prunus laurocerasus
lavalleei named for Pierre Lavalle (1836–1884), a French botanist
  Crataegus × *lavalleei*
lavandulifolius with leaves like *Lavandula* (lavender)
  Salvia lavandulifolia

lawsonianus named for the Scottish
  botanical author and nurseryman
  Charles Lawson (1794–1873)
  Chamaecyparis lawsoniana

---

laxiflorus loose-flowered
  Campanula laxiflora
  Lathyrus laxiflorus
  Lobelia laxiflora

---

laxifolius loose-leaved
  Athrotaxis laxifolia
laxus loose, open
  Triteleia laxa 'Koningin Fabiola'
lazicus from Lazistan, on the
  Black Sea
  Iris lazica
ledifolius with leaves like the
  aromatic evergreen shrub *Ledum*
  Ozothamnus ledifolius

WHAT'S IN A NAME?

ANIMAL CONNECTIONS

anguilliformis eel-shaped
anguinus snakelike
anserinus relating to geese
apianus of bees
aquilinus eagle-like
arachnoides like a spider or its web
aucuparius bird-catching
avicularis relating to small birds
avium of birds
bufonius relating to toads; growing in
  damp places
caninus relating to dogs
caprea a nanny goat; relating to goats
caprifolius with goatlike leaves
cochleatus shaped like a snail-shell, in
  a spiral
colombinus like a dove
colubrinus snakelike
crista-galli a cockerel's comb
crus-galli a cockerel's spur
dens-canis a dog's tooth
dracocephalus with a dragon 's head
echiniformis shaped like a hedgehog or
  sea-urchin (*echinus*)
elephantipes like an elephant's foot

erinaceus like a hedgehog
formicarius attractive to ants; of ants
gruinus like a crane
lagocephalus with a head like a hare
lagopus hare-footed
leonensis like a lion
leonurus like a lion's tail
lupulus a small wolf
meleagris a guinea-fowl (spotted)
muricatus rough with sharp points (like
  the purple mollusc *murex*)
ophiocarpus with snakelike fruits
ornithopodus like a bird's foot
ovinus for sheep
papilio butterfly
pardalinus like a leopard (spotted)
perdicarius of partridges
psittacinus like a parrot
scolopendrius millipede
scorpioides like a scorpion
sphegodes like a wasp
tragophyllus with goatlike leaves
urophyllus with leaves like an ox's tail
ursinus bearlike
vulpinus relating to foxes

GENUS NAMES
L

Lathyrus from Greek *lathyros,* pea or pulse

Lavandula from Latin *lavare,* to wash

Leptospermum from Greek *leptos,* slender, and *sperma,* seed

Leucanthemum from Greek *leukos,* white, and *anthemon,* flower

Lewisia named for Captain Meriwether Lewis (1774–1809), explorer in North America

Libertia named for Marie Libert (1782–1863), Belgian botanist

Ligularia from Latin *ligula,* strap

Limnanthes from Greek *limne,* marsh, and *anthos,* flower

Linnaea named for Carl Linnaeus (see page 123)

Liriope in Greek mythology, a nymph who was the mother of Narcissus

Lithospermum from Greek *lithos,* stone, and *sperma,* seed

Lobelia named for Mathias de l'Obel (1538–1616), Flemish botanist

Lonicera named for Adam Lonitzer (1528–1586), German botanist

Lunaria from Latin *luna,* the moon

---

leichtlinii named for the German plantsman Max Leichtlin (1831–1910)

  Camassia leichtlinii

lemoinei named for the French plant breeder and nurseryman Victor Lemoine (1823–1911) and his son Emile (1862–1942)

  Philadelphus × lemoinei

leonurus like a lion's tail

  Leonotis leonurus

leonensis like a lion

  Penstemon leonensis

lepido- scaly

lepto- slender (see below)

leptophyllus with slender leaves

leptorrhizus with slender rhizomes

  Epimedium leptorrhizum

leucanthus white-flowered

  Lilium leucanthum

leuco- white

leucocarpus with white fruit

  Callicarpa japonica 'Leucocarpa'

leucodermis with white skin or bark

  Acer saccharum subsp. *leucoderme*

leuconeurus white-veined

leucophaeus light gray

  Digitalis leucophaea

leylandii named after C.J. Leyland, a 19th-century owner of Haggerston Hall in Northumberland, UK, where the popular hybrid hedging conifer was bred

  × *Cupressocyparis leylandii*

COMMON DESCRIPTIVE TERMS

libani, libanotis, libanoticus

  Lebanese; from Mount Lebanon

Cedrus libani

Cistus libanotis

Cyclamen libanoticum

Geranium libani

Puschkinia scilloides var. *libanotica*

Labrador tea *Ledum groenlandicum*
Lad's love *Artemisia abrotanum*
Lady fern *Athyrium filix-femina*
Lady's mantle *Alchemilla mollis*
Lady's smock *Cardamine pratensis*
Ladybird poppy *Papaver commutatum*
Lamb's ears, Lamb's lugs, Lamb's tails
   Stachys byzantina
Larch *Larix*
Larkspur *Consolida ambigua*
Laurel, bay *Laurus nobilis*
Laurel, cherry *Prunus laurocerasus*
Laurel, Portugal *Prunus lusitanica*
Laurel, spotted *Aucuba japonica*
Laurustinus *Viburnum tinus*
Lavender *Lavandula*
Lavender cotton *Santolina*
Lawson cypress *Chamaecyparis
   lawsoniana*
Leadwort *Plumbago*
Lemon balm *Melissa officinalis*
Lemon verbena *Aloysia triphylla*
Lent lily *Narcissus pseudonarcissus*
Lenten rose *Helleborus orientalis;
   Helleborus* × *hybridus*
Leopard's bane *Doronicum orientale*
Leyland cypress   × *Cupressocyparis
   leylandii*
Lilac *Syringa vulgaris*
Lily *Lilium*
Lily-of-the-valley *Convallaria majalis*
Lilyturf *Liriope; Ophiopogon*
Lime, Linden *Tilia*
Ling *Calluna vulgaris*
Lobster claw *Clianthus puniceus*
Locust *Robinia*
Lombardy poplar *Populus nigra* 'Italica'
London pride *Saxifraga* × *urbium*

LILY-OF-THE-VALLEY

Looking-glass plant *Coprosma repens*
Loquat *Eriobotrya japonica*
Lord Anson's blue pea *Lathyrus
   nervosus*
Lords and ladies *Arum italicum*
Lotus *Nelumbo*
Love-grass *Eragrostis*
Love-in-a-mist *Nigella damascena*
Love-lies-bleeding *Amaranthus
   caudatus*
Lucerne *Medicago sativa*
Lucombe oak *Quercus* × *hispanica*
   'Lucombeana'
Lungwort *Pulmonaria*
Lupin *Lupinus*

WHAT'S IN A NAME?

PLANT USES

catharticus purgative, purifying
coronarius used for wreaths or garlands
domestica domesticated
dysentericus for the treatment of dysentery
edulis edible
emeticus emetic, causing vomiting
esculentus edible
febrifugus driving out fever
ferax fruit-bearing, fruitful, fertile
fructifer, frugifer fruit-bearing
frumentaceus grain-bearing
fullonum of fullers
funebris funereal; of cemeteries
medicus medicinal
officinalis sold in (apothecaries') shops; used in medicine
oleraceus relating to vegetables and herbs; of the kitchen garden (also *holeraceus*)
papyriferus paper-bearing
pulegius, pulegioides flea-repelling
ritualis ritual, of ceremonies
sativus sown, planted, cultivated
somnifer sleep-bringing
tinctorius used in dyeing
topiarius of or for topiary
torminalis curing gripe or colic
trachelius curing throat ailments
tranquillans calming
usitatissimus very useful
utilis useful
vesicarius relating to the bladder (or a remedy for bladder ailments)
vinifer wine-producing
vomitorius causing vomiting
vulnerarius of wounds; for wounds

liburnicus from the Croatian coast
  Asphodeline liburnica
lichiangensis from the area around Lijiang in Yunnan Province, China
  Lysimachia lichiangensis
ligustrinus like *Ligustrum* (privet)
  Eupatorium ligustrinum
lilacinus lilac-colored
  Primula vulgaris 'Lilacina Plena'
liliago lily-like
  Anthericum liliago
liliiflorus lily-flowered
  Magnolia liliiflora
limosus of marshes
linarioides like *Linaria* (toadflax)
  Penstemon linarioides
lindheimeri named for Ferdinand Lindheimer (1802–1879), a German botanist in Texas
  Gaura lindheimeri
linearifolius with linear leaves
  Cotoneaster linearifolius
linearis linear, narrow
  Callistemon linearis
lineatus with lines, in a straight line
  Convolvulus lineatus

COMMON DESCRIPTIVE TERMS

linifolius with leaves like *Linum* (flax)
Anagallis monellii subsp. *linifolia*
Erysimum linifolium
Lathyrus linifolius
Tulipa linifolia

linnaeoides named for the Swedish taxonomist Carl Linnaeus (1707–1778), the father of botanical classification and naming
   Lobelia linnaeoides

lissospermus with smooth seeds
   Hakea lissosperma

litho- stone (see below)

lithophilus stone-loving, growing in stony places
   Paeonia tenuifolia subsp. *lithophila*

lithospermus with hard seeds, like stones

littoralis of the seashore
   Griselinia littoralis

lividus leaden blue-gray
   Helleborus lividus

lizei named for the nursery of Lizé Frères in Nantes, France
   × *Fatshedera lizei*

lobatus lobed
   Ipomoea lobata

lobularis, lobulatus with small lobes
   Narcissus pseudonarcissus 'Lobularis'

locellatus divided into subsidiary compartments

locularis with cavities or chambers

lomariifolius with leaves like *Blechnum* (ferns formerly named *Lomaria*)
   Mahonia lomariifolia

longaevus long-lived
   Furcraea longaeva

CULTIVAR NAMES
Strange but True
L

IRIS ENSATA 'LAUGHING LION'

FUCHSIA 'LECHLADE CHINAMAN'

PULMONARIA SACCHARATA 'LEOPARD'

LARIX DECIDUA 'LITTLE BOGLE'

HEMEROCALLIS 'LITTLE BUMBLE BEE'

PENNISETUM ALOPECUROIDES 'LITTLE BUNNY'

HEMEROCALLIS 'LITTLE FAT DAZZLER'

PENNISETUM ALOPECUROIDES 'LITTLE HONEY'

MISCANTHUS SINENSIS 'LITTLE KITTEN'

LEWISIA COTYLEDON 'LITTLE PLUM'

OPHIOPOGON PLANISCAPUS 'LITTLE TABBY'

NEPETA RACEMOSA 'LITTLE TITCH'

HEMEROCALLIS 'LITTLE WART'

SEMPERVIVUM 'LIVELY BUG'

IRIS 'LOOP THE LOOP'

FUCHSIA 'LOTTIE HOBBY'

CROCOSMIA 'LUCIFER'

ROSA LUCKY DUCK ('DICZEST')

---

longibarbatus with a long beard

longibracteatus with long bracts
   Ornithogalum longibracteatum

longicaudatus long-tailed
   Polypodium glycyrrhiza 'Longicaudatum'

longiflorus with long flowers
   Lilium longiflorum

Common descriptive terms

longifolius long-leaved
Mentha longifolia
Morina longifolia
Pulmonaria longifolia

longipes with a long stalk
Nepeta longipes
longipetalus with long petals
Lewisia longipetala

longissimus very long
Hosta longissima
lophanthus with crested flowers
Paraserianthes lophantha
lucidus shining, clear, transparent
Ligustrum lucidum
ludlowii named for Frank Ludlow (1885–1972), a British teacher and plant collector in Tibet
Paeonia delavayi var. *ludlowii*

CULTIVAR NAMES
Natural Features

Malus 'Adirondack'
Fuchsia 'Airedale'
Juniperus chinensis 'Blue Alps'
Alstroemeria 'Glory of the Andes'
Iris 'River Avon'
Griselinia littoralis 'Bantry Bay'
Helianthemum 'Ben More' (also 'Ben Fhada', 'Ben Ledi' etc.)
Hyacinthus orientalis 'Ben Nevis'
Hydrangea macrophylla 'Bodensee'
Geranium × *oxonianum* 'Breckland Sunset'
Gentiana 'Cairngorm'
Helianthemum 'Cheviot'
Iris 'Derwentwater'
Erysimum 'Cotswold Gem'
Iris 'Cliffs of Dover'
Buddleia davidii 'Dartmoor'
Pulmonaria longifolia 'Dordogne'
Astilbe 'Etna'
Hosta 'Mount Everest'
Phlox paniculata 'Mount Fuji'

Hebe 'Great Orme'
Dianthus 'Haytor White'
Polygonatum verticillatum 'Himalayan Giant'
Iris 'Kangchenjunga'
Penstemon Kilimanjaro ('Yajaro')
Delphinium 'Loch Leven'
Philadelphus 'Mont Blanc'
Hemerocallis 'Nile Crane'
Iris 'Orinoco Flow'
Hosta 'Pacific Blue Edger'
Helleborus argutifolius 'Pacific Frost'
Geranium macrorrhizum 'Pindus'
Mimulus 'Popacatapetl'
Narcissus 'Purbeck'
Pelargonium 'Rio Grande'
Stachys officinalis 'Saharan Pink'
Geranium × *oxonianum* 'Sherwood'
Pelargonium 'Solent Waves'
Gentiana 'Strathmore'
Lychnis × *arkwrightii* 'Vesuvius'

ludoviciana from Louisiana
   Artemisia ludoviciana
lunulatus shaped like a small crescent
   moon
   Helianthemum lunulatum
lupulus a small wolf
   Humulus lupulus
luridus dirty yellow
   Carex lurida

COMMON DESCRIPTIVE TERMS
lusitanicus from Portugal (the
   Roman province of Lusitania)
Echium lusitanicum
Fritillaria lusitanica
Lavandula stoechas subsp. *lusitanica*
Prunus lusitanica

---

luteolus yellowish
   Primula luteola
luteovenosus with yellow veins
   Hydrangea luteovenosa
lutetianus from Paris
   Circaea lutetiana (enchanter's
   nightshade)

COMMON DESCRIPTIVE TERMS
luteus yellow
Asphodeline lutea
Corydalis lutea
Digitalis lutea
Fritillaria imperialis 'Maxima Lutea'
Gentiana lutea
Mimulus luteus

---

lyallii named for David Lyall
   (1817–1895), a Scottish naval
   surgeon and naturalist who
   collected plants in New Zealand
   Hoheria lyallii
lycoctonus from *lykos* (wolf) and
   ktonos (murder)
   Aconitum lycoctonum (wolfsbane)
lydius from Lydia in Asia Minor
   Genista lydia
lyonii named for the Scottish
   gardener and botanist John Lyon
   (1765–1814), who collected plants
   in North America
   Chelone lyonii
lyratus lyre-shaped
lysolepis with loose scales

CIRCAEA LUTETIANA

M

maackii named for the Russian naturalist and traveler Richard Maack (1825–1886)
Prunus maackii

macedonicus Macedonian
Knautia macedonica

macranthus with large flowers
Exochorda × *macrantha*

macro, macra large
Hakonechloa macra

macrocalyx with a large calyx
Cyananthus macrocalyx

WHAT'S IN A NAME?

COLOR: GRAY AND SILVER

argentatus silvered
argenteus silvery, lustrous
argyrotrichon silver-haired
canescens rather hoary, whitish gray
cinereus, cineraceus ash gray
ferreus iron gray
fulmineus lightning-colored
fumeus, fumidus, fumosus smoky gray
glaucescens rather glaucous, becoming glaucous
glaucus glaucous
griseus pure pearly gray
incanus pale, whitish gray; hoary
leucophaeus light gray
murinus mousy gray
plumbeus leaden
schistaceus slate gray

COMMON DESCRIPTIVE TERMS

macrocarpus with large fruit
Cupressus macrocarpa
Hebe macrocarpa
Muscari macrocarpum
Oenothera macrocarpa
Quercus macrocarpa

macrocephalus with a large head
Carex macrocephala

macrodontus with large teeth
Olearia macrodonta

macropetalus with large petals
Clematis macropetala

COMMON DESCRIPTIVE TERMS

macrophyllus with large leaves
Brunnera macrophylla
Cornus macrophylla
Hydrangea macrophylla
Magnolia macrophylla
Pachyphragma macrophyllum
Persicaria macrophylla
Primula macrophylla

macropodus with a large stalk
Daphniphyllum himalaense subsp. *macropodum*

macrorrhizus with large roots
Geranium macrorrhizum

macrostachyus with a large spike
Pennisetum macrostachyum

macrostylus with a large style
Geranium macrostylum

CULTIVAR NAMES
Personal Names
M

SEMPERVIVUM 'MADELEINE'

CANNA 'MAGGIE'

FUCHSIA 'AMAZING MAISIE'

FUCHSIA 'MARCIA'

FUCHSIA 'MARGARET'

HELENIUM 'MARGOT'

CORREA 'MARIAN'S MARVEL'

HEBE 'BABY MARIE'

ACHILLEA 'MARIE ANN'

TULIPA 'MARIETTE'

TULIPA 'MARILYN'

ARBUTUS 'MARINA'

ABUTILON 'MARION'

PRUNUS DOMESTICA (PLUM) 'MARJORIE'S SEEDLING'

PRIMULA AURICULA 'MARK'

OSTEOSPERMUM 'SUNNY MARTHA'

VIOLA 'MARTIN'

ACHILLEA 'MARTINA'

FUCHSIA 'MARY'

HEDERA HELIX 'MATHILDE'

CLEMATIS 'MAUREEN'

NARCISSUS 'MAX'

PELARGONIUM 'MAXINE'

SISYRINCHIUM STRIATUM 'AUNT MAY'

CLEMATIS 'MAYLEEN'

ROSA 'MEG'

RHODODENDRON 'MEGAN'

HEDERA HELIX 'MELANIE'

PARAHEBE 'MERVYN'

OLEARIA × *SCILLONIENSIS* 'MASTER MICHAEL'

PRIMULA AURICULA 'MILLICENT'

RHODODENDRON 'MIMI'

HYDRANGEA SERRATA 'MIRANDA'

PELARGONIUM 'SWEET MIRIAM'

ALSTROEMERIA PRINCESS MONICA 'STAPRIMON'

PELARGONIUM 'MORWENNA'

FUCHSIA 'MOYRA'

FUCHSIA 'MURIEL'

COMMON DESCRIPTIVE TERMS

maculatus, maculifer spotted, blotched

Arum maculatum

Dactylorhiza maculata

Elaeagnus pungens 'Maculata'

Geranium maculatum

Lamium maculatum

Phlox maculata

Rhododendron maculiferum

madagascariensis from the island of Madagascar

Buddleia madagascariensis

COMMON DESCRIPTIVE TERMS

maderensis from Madeira

Argyranthemum maderense

Geranium maderense

Hedera maderensis

Ilex × *altaclerensis* 'Maderensis'

CULTIVAR NAMES
Foreign Expressions
M

MAIGRÜN (*German*) MAY GREEN
(*LONICERA NITIDA* 'MAIGRÜN')

MAINACHT (*German*) MAY NIGHT
(*SALVIA* × *SYLVESTRIS* 'MAINACHT')

MAISCHNEE (*German*) MAY SNOW
(*PHLOX SUBULATA* 'MAISCHNEE')

MANTEAU D'HERMINE (*French*)
ERMINE CLOAK
(*PHILADELPHUS* 'MANTEAU
D'HERMINE')

MARÉE D'OR (*French*) GOLD TIDE
(*FORSYTHIA* MARÉE D'OR
('COURTASOL')

MATKA TERESA (*Polish*)
MOTHER TERESA
(*CLEMATIS* 'MATKA TERESA')

MILCHSTRASSE (*German*)
THE MILKY WAY
(*PULMONARIA* 'MILCHSTRASSE')

MIYAMA-YAE-MURASAKI (*Japanese*)
MOUNTAIN DOUBLE PURPLE
(*HYDRANGEA SERRATA*
'MIYAMA-YAE-MURASAKI')

MOORHEXE (*German*)
MOORLAND WITCH
(*MOLINIA CAERULEA* SUBSP. *CAERULEA*
'MOORHEXE')

MORGENRÖTE (*German*)
MORNING RED
(*BERGENIA* 'MORGENRÖTE')

MÖWE (*German*) SEAGULL
(*HYDRANGEA MACROPHYLLA* 'MÖWE')

COMMON DESCRIPTIVE TERMS

magellanicus from the southern
tip of South America, around the
Straits of Magellan
Elymus magellanicus
Fuchsia magellanica
Gunnera magellanica
Philesia magellanica

magnificus magnificent, splendid
Geranium × *magnificum*
magniflorus large-flowered
Geranium magniflorum
magnus large
Ornithogalum magnum
majalis of May, flowering in May
Convallaria majalis

COMMON DESCRIPTIVE TERMS
major, majus greater
Ammi majus
Antirrhinum majus
Astrantia major
Cerinthe major
Fothergilla major
Lagarosiphon major
Melianthus major
Tropaeolum majus
Vinca major

makinoi named for the Japanese
botanist Tomitaro Makino
(1863–1957)
Rhododendron makinoi

malacoides soft, supple
  Primula malacoides
malviflorus with flowers like *Malva*
  (mallow)
  Sidalcea malviflora

COMMON DESCRIPTIVE TERMS
**mandschuricus, mandshuricus,
  manshuriensis** from Manchuria
Acer mandschuricum
Betula mandshurica
Clematis mandschurica
Malus baccata var. *mandshurica*
Prunus mandshurica

---

manicatus long-sleeved
  Gunnera manicata
marantinus like *Maranta* (arrowroot)
  Globba marantina
margaritaceus pearly
  Anaphalis margaritacea (pearl
  everlasting)

COMMON DESCRIPTIVE TERMS
marginalis, marginatus with a
  distinct margin, edge or border
Buxus sempervirens 'Marginata'
Dryopteris marginalis
Ilex aquifolium 'Argentea Marginata'
Luzula sylvatica 'Marginata'
Primula marginata
Sambucus nigra 'Marginata'
Teucrium scorodonia 'Crispum
  Marginatum'

WHAT'S IN A NAME?
SIZE

altissimus very tall
altus tall
decumanus very large
diminutus small, diminished
elatus tall; *elatior, elatius* taller
excelsus lofty, high
exiguus small, weak
giganteus giant, gigantic, very large
gigas giant
grandis big
magnus large
major, majus greater
maximus largest, very large
mega-, megalo- large
minimus smallest, very small
minor smaller
minutissimus most minute, very
  minute
nanus dwarf
parvi- small
procerus high, tall
pumilus dwarf
pygmaeus pygmy, dwarf, very small
vescus small, feeble

marianus named for the Virgin Mary
  Silybum marianum

COMMON DESCRIPTIVE TERMS
mariesii named for the British plant
collector Charles Maries (1851–
1902)
Ilex crenata 'Mariesii'
Platycodon grandiflorus 'Mariesii'
Viburnum plicatum 'Mariesii

CULTIVAR NAMES
Strange but True
M

Iris 'Making Eyes'

Iris 'Marmalade Skies'

Knautia macedonica 'Mars Midget'

Potentilla fruticosa 'Medicine Wheel Mountain'

Iris 'Mesmerizer'

Fuchsia 'Microchip'

Veronica chamaedrys 'Miffy Brute'

Galanthus 'Mighty Atom'

Hemerocallis 'Milanese Mango'

Pinus mugo 'Minikin'

Rosa 'Minnehaha'

Juniperus × *pfitzeriana* 'Mint Julep'

Paeonia lactiflora 'Mischief'

Rosa Miss Flippins ('Tuckflip')

Lavandula angustifolia Miss Muffet ('Scholmis')

Primula auricula 'Mr "A"'

Narcissus 'Mite'

Penstemon 'Modesty'

Pelargonium 'The Mole'

Pinus mugo 'Mops' (and 'Mini Mops')

Calluna vulgaris 'Mousehole'

Hosta 'Mr Big'

Geranium × *monacense* var. *monacense* 'Muldoon'

Hemerocallis 'Mumbo Jumbo'

Begonia 'Munchkin'

Lupinus 'My Castle'

marilandicus from Maryland

  Spigelia marilandica 'Wisley Jester'

COMMON DESCRIPTIVE TERMS

maritimus coastal, growing
  by the sea

Armeria maritima (thrift)

Crambe maritima (seakale)

Eryngium maritimum (sea holly)

Lavatera maritima

Lobularia maritima (sweet alyssum)

CRAMBE MARITIMA

marmorarius of marble

marmoratus marbled

  Arum italicum subsp. *italicum*
  'Marmoratum'

mas, masculus male, masculine

  Cornus mas

  Paeonia mascula

WHAT'S IN A NAME?

PLANT HABIT

apodus without a foot or stalk; sessile

arborescens growing to be a tree; woody

arboreus treelike, woody

arbusculus like a small tree

caespitosus, cespitosus clump-forming

cernuus drooping, downturned

columnaris columnar

contortus twisted, contorted

decumbens decumbent; prostrate but with upright tips

dependens hanging down

dilatatus spread out, expanded

divaricatus spreading, straggling

dumosus bushy

effusus spreading, straggly

erectus erect, upright

fastigiatus fastigiate; with an upright habit

fruticosus, frutescens, fruticans shrubby

gracilis slender

ortho- straight, upright (see below)

patens spreading

patulus spreading

pendulus pendulous, hanging

procumbens prostrate

procurrens spreading, running

prostratus prostrate

ramosus branched

ramulosus twiggy

rectus upright

repens, reptans creeping

scandens climbing

sessilis sessile, stalkless

sobolifer with creeping stems that form roots

socialis growing in colonies

spiralis spiral

stans upright

sten-, steno- narrow

stolonifer with stolons (rooting runners)

stragulus, stragulatus mat-forming

strictus upright, erect, tight

suffruticosus somewhat shrubby

suspensus hanging

tenuis thin, fine, slender

tenuissimus very thin

tortuosus, tortus, tortilis tortuous, winding

verticillatus verticillate; arranged in whorls

viminalis, vimineus with long, thin shoots; like osiers

virgatus twiggy

volubilis winding, revolving

---

matronalis named for *Matronalia*, a Roman festival on 1 March *Hesperis matronalis*

maxillaris relating to jaws

maximowiczianus, maximowiczii named after a Russian botanist, Carl Maximowicz (1827–1891) *Geranium maximowiczii*

COMMON DESCRIPTIVE TERMS

maximus largest, very large, *Astrantia maxima*

Briza maxima

Corylus maxima

Glyceria maxima

Hepatica maxima

Rhododendron maximum

Macleaya named for Alexander Macleay (1767–1848), one-time secretary of the Linnaean Society

Magnolia named for Pierre Magnol (1638–1715), French botanist

Mahonia named for Bernard M'Mahon (1775–1816), American horticulturist

Malus from Greek *melon*, apple

Matteucia named for Carlo Matteuci (1811–1868), Italian scientist

Matthiola named for Pietro Andrea Mattioli (1500–1577), Italian botanist and doctor

Melianthus from Greek *meli*, honey, and *anthos*, flower

Melissa in Greek, a bee

Miscanthus from Greek *miskos*, stem, and *anthos*, flower

Monarda named for Nicolas Monardes (1493–1588), Spanish botanist

Myosotis from Greek *mus*, mouse, and *otos*, ear

medicus medicinal

COMMON DESCRIPTIVE TERMS

medius mid, in the middle, intermediate

Briza media

Campanula medium

Dierama media

Mahonia × media

Plantago media

mega-, megalo- large (see below)

megacalyx with a large calyx
  Rhododendron megacalyx

megalanthus with large flowers
  Potentilla megalantha

megalocarpus with large fruits
  Sorbus megalocarpa

megalophyllus with large leaves
  Ampelopsis megalophylla

megapotamicus (literally) from the big river; from the Rio Grande
  Abutilon megapotamicum

mela-, melano- black

melanocarpus with black fruit
  Aronia melanocarpa

melanostictus spotted with black

meleagris a guinea-fowl; hence, spotted
  Fritillaria meleagris

meliodorus honey-scented

melissifolius, melissophyllus with leaves like *Melissa* (lemon balm)
  Melittis melissophyllum

melleus, mellitus sweet like honey

mellifer honey-bearing
  Euphorbia mellifera

membranaceus like skin or membrane
  Epimedium membranaceum

meniscifolius with concave leaves

menthifolius with leaves like *Mentha* (mint)
  Calamintha menthifolia

Madonna lily *Lilium candidum*

Maidenhair fern *Adiantum*

Maidenhair spleenwort *Asplenium trichomanes*

Maidenhair tree *Ginkgo biloba*

Maize *Zea mays*

Male fern *Dryopteris filix-mas*

Mallow *Lavatera; Malope; Malva*

Maltese cross *Lychnis chalcedonica*

Manchurian cherry *Prunus maackii*

Mandrake *Mandragora*

Manzanita *Arbutus; Arctostaphylos*

Maple *Acer*

Marguerite *Argyranthemum frutescens; Leucanthemum vulgare*

Marigold *Calendula; Tagetes*

Mariposa tulip *Calochortus*

Marjoram *Origanum*

Marsh marigold *Caltha palustris*

Marvel of Peru *Mirabilis jalapa*

Masterwort *Astrantia*

Mastic tree *Pistacia lentiscus*

May *Crataegus monogyna; Crataegus laevigata*

Meadow cranesbill *Geranium pratense*

Meadow foxtail *Alopecurus pratensis*

Meadow rue *Thalictrum*

Meadow saffron *Colchicum*

Meadowsweet *Filipendula ulmaria*

Medick *Medicago*

Medlar *Mespilus germanica*

Melick grass *Melica*

Mexican breadfruit *Monstera deliciosa*

Mexican hat plant *Kalanchoe daigremontiana*

Mexican orange blossom *Choisya ternata*

Mezereon *Daphne mezereum*

Michaelmas daisy *Aster*

Midland hawthorn *Crataegus laevigata*

Mignonette *Reseda odorata*

Mile-a-minute vine *Fallopia baldschuanica*

Milk thistle *Silybum marianum*

Milkweed *Asclepias*

Milkwort *Polygala*

Mimosa *Acacia dealbata*

Mind-your-own-business *Soleirolia soleirolii*

Mint *Mentha*

Mint bush *Prostanthera*

Mintleaf *Plectranthus madagascariensis*

Miss Willmott's ghost *Eryngium giganteum*

Missey-moosey *Sorbus americana*

Mistletoe *Viscum album*

Mock orange *Philadelphus*

Mole plant *Euphorbia lathyris*

Monkey flower *Mimulus*

Monkey-puzzle tree *Araucaria araucana*

Monkshood *Aconitum*

Montbretia *Crocosmia*

Moon daisy *Leucanthemum vulgare*

Morning glory *Ipomoea tricolor*

Moss rose *Rosa* × *centifolia* 'Muscosa'

Mount Etna broom *Genista aetnensis*

Mountain ash *Sorbus aucuparia*

Mourning widow *Geranium phaeum*

Moutan *Paeonia suffruticosa*

Mulberry *Morus*

Mullein *Verbascum*

Musk mallow *Malva moschata*

Musk rose *Rosa moschata*

Myrobalan *Prunus cerasifera*

Myrtle *Myrtus communis*

Monterey cypress *Cupressus macrocarpa*

CULTIVAR NAMES
Plants for all Seasons

SPRING

CALLUNA VULGARIS 'SPRING CREAM'

CHAMAECYPARIS LAWSONIANA 'SPRINGTIME'

CLEMATIS 'FRAGRANT SPRING'

CORNUS FLORIDA 'SPRING SONG'

DICENTRA 'SPRING MORNING'

LATHYRUS VERNUS 'SPRING MELODY'

PAPAVER ORIENTALE 'SPRINGTIME'

PELARGONIUM 'FLOWER OF SPRING'

PRIMULA AURICULA 'SPRING MEADOWS'

PRUNUS CERASIFERA 'SPRING GLOW'

TIARELLA 'SPRING SYMPHONY'

SUMMER

CANNA 'SUMMER GOLD'

CHAMAECYPARIS LAWSONIANA 'SUMMER SNOW'

DIGITALIS 'SALTWOOD SUMMER'

GERANIUM PYRENAICUM 'SUMMER SNOW'

GERANIUM SUMMER SKIES ('GERNIC')

GERANIUM × *OXONIANUM* 'SUMMER SURPRISE'

HEBE 'MIDSUMMER BEAUTY'

HEBE ODORA 'SUMMER FROST'

HEMEROCALLIS 'SUMMER WINE'

LAVATERA OLBIA 'SUMMER KISSES'

LEUCANTHEMUM × *SUPERBUM* 'SUMMER SNOWBALL'

OENOTHERA 'SUMMER SUN'

PHYSOSTEGIA VIRGINIANA 'SUMMER SNOW'

RHODODENDRON 'HIGH SUMMER'

ROSA SUMMER WINE ('KORIZONT')

AUTUMN

ASTER NOVI-BELGII 'AUTUMN GLORY'

COLCHICUM 'AUTUMN QUEEN'

CAMPSIS RADICANS 'INDIAN SUMMER'

DAHLIA 'AUTUMN LUSTRE'

GINKGO BILOBA 'AUTUMN GOLD'

HEBE 'AUTUMN GLORY'

HELENIUM 'AUTUMN LOLLIPOP'

HEMEROCALLIS 'AUTUMN RED'

LEPTOSPERMUM SCOPARIUM 'AUTUMN GLORY'

MISCANTHUS SINENSIS 'AUTUMN LIGHT'

ROSA 'AUTUMN DELIGHT'

RUBUS IDAEUS (RASPBERRY) 'AUTUMN BLISS'

SORBUS AUTUMN SPIRES ('FLANROCK')

WINTER

BUXUS SINICA VAR. *INSULARIS* 'WINTER GEM'

CORNUS SANGUINEA 'MIDWINTER FIRE'

ERICA CARNEA 'WINTER BEAUTY'

EUONYMUS HAMILTONIANUS 'WINTER GLORY'

GAULTHERIA MUCRONATA 'WINTERTIME'

HEBE 'WINTER GLOW'

ILEX VERTICILLATA 'WINTER RED'

LEPTOSPERMUM SCOPARIUM 'WINTER CHEER'

LONICERA × *PURPUSII* 'WINTER BEAUTY'

MAHONIA × *MEDIA* 'WINTER SUN'

MALUS DOMESTICA (APPLE) 'WINTER BANANA'

menziesii named for the Scottish
plant collector, surgeon and
naturalist Archibald Menzies
(1754–1842)
Arbutus menziesii
Nothofagus menziesii
Pseudotsuga menziesii (Douglas fir)
Sanguisorba menziesii
Tolmiea menziesii

meridionalis (flowering at) midday,
noon
Globularia meridionalis
meserveae named for Kathleen
Meserve, who in the 1950s bred
hollies on Long Island, New
York
Ilex × *meserveae*
messanensis from Messina, Sicily
Fritillaria messanensis
metallicus metallic
Begonia metallica

mexicanus Mexican
Agastache mexicana
Penstemon mexicanus
Philadelphus mexicanus
Quercus mexicana

michiganensis from Michigan
Lilium michiganense
micr-, micro- small

micranthus with small flowers
Acer micranthum
Colchicum micranthum
Dichondra micrantha
Heuchera micrantha
Rhododendron micranthum

microcarpus with small fruits
Macleaya microcarpa
microcephalus with a small head
Persicaria microcephala
microlepis with small scales
Dianthus microlepis

microphyllus with small leaves
Azara microphylla
Buxus microphylla
Cotoneaster microphyllus
Euonymus japonicus 'Microphyllus'
Fuchsia microphylla
Helichrysum microphyllum
Myrtus communis 'Microphylla
Variegata'
Origanum microphyllum
Philadelphus microphyllus
Sophora microphylla

middendorffianus, middendorfii
named for Alexander von
Middendorff (1815–1894), a plant
collector and zoologist in Siberia
Sedum middendorffianum

WHAT'S IN A NAME?

PLANTS OF DISTINCTION

admirabilis admirable, wonderful
amabilis lovely
amoenus lovely, pleasant
augustus venerable, majestic
basilicus princely, royal
benedictus well spoken of; blessed
concinnus neat
decoratus, decorus decorative
elegans elegant
elegantissimus very elegant
erromenus vigorous, healthy
eucharis pleasing, agreeable
eudoxus of good repute
eximius distinguished, extraordinary
facetus choice, fine
formosissimus very beautiful
formosus finely formed, handsome, beautiful
fortis strong, vigorous
generosus noble, eminent
gloriosus glorious
imperialis imperial, showy
insignis distinguished
jucundus pleasant, delightful
magnificus magnificent, splendid
mirabilis marvelous
nobilis noble, renowned
ornatus showy
praestans distinguished, excellent
princeps princely, most distinguished
pulcher, pulchellus beautiful, pretty
regalis royal; fit for a king
robustus robust, strong
speciosus showy, splendid
spectabilis spectacular
superbus superb
validus strong, robust, powerful
venustus lovely, charming, pleasing

miliaceus like millet
millefolius, millefoliatus (literally)
    with a thousand leaves
    Achillea millefolium (yarrow)
miniatus the color of red-lead
    or cinnabar
    Clivia miniata
minimus smallest, very small
    Ocimum minimum (bush basil)

COMMON DESCRIPTIVE TERMS

minor smaller
Hemerocallis minor
Hosta minor
Rhinanthus minor (yellow rattle)
Vinca minor

---

minutiflorus with very small flowers
    Origanum minutiflorum
minutissimus most minute, very
    minute
    Athyrium filix-femina
    'Minutissimum'
minutus minute, very small
    Fritillaria minuta
mirabilis marvelous
    Cyclamen mirabile
mischtschenkoanus named for
    P.I. Misczenko (1869–1938),
    a Russian botanist
    Scilla mischtschenkoana
missouriensis from Missouri or
    the Missouri River
    Iris missouriensis

mitriformis shaped like a cap or hat
  Aloe mitriformis
mlokosewitschii named for Ludwik
  Mlokosiewicz (1831–1909),
  a Polish naturalist
  Paeonia mlokosewitschii
modestus modest

COMMON DESCRIPTIVE TERMS
mollis soft
Acanthus mollis
Alchemilla mollis
Hamamelis mollis
Helianthus mollis
Holcus mollis
Olearia × *mollis*
Pulmonaria mollis

---

mollissimus very soft
  Passiflora mollissima
monacensis of or from Munich,
  Germany
  Geranium × *monacense*
mongolicus Mongolian
  Tilia mongolica
mono- single
monocephalus with one head
  Anaphalis nepalensis var.
  monocephala
monogynus with one pistil
  Crataegus monogyna (hawthorn)
monopetalus with one petal
monostictus with one spot
  Galanthus elwesii var. *monostictus*

COMMON DESCRIPTIVE TERMS
monspeliensis, monspessulanus
  from Montpellier, France
Acer monspessulanum
Aphyllanthes monspeliensis
Cistus monspeliensis
Dianthus monspessulanus

CULTIVAR NAMES
Colors: Orange

ALSTROEMERIA 'ORANGE GLORY'
BERBERIS LINEARIFOLIA 'ORANGE KING'
CANNA 'ORANGE PERFECTION'
ERICA × STUARTII 'IRISH ORANGE'
ERYSIMUM 'ORANGE FLAME'
GEUM 'PRINCE OF ORANGE'
HAMAMELIS × INTERMEDIA 'ORANGE PEEL'
HEDYCHIUM DENSIFLORUM 'ASSAM ORANGE'
HELENIUM 'CHIPPERFIELD ORANGE'
IRIS 'ORANGE CAPER'
LILIUM 'ORANGE PIXIE'
MALUS DOMESTICA (APPLE) 'ELLISON'S ORANGE'
MIMULUS 'HIGHLAND ORANGE'
OSTEOSPERMUM ORANGE SYMPHONY ('SEIMORA')
PHLOX PANICULATA 'PRINCE OF ORANGE'
POTENTILLA FRUTICOSA 'HOPLEYS ORANGE'
PYRACANTHA 'ORANGE GLOW'
RHODODENDRON 'ORANGE BEAUTY'
TULIPA 'ORANGE EMPEROR'

SCENT AND TASTE

agathosmus smelling good, fragrant
aromaticus fragrant, aromatic, spicy
blandus mild, not bitter; pleasing
citriodorus lemon-scented
deliciosus delicious
dulcis sweet, pleasant
foetidus evil-smelling
fragrans fragrant
glycyrrhizus like liquorice
graveolens strongly scented
inodorus scentless
meliodorus honey-scented
moschatus musk-scented
odoratus, odorus scented, fragrant
oxycarpus with sour fruits
phu rotten-smelling; acrid
saccharatus, saccharinus sweet, sugary
salsillus salted
suaveolens fragrant, smelling sweetly

COMMON DESCRIPTIVE TERMS

montanus of mountains
Arenaria montana
Centaurea montana
Clematis montana
Fritillaria montana
Geum montanum
Lathyrus montanus

montevidensis from Montevideo
  Lantana montevidensis
monticola a mountain-dweller
  Pinus monticola
morifolius mulberry-leaved

COMMON DESCRIPTIVE TERMS

moschatus musk-like, musk-scented
Chelonopsis moschata
Malva moschata
Narcissus moschatus
Olearia moschata
Rosa moschata

moupinensis from Baoxing (Mupin)
  in Sichuan, China
  Primula moupinensis
moyesii named for an early 20th-
  century missionary in China,
  the Rev. J. Moyes
  Rosa moyesii
mucosus slimy
mucronatus pointed
  Gaultheria mucronata
mucronifolius with pointed leaves
  Androsace mucronifolia
multi- many (see below)
multiceps many-headed

COMMON DESCRIPTIVE TERMS

multifidus with many divisions,
  much-divided
Anemone multifida
Brachyscome multifida
Helleborus multifidus
Lavandula multifida

multiflorus with many flowers
  Polygonatum multiflorum
  (Solomon's seal)

multijugus 'many yoked together' (e.g. a leaf with many leaflets)

multiscapoideus with many scapes (bare flower stems)
  Erythronium multiscapoideum

multisectus with many cuts

munitus fortified; protected
  Polystichum munitum

muralis of walls, growing on walls
  Cymbalaria muralis

muricatus rough with sharp points: a term derived from the purple mollusc *Murex*
  Pinus muricata

murielae named by the plant hunter E.H. Wilson (see page 212) after his daughter Muriel
  Fargesia murielae

musaceus like Musa (banana)

musaicus like a mosaic

muscosus mossy, like moss
  Rosa × centifolia 'Muscosa'

musifolius with leaves like *Musa* (banana)
  Canna 'Musifolia'

mutabilis changing, changeable (e.g. in color)
  Rosa × odorata 'Mutabilis'

myiagrus sticky (named for Myiagros, a fly-catching deity of the ancient Greeks)

myosotidifolius with leaves like *Myosotis* (forget-me-not)
  Buxus sempervirens 'Myosotidifolia'

MALVA MOSCHATA

myri- many

myrsinites like myrtle
  Euphorbia myrsinites

COMMON DESCRIPTIVE TERMS

myrtifolius with leaves like *Myrtus* (myrtle)

Buxus sempervirens 'Myrtifolia'
Ilex aquifolium 'Myrtifolia'
Leptospermum myrtifolium
Polygala myrtifolia
Quercus myrtifolia

---

myrtinervius with veins like *Myrtus* (myrtle)
  Dianthus myrtinervius

N

nankingensis from Nanjing, China
  Chrysanthemum nankingense

COMMON DESCRIPTIVE TERMS
nanus dwarf
Betula nana
Cryptomeria japonica 'Elegans nana'
Larix kaempferi 'Nana'
Lilium nanum

---

napaulensis from Nepal (see also
  nepalensis)
  Meconopsis napaulensis
napellus little turnip
  Aconitum napellus
napolitanus from Naples, Italy
  (see also *neapolitanus*)
  Daphne napolitana
narbonensis from Narbonne, France
  Linum narbonense
narcissiflorus with flowers like
  Narcissus
  Anemone narcissiflorus
neapolitanus (see also *napolitanus*)
  from Naples, Italy
  Allium neapolitanum
nebulosus like a cloud
nectarifer nectar-bearing
neglectus neglected, overlooked
  Muscari neglectum

ACONITUM NAPELLUS

nemorosus growing in woods
  Anemone nemorosa

COMMON DESCRIPTIVE TERMS
nepalensis from Nepal (see also
  napaulensis)
Anaphalis nepalensis var. *monocephala*
Lilium nepalense
Miscanthus nepalensis
Potentilla nepalensis
Piptanthus nepalensis

---

nepenthoides like *Nepenthes* (pitcher
  plant)
  Arisaema nepenthoides

nephro- kidney-
nephrolepis with kidney-shaped scales

---

nervosus fibrous, sinewy; with
  conspicuous veins
Astelia nervosa
Cynoglossum nervosus
Lathyrus nervosus
Mahonia nervosa
Nepeta nervosa
Onopordum nervosum

CULTIVAR NAMES
Strange but True
N, O
PRIMULA AURICULA 'NEAT AND TIDY'
PELARGONIUM 'NERVOUS MABEL'
ARMERIA 'NIFTY THRIFTY'
PITTOSPORUM TENUIFOLIUM 'NUTTY'S
  LEPRECHAUN'
SEMPERVIVUM 'ODDITY'
DIANTHUS 'OLD MOTHER
  HUBBARD'
PRIMULA AURICULA 'OLD RED DUSTY
  MILLER'
PRIMULA AURICULA 'OLD SMOKEY'
PELARGONIUM 'OLD SPICE'
DIANTHUS 'OLD SQUARE EYES'
CAREX NIGRA 'ON-LINE'
HEBE 'ORPHAN ANNIE'
PENSTEMON 'OSPREY'
FUCHSIA 'OTHER FELLOW'
NARCISSUS 'OZ'

---

neso- of islands
nesophilus island-loving, growing
  on islands
  Melaleuca nesophila
neurolobus with veined lobes
  Lathyrus neurolobus
nevadensis from Nevada, USA, or
  from the Sierra Nevada, California,
  or the Sierra Nevada, Spain
  Lewisia nevadensis
nicaeensis from Nice, France; or
  Nicaea (now Iznik), Turkey
  Euphorbia nicaeensis
nidiformis nest-shaped
  Picea abies 'Nidiformis'
nidulans (literally) nesting; partially
  enclosed
nidularius like a little nest
  Phyllostachys nidularia

---

niger black
Allium nigrum
Carex niger
Helleborus niger (Christmas rose)
Hydrangea macrophylla 'Nigra'
Juglans nigra (walnut)
Morus nigra (black mulberry)
Lathyrus nigra
Phyllostachys nigra (black bamboo)
Prunus cerasifera 'Nigra'
Sambucus nigra (elder)
Veratrum nigrum
Verbascum nigrum

HOW MANY?

aequitrilobus with three equal lobes
bicornis with two horns
bicuspidatus with two points
bidentatus with two teeth
biflorus with two flowers
bifolius with two leaves
bilobus, bilobatus with two lobes
bisectus divided into two equal parts
biternatus twice ternate
decapetalus with ten petals
decaphyllus with ten leaves or leaflets
dichotomus dividing repeatedly in two
didymus paired, two-lobed
digynus with two styles or carpels
diphyllus two-leaved
dipterus two-winged
distachyus with two spikes
distichus in two rows
distylus with two styles
dodecandrus with 12 stamens
enneaphyllus with nine leaflets or leaves
mono- single
monocephalus with one head
monogynus with one style or carpel
monopetalus with one petal
oct-, octo- eight
octopetalus with eight petals
olig-, oligo- few
oligophyllus with few leaves
pauci- few
pauciflorus with few flowers
penta- five
pentapetalus with five petals
pentaphyllus with five leaves or leaflets
poly- many
quadrangularis, quadrangulatus with four angles
quadratus square; in fours; in four
quadridentatus with four teeth

quadrifolius with four leaves or leaflets
quinatus in fives
quinquefolius with five leaves
quinquelobatus with five lobes
quintuplinervius with five veins
septem- seven
septemfidus divided into seven
septemlobus with seven lobes
sexstylosus with six styles
ternatus in threes
terniflorus with flowers in threes
ternifolius with three leaves or leaflets
tetra- four
tetragonus with four angles
tetrandrus with four stamens
tetraphyllus with four leaves or leaflets
tetrapterus four-winged
triacanthos three-thorned
triandrus with three stamens
triangularis three-angled
trichotomum with divisions in threes
tricornis with three horns
tricuspidatus three-pointed
trifidus divided or cleft into three
triflorus three-flowered
trifolius; trifoliatus three-leaved
trifurcatus three-pronged
trilobus, trilobatus three-lobed
trinervis, triplinervis three-veined
tripartitus divided into three parts
tripetalus with three petals
triphyllus three-leaved
tripinnatus thrice pinnate
tripteris three-winged
triquetrus three-cornered
triternatus thrice ternate
uni- one
uniflorus with one flower
unifolius with one leaf

nigercors a hybrid between
   Helleborus niger and *Helleborus*
   argutifolius (*Helleborus corsicus*)
   Helleborus × *nigercors*

COMMON DESCRIPTIVE TERMS

nigrescens, nigricans blackish
Cistus × *nigricans*
Cytisus nigricans
Fuchsia nigricans
Hosta nigrescens
Ophiopogon planiscapus
   'Nigrescens'

---

nigropunctatus black-spotted
niloticus from the River Nile, Egypt
niphophilus snow-loving
   Eucalyptus pauciflora subsp.
   niphophila

COMMON DESCRIPTIVE TERMS

niponicus, nipponicus Japanese
Athyrium niponicum
Nipponanthemum nipponicum
Phyllodoce nipponica
Prunus nipponica
Spiraea nipponica

---

nitens, nitidus shining
Dianthus nitidus
Eucalyptus nitens
Fargesia nitida
Lonicera nitida
Potentilla nitida

CULTIVAR NAMES
Foreign Expressions
N, O

NACHTHIMMEL (*German*)
NIGHT SKY
(*ERIGERON* 'NACHTHIMMEL')

NACHTIGALL (*German*)
NIGHTINGALE
(*HYDRANGEA MACROPHYLLA*
'NACHTIGALL')

OCHSENBLUT (*German*)
OX BLOOD
(*PHLOX DOUGLASII* 'OCHSENBLUT')

OEIL DE POURPRE (*French*)
PURPLE EYE
(*PHILADELPHUS* 'OEIL DE POURPRE')

OISEAU BLEU (*French*)
BLUE BIRD
(*HIBISCUS SYRIACUS* 'OISEAU BLEU')

OKAME (*Japanese*)
A MASK USED IN TRADITIONAL
JAPANESE COMEDY
(*PRUNUS* 'OKAME')

ORANJE BOVEN (*Dutch*)
ORANGE TOP
(*HYACINTHUS ORIENTALIS*
'ORANJE BOVEN')

ORO DI BOGLIASCO (*Italian*)
BOGLIASCO GOLD
(*HEDERA HELIX* 'ORO DI BOGLIASCO')

OSAKAZUKI (*Japanese*)
SAKE (RICE WINE) CUP
(*ACER PALMATUM* 'OSAKAZUKI')

OSHIDORI (*Japanese*)
MANDARIN DUCK
(*PRUNUS INCISA* 'OSHIDORI')

CULTIVAR NAMES
Colors: Silver

ARTEMISIA ABSINTHIUM
'LAMBROOK SILVER'

CLEMATIS 'SILVER MOON'

CORTADERIA SELLOANA
'SUNNINGDALE SILVER'

DICHONDRA MICRANTHA
'SILVER FALLS'

ELAEAGNUS 'QUICKSILVER'

EUONYMUS FORTUNEI
'SILVER QUEEN'

HEBE PIMELEOIDES 'QUICKSILVER'

HEBE 'SILVER DOLLAR'

HELLEBORUS ARGUTIFOLIUS
'SILVER LACE'

HOSTA 'SILVERY SLUGPROOF'

ILEX AQUIFOLIUM 'SILVER MILKMAID'

IRIS SIBIRICA 'SILVER EDGE'

JUNIPERUS VIRGINIANA SILVER SPREADER
('MONA')

LAMIUM MACULATUM
'BEACON SILVER'

LAVATERA TRIMESTRIS 'SILVER CUP'

LONICERA NITIDA 'SILVER BEAUTY'

NARCISSUS 'SILVER CHIMES'

OZOTHAMNUS ROSMARINIFOLIUS
'SILVER JUBILEE'

PHLOX PANICULATA 'SILVERMINE'

PIERIS 'FLAMING SILVER'

PITTOSPORUM TENUIFOLIUM
'SILVER QUEEN'

PRIMULA AURICULA 'SILVERWAY'

PULMONARIA SACCHARATA
'SILVERADO'

SENECIO CINERARIA 'SILVER DUST'

THYMUS VULGARIS 'SILVER POSIE'

COMMON DESCRIPTIVE TERMS

nivalis, niveus snowy, snow-like
Epimedium × youngianum 'Niveum'
Galanthus nivalis
Luzula nivea
Phlox nivalis
Podocarpus nivalis
Rhododendron niveum

---

nobilis noble, renowned
  Laurus nobilis
noctiflorus night-flowering
nodiflorus with flowers at the
  nodes
  Phyla nodiflora
nodosus with conspicuous nodes
  Geranium nodosum
non-scriptus unmarked
  Hyacinthoides non-scripta (English
  bluebell)
nootkatensis from the Nootka Sound,
  British Columbia
  Chamaecyparis nootkatensis
nordmannianus named for Alexander
  von Nordmann (1803–1866),
  a German botanist
  Abies nordmanniana
normalis normal (e.g. not variegated,
  double-flowered etc.)
  Allium paradoxum var. *normale*
northiae named for the British
  botanical artist and traveler
  Marianne North (1830–1890)
  Kniphofia northiae

WHAT'S IN A NAME?

SOME AMERICAN NAMES

alabamensis Alabama
arizonicus Arizona
arkansanus Arkansas
californicus California
carolinianus North Carolina or
  South Carolina
coloradoensis Colorado
floridanus Florida
georgianus Georgia
idahoensis Idaho
illinoinensis Illinois
kentuckiensis Kentucky
ludovicianus Louisiana
marilandicus Maryland
michiganensis Michigan
missouriensis Missouri or the
  Missouri River
nevadensis Nevada or the Sierra
  Nevada (California or Spain)
novae-angliae New England
novi-belgii New York
ohiensis Ohio
oreganus, oregonus Oregon
pensylvanicus Pennsylvania
philadelphicus Philadelphia
tennesseensis Tennessee
texanus, texensis Texas
utahensis Utah
virginianus, virginicus Virginia

novae-zelandiae from New Zealand
  Festuca novae-zelandiae
novi-belgii from New York
  Aster novi-belgii
nucifer nut-bearing
nudicaulis with a bare stem
  Papaver nudicaule
nudiflorus with naked flowers (i.e.
  flowering before the leaves open)
  Jasminum nudiflorum
nudus, nudatus naked
  Nepeta nuda
numidicus from Algeria (the Roman
  province of Numidia)
nummularius like a coin (*nummus*)
  Lysimachia nummularia
nummariifolius with round leaves,
  like a coin
  Olearia nummulariifolia

COMMON DESCRIPTIVE TERMS
nutans nodding
Allium nutans
Billbergia nutans
Melica nutans
Ornithogalum nutans

---

norvegicus Norwegian
notho- false (e.g. *Nothofagus,*
  southern beech*)*
nova-anglica, novae-angliae from
  New England
  Aster novae-angliae
  Eucalyptus nova-anglica

nuttallii named for English botanist,
  Thomas Nuttall (1786–1859)
  Cornus nuttallii
nyctagineus night-flowering
nymansensis from Nymans Garden,
  West Sussex, UK
  Eucryphia × *nymansensis*

O

ob- inverted, reversed

obconicus like an inverted cone
  Primula obconica

obliquus oblique, awry, lopsided
  Nothofagus obliqua

oblongifolius with oblong leaves
  (see below)
  Aster oblongifolius

oblongus, oblongatus oblong
  Cydonia oblonga (quince)

obovatus obovate; inversely ovate
  Paeonia obovata

obscurus obscure, indistinct, dark
  Digitalis obscura

obtusatus blunted
  Hebe obtusata

obtusifolius with blunt leaves
  Cistus × *obtusifolius*

obtusilobus with blunt lobes
  Anemone obtusiloba

obtusus blunt, obtuse
  Chamaecyparis obtusa

obvallaris (literally) walled around
  Narcissus obvallaris

occidentalis western
  Gentiana occidentalis

ocellatus with an eye
  Geranium ocellatum

ochraceus ochre
  Hebe ochracea

ochroleucus yellowish white
  Corydalis ochroleuca

oct-, octo- eight

octopetalus with eight petals
  Dryas octopetala

oculatus with an eye
  Lychnis coronaria Oculata Group

oculus-christi Christ's eye
  Inula oculus-christi

oculus-draconis dragon's eye
  Pinus densiflora 'Oculus-draconis'

ocymoides like *Ocimum* (basil)
  Halimium ocymoides

COMMON DESCRIPTIVE TERMS

odoratus, odorus scented, fragrant

Daphne odora

Galium odoratum (sweet woodruff)

Lathyrus odoratus (sweet pea)

Myrrhis odorata (sweet cicely)

Nymphaea odorata

Reseda odorata (mignonette)

Rosa × *odorata* 'Mutabilis'

Viola odorata (sweet violet)

VIOLA ODORATA

WHAT'S IN A NAME?

HABITATS

acraeus living on the heights
agrarius of fields
agrestis rural, rustic; of fields
alpestris growing just below the alpine zone
alpinus alpine, of high mountains
ammophilus sand-loving
amphibius amphibious, growing in water and on land
aquaticus, aquatilis of water; growing by water
arcticus arctic
arenarius of sandy places
arvensis of fields
calcareus chalky, of limestone
calcicola growing on limy soil
campestris, camporum of fields or plains
clivorum of slopes
collinus of hills
cultorum of cultivated land such as gardens
dumetorum of thickets and hedgerows
eremicus of deserts
fluminalis, flumineus, fluviatilis of rivers
fontanus; fontinalis growing in or by springs
frigidus cold; growing in cold locations
glacialis glacial, from cold places
glareosus of gravel
hortensis of gardens
hylaeus of woods
insularis of islands
lacustris of lakes
limosus of marshes

lithophilus stone-loving, growing in stony places
littoralis pertaining to the seashore
maritimus coastal, found near the sea
montanus of mountains
muralis of walls, growing on walls
nemorosus growing in woods
nesophilus island-loving
niphophilus snow-loving
oreophilus mountain-loving
paludosus marshy
palustris of marshes
petraeus growing among rocks
petrophilus rock-loving
pratensis of meadows
riparius of riverbanks
rivalis, rivularis found near brooks
rupestris growing among rocks
rusticanus, rusticus rural, of the country
salinus salty, growing in salty locations
saxatilis, saxosus stony, found among rocks
scopulorum of rocks, cliffs or crags
siliceus growing in sand
spelunca a cave; growing in caves
subalpinus growing below the timber line
sylvaticus, sylvestris of woods
tectorum of roofs
uliginosus marshy, growing in wet places
umbrosus growing in shade
urbanus, urbium urban, of towns
vulcanicus of volcanoes, growing in volcanic soil

CULTIVAR NAMES
Colors: Pink

ASTER ERICOIDES 'PINK CLOUD'

ASTER NOVAE-ANGLIAE
'HARRINGTON'S PINK'

AUBRIETA 'BRESSINGHAM PINK'

CANNA 'PINK SUNBURST'

CLEMATIS 'PINK FLAMINGO'

CLETHRA ALNIFOLIA 'PINK SPIRE'

COLCHICUM 'PINK GOBLET'

CORDYLINE AUSTRALIS 'PINK STRIPE'

DAHLIA 'PINK PASTELLE'

DIANTHUS 'PIKE'S PINK'

ERICA CARNEA 'PINK SPANGLES'

EUCRYPHIA LUCIDA 'PINK CLOUD'

FUCHSIA 'PINK MARSHMALLOW'

GAURA LINDHEIMERI 'SISKIYOU PINK'

GERANIUM SYLVATICUM F. *ROSEUM*
'BAKER'S PINK'

HEBE 'PINK ELEPHANT'

HEMEROCALLIS 'PINK DAMASK'

HYACINTHUS ORIENTALIS 'PINK PEARL'

KOLKWITZIA AMABILIS 'PINK CLOUD'

LAVANDULA ANGUSTIFOLIA 'LODDON
PINK'

LILIUM PINK PERFECTION GROUP

MAGNOLIA 'PINKIE'

MONARDA 'CROFTWAY PINK'

PENSTEMON 'HEWELL PINK BEDDER'

PHYGELIUS AEQUALIS 'TREWIDDEN
PINK'

POTENTILLA FRUTICOSA 'PINK
BEAUTY'

PRUNUS 'PINK PERFECTION'

RIBES SANGUINEUM 'POKY'S PINK'

SORBUS 'PINK-NESS'

CALENDULA OFFICINALIS

COMMON DESCRIPTIVE TERMS

officinalis sold in (apothecaries')
shops; used in medicine

Borago officinalis (borage)

Calendula officinalis (pot marigold)

Hyssopus officinalis (hyssop)

Jasminum officinale (jasmine)

Levisticum officinale (lovage)

Melissa officinalis (lemon balm)

Paeonia officinalis (paeony)

Rosmarinus officinalis (rosemary)

Salvia officinalis (sage)

ogisui named for the Japanese
botanist Mikinori Ogisu

Epimedium ogisui

ohiensis from Ohio

olbius, olbiensis from the Iles
d'Hyères, off the Mediterranean
coast of France

Lavatera olbia

oleoides like *Olea* (olive)
 Daphne oleoides
oleifolius with leaves like olive
 Lithodora oleifolia
oleraceus relating to vegetables
 and herbs; of the kitchen garden
 (alternative form of *holeraceus*)
 Brassica oleracea
olig-, oligo- few (see below)
oligophyllus with few leaves
 Ornithogalum oligophyllum
olympicus from Olympus (referring
 to several high mountains: in
 Greece, Asia Minor and America)
 Verbascum olympicum
omeianus, omeiensis from Emei Shan
 (Mount Omei) in Sichuan, China
 Impatiens omeiana
opacus shady, dark
 Ilex opaca
ophiocarpus with snakelike fruits
 Corydalis ophiocarpa
oppositiflorus opposite-flowered
 Gladiolus oppositiflorus
oppositifolius opposite-leaved
 Chrysosplenium oppositifolium
opulifolius with maple-like leaves
 Physocarpus opulifolius
opulus old term for a kind of
 maple tree
 Viburnum opulus
orbiculatus, orbicularis disc-shaped,
 round
 Celastrus orbiculatus

CULTIVAR NAMES
Personal Names
N, O

Iris 'Broadleigh Nancy'
Rhododendron 'Naomi'
Clematis 'Natacha'
Geranium 'Natalie'
Phlox maculata 'Natascha'
Erica carnea 'Nathalie'
Hebe 'Neil's Choice'
Hebe 'Nicola's Blush'
Primula auricula 'Nigel'
Clematis 'Olga'
Delphinium 'Oliver'
Lilium 'Olivia'

---

orcadensis from Orkney, Scotland
orchidiflorus with flowers like orchid
 Gladiolus orchidiflorus
orchioides orchid-like
 Iris orchioides

Common descriptive terms
oreganus, oregonensis, oregonus
 from the north-western USA: the
 state of Oregon, or the Oregon
 division of the Hudson's Bay
 Company, which also included
 Washington State
Erythronium oregonum
Geranium oreganum
Oxalis oregana
Sedum oreganum
Sedum oregonense

---

oreophilus mountain-loving

oreoprasum mountain leek

   Allium oreoprasum

COMMON DESCRIPTIVE TERMS

orientalis eastern; from the Orient

Crataegus orientalis

Doronicum orientale

Helleborus orientalis

Hyacinthus orientalis

Iris orientalis

Papaver orientale

Pennisetum orientale

Platanus orientalis

---

ornatus showy

   Musa ornata

ornithopodus like a bird's foot

   Carex ornithopoda 'Variegata'

ortho- straight, upright

orthophyllus with straight leaves

ottawensis from Ottawa, Canada

   Berberis × *ottawensis*

ovalifolius with oval leaves

   Ligustrum ovalifolium

ovalis oval, broadly elliptic

   Carex ovalis

GENUS NAMES
N,O

Nectaroscordum from Greek *nektar,*
   nectar, and *scorodon*, garlic

Nemophila from Greek *nemos*, wood
   pasture, and *philo*, to love

Nerine named for a mythical sea-
   nymph

Nicotiana named for Jean Nicot
   (1530–1600), a French ambassador
   in Portugal

Nigella from Latin, a diminutive
   of *niger*, black

Nymphaea from Greek *nymphaia*,
   a water-nymph

Olearia Latinized name for Johann
   Ölschläger (1635–1711), a German
   horticulturist

Omphalodes from Greek *omphalos*,
   navel

Onopordum from Greek *onos*, ass,
   and *porde*, breaking wind

Ophiopogon from Greek *ophis*, snake,
   and *pogon*, beard

Ornithogalum from Greek *ornis*, bird,
   and *gala*, milk

Osmanthus from Greek *osme*,
   fragrance, and *anthos*, flower

Oxalis from Greek *oxys*, acid

Naked ladies *Colchicum*
Nasturtium *Tropaeolum majus*
Navelwort *Omphalodes*
Nettle tree *Celtis*
New England aster *Aster novae-angliae*
New York aster *Aster novi-belgii*
New Zealand flax *Phormium tenax*
Night-scented stock *Matthiola bicornis*
Nightshade *Solanum*
Ninebark *Physocarpus*
Norfolk Island pine *Araucaria heterophylla*
Norway maple *Acer platanoides*
Norway spruce *Picea abies*
Oak *Quercus*
Obedient plant *Physostegia virginiana*
Old man's beard *Clematis vitalba*
Oleander *Nerium oleander*
Oleaster *Elaeagnus angustifolia*
Olive *Olea europaea*
Opium poppy *Papaver somniferum*
Orache *Atriplex hortensis*
Orchid *Dactylorhiza, Orchis, Ophrys, etc.*
Oregon grape *Mahonia aquifolium*

OPIUM POPPY

Oriental poppy *Papaver orientale*
Orpine *Sedum telephium*
Osier *Salix viminalis*
Ostrich fern *Matteuccia struthiopteris*
Oswego tea *Monarda didyma*
Oxeye daisy *Leucanthemum vulgare*
Oxlip *Primula elatior*

COMMON DESCRIPTIVE TERMS

ovatus ovate, egg-shaped
Asteranthera ovata
Codonopsis ovata
Crassula ovata
Forsythia ovata
Penstemon ovatus

---

ovifer bearing eggs or egg-shaped structures (seeds, etc.)

ovinus for sheep
Festuca ovina
oxonianus, oxoniensis from Oxford, UK
Geranium × *oxonianum*
oxy- sharp-; sour, acidic (see below)
oxyacanthus with sharp thorns
Fraxinus angustifolia subsp. *oxycarpa*
oxypetalus with sharp petals
oxysepalus with sharp sepals
Aquilegia oxysepala

P

pachy- thick

pachycarpus with a thick (thick-shelled) fruit

pachypodus with a thick stalk

pacifica of the Pacific Ocean
  Gypsophila pacifica

padus wild cherry
  Prunus padus

pallescens rather pale, becoming pale

pallidiflorus pale-flowered
  Fritillaria pallidiflora

COMMON DESCRIPTIVE TERMS

pallidus pale
Callistemon pallidus
Hamamelis × *intermedia* 'Pallida'
Iris pallida
Juncus pallidus
Mahonia pallida

palmatus palmate
Acer palmatum
Filipendula palmata
Geranium palmatum
Kirengeshoma palmata
Primula palmatum
Rheum palmatum

---

paludosus marshy
  Epacris paludosa

GENUS NAMES

P

Pachysandra from Greek *pachys*, thick, and *andros*, stamen

Parrotia named for F.W. Parrot (1792–1841), a German naturalist

Parthenocissus from Greek *parthenos*, virgin, and *kissos*, ivy

Paulownia named for Princess Anna Paulowna (1795–1865), daughter of the Czar of Russia

Pelargonium from Greek *pelargos*, a stork

Pennisetum from Latin *penna*, feather, and *seta*, bristle

Penstemon from Greek *pente*, five, and *stemon*, stamen

Perovskia named for V.A. Perovski (1794–1857), a Russian general

Philadelphus from Greek *philadelphos*, brotherly love

Phlox in Greek, a flame

Phormium from Greek *phormion*, mat

Photinia from Greek *phos*, light

Phyllostachys from Greek *phyllon*, leaf, and *stachys*, spike

Physocarpus from Greek *physa*, a bladder, and *karpos*, fruit

Pittosporum from Greek *pitta*, pitch, and *spora*, seed

Platycodon from Greek *platys*, broad, and *kodon*, bell

Polypodium from Greek *polys*, many, and *pous*, foot

Potentilla from Latin *potens*, powerful

Primula from Latin *primus*, first

Pulmonaria from Latin *pulmo*, lung

Pyracantha from Greek *pyr*, fire, and *akantha*, thorn

COMMON DESCRIPTIVE TERMS

palustris of marshes
Calla palustris
Caltha palustris
Epipactis palustris
Euphorbia palustris
Hottonia palustris
Ledum palustre
Pinus palustris
Quercus palustris

pandanifolius with leaves like
    Pandanus (screw pine)
    Eryngium pandanifolium

COMMON DESCRIPTIVE TERMS

paniculatus with flowers arranged
    in panicles
Fuchsia paniculata
Gypsophila paniculata
Hydrangea paniculata
Kolreuteria paniculata
Phlox paniculata

papilio butterfly
    Gladiolus papilio
papyraceus papery
    Narcissus papyraceus
papyrifer paper-bearing
    Betula papyrifera
paradoxus paradoxical; unexpected
    Gentiana paradoxa
paraguayensis from Paraguay
    Azara paraguayensis

CULTIVAR NAMES
World of Music

PELARGONIUM 'ABBA'
CAREX CARYOPHYLLEA 'THE BEATLES'
RHODODENDRON 'BEETHOVEN'
HEMEROCALLIS 'LEONARD BERNSTEIN'
ROSA BENJAMIN BRITTEN ('AUSENCART')
PELARGONIUM 'BOLERO'
RHODODENDRON 'CARMEN'
TULIPA 'CHOPIN'
PRIMULA AURICULA 'CHORISTER'
× *PHYLLIOPSIS* 'COPPELIA'
NARCISSUS 'DÉLIBES'
PHORMIUM 'DUET'
CLEMATIS 'JACQUELINE DU PRÉ'
PAEONIA LACTIFLORA 'SIR EDWARD ELGAR'
PRIMULA AURICULA 'FIGARO'
ROSA 'KATHLEEN FERRIER'
ROSA HANDEL ('MACHA')
PELARGONIUM 'JOSEF HAYDN'
PELARGONIUM 'JAZZ'
CLEMATIS 'KIRI TE KANAWA'
CHAENOMELES 'MADAME BUTTERFLY'
ROSA 'MOZART'
PAPAVER ORIENTALE 'PIZZICATO'
IRIS 'RINGO'
PRUNUS VIRGINIANA 'SCHUBERT'
SAXIFRAGA 'FRANK SINATRA'
TULIPA 'JOHANN STRAUSS'
PRIMULA AURICULA 'SYMPHONY'
PHLOX PANICULATA 'TENOR'
PRIMULA AURICULA 'TOSCA'
CANNA 'VERDI'

pardalianches (literally) poisonous
  to panthers; hence leopard's bane
  Doronicum pardalianches
pardalinus spotted like a leopard
  Lilium pardalinum
parnassicus from Mt Parnassus, Greece
  Colchicum parnassicum

COMMON DESCRIPTIVE TERMS
parviflorus with small flowers
Aesculus parviflora
Agave parviflora
Cistus parviflorus
Digitalis parviflora
Lithophragma parviflorum
Pinus parviflora

---

parvifolius with small leaves
  Eucalyptus parvifolia
patagonicus from Patagonia
  Oxalis patagonica
patens spreading
  Salvia patens
patulus spreading
  Tagetes patula
pauci- few (see below)

COMMON DESCRIPTIVE TERMS
pauciflorus with few flowers
Corylopsis pauciflora
Dierama pauciflorum
Eucalyptus pauciflora
Kniphofia pauciflora
Polemonium pauciflorum

---

paucinervis with few veins
pauciramosus with few branches
  Hebe pauciramosa
pauculus very few
pausiacus olive green
pavoninus like a peacock (in color
  – peacock blue – or with an "eye")
  Anemone pavonina
pectinatus like a comb, combed
  Euryops pectinatus
pedatisectus cut like a foot
  Pinellia pedatisecta
pedatus like a foot (usually meaning
  a bird's foot)
  Adiantum pedatum
pedemontanus from Piedmont, Italy
  Primula pedemontana
peduncularis, pedunculatus with
  a peduncle (flower stalk)
  Veronica peduncularis
pekinensis from Beijing, China
  Phyllostachys aureosulcata f.
  pekinensis
pelagicus of the sea
pelargoniiflorus with flowers like
  Pelargonium
  Erodium pelargoniiflorum
pellucidus translucent
peloponnesiacus from the
  Peloponnese region of Greece
  Cyclamen peloponnesiacum
peltatus like a *pelta*, a small, half-
  moon-shaped shield
  Darmera peltata

Paeony, peony *Paeonia*
Pagoda dogwood *Cornus alternifolia*
Palm *Phoenix, Trachycarpus* etc.
Pampas grass *Cortaderia selloana*
Pansy *Viola × wittrockiana*
Paper birch *Betula papyrifera*
Paperbark maple *Acer griseum*
Pasque flower *Pulsatilla vulgaris*
Passion flower *Passiflora*
Peach-leaved bellflower *Campanula persicifolia*
Pear *Pyrus communis*
Pearl everlasting *Anaphalis margaritacea*
Pearlbush *Exochorda*
Pebble plants *Lithops*
Pecan *Carya illinoinensis*
Pendulous sedge *Carex pendula*
Père David's maple *Acer davidii*
Periwinkle *Vinca*
Pheasant's eye *Narcissus poeticus* var. *recurvus*
Pickerel weed *Pontaderia cordata*
Piggyback plant *Tolmiea menziesii*
Pimpernel *Anagallis*
Pine *Pinus*

Pineapple broom *Cytisus battandieri*
Pink *Dianthus*
Pitcher plant *Nepenthes; Sarracenia*
Plane *Platanus* (in Scotland: *Acer pseudoplatanus*)
Plantain *Plantago*
Plantain lily *Hosta*
Plume poppy *Macleaya*
Poached-egg flower *Limnanthes douglasii*
Poinsettia *Euphorbia pulcherrima*
Poison ivy *Rhus radicans*
Pokeberry, pokeweed *Phytolacca americana*
Polyanthus *Primula polyantha*
Poplar *Populus*
Poppy *Papaver*
Portugal laurel *Prunus lusitanica*
Pot marigold *Calendula officinalis*
Prickly pear *Opuntia*
Primrose *Primula vulgaris*
Privet *Ligustrum*
Purple loosestrife *Lythrum salicaria*
Purple moor grass *Molinia caerulea*
Purslane *Portulaca*

PINK

WHAT'S IN A NAME?

FLOWER CHARACTERISTICS

acutiflorus with sharply pointed flowers

albiflorus, albiflos white-flowered

amblyanthus with blunt flowers

angustipetalus narrow-petaled

anopetalus with upright petals

apetalus without petals

brevipedunculatus with a short flower-stalk

brevipetalus with short petals

callianthus with beautiful flowers

campaniflorus with bell-shaped flowers

chasmanthus with wide-open flowers

chrysanthus with golden flowers

congestiflorus with closely packed flowers

corymbiflorus with flowers in a corymb

curviflorus with curved flowers

densiflorus densely flowered

dolichostachyus with a long spike

erianthus with woolly flowers

fasciculiflorus with flowers in clusters

flore pleno with double flowers

floridus flowering abundantly

geminiflorus with twin flowers

globiferus bearing globe-shaped clusters

globispicus with globose spikes

glomeratus clustered in a head

grandiflorus large-flowered

lactiflorus with milky-colored flowers

laetiflorus with bright flowers

latisepalus with broad sepals

laxiflorus loose-flowered

longiflorus with long flowers

longipetalus with long petals

lophanthus with crested flowers

macranthus with large flowers

macropetalus with large petals

megalanthus with large flowers

micranthus with small flowers

nudiflorus with naked flowers (i.e. flowering before the leaves open)

oppositiflorus opposite-flowered

oxypetalus with sharp petals

pallidiflorus pale-flowered

paniculatus with flowers arranged in panicles

parviflorus with small flowers

platyanthus with broad flowers

platypetalus with broad (or flat) petals

pleniflorus with double (full) flowers

plenus double (full)

pogonanthus with bearded flowers

polyandrus with many anthers

polyanthus with many flowers

psilostemon with bare or smooth stamens

racemosus with flowers in racemes

radiatus with rays; radiating in form

rariflorus with scattered flowers

recurvus, recurvatus recurved, curved backwards

reflexus bent back

sessiliflorus with sessile flowers

stenanthera with narrow anthers

stylosus with a conspicuous or large style

thyrsiflorus with flowers in a thyrse

thyrsoides like a thyrse

umbellatus umbelliferous

viridiflorus with green flowers

COMMON DESCRIPTIVE TERMS

pendulus pendulous, hanging
Betula pendula (silver birch)
Carex pendula (pendulous sedge)
Cercidiphyllum japonicum f. *pendulum*
Dierama pendulum
Fraxinus excelsior 'Pendula'
Pyrus salicifolia 'Pendula'

penicillaris with a paintbrush-like
  tuft of hair
  Melica penicillaris
pensylvanicus from Pennsylvania
  Acer pensylvanicum
penta- five (see below)
pentapetalus with five petals
  Geum pentapetalum
pentaphyllus with five leaves
  or leaflets
  Acer pentaphyllum
perdicarius of partridges
  Oxalis perdicaria
peregrinans wandering abroad, in
  foreign parts
  Libertia peregrinans
peregrinus foreign, exotic
  Tropaeolum peregrinum

COMMON DESCRIPTIVE TERMS

perennis perennial
Bellis perennis
Linum perenne
Oenothera perennis
Pterocephalus perennis

CULTIVAR NAMES
Personal Names
P

DIGITALIS PURPUREA 'PAM'S CHOICE'
CLEMATIS 'PAMELA'
PRIMULA 'OUR PAT'
GERANIUM 'PATRICIA'
PAPAVER ORIENTALE 'PATTY'S PLUM'
CRATAEGUS LAEVIGATA 'PAUL'S
  SCARLET'
HEBE 'PAULA'
CLEMATIS 'PAULINE'
FUCHSIA 'PEGGY'
ROSA 'PENELOPE'
PELARGONIUM 'PENNY'
DAHLIA 'PETER'
GENTIANA ASCLEPIADEA 'PHYLLIS'
FUCHSIA 'PEGGY'
HYDRANGEA MACROPHYLLA 'PIA'
ROSA 'POLLY'

COMMON DESCRIPTIVE TERMS

perfoliatus perfoliate (with the
  leaf surrounding the stem)
Claytonia perfoliata
Eupatorium perfoliatum
Parahebe perfoliata
Smyrnium perfoliatum

---

perforatus pierced with holes or pores
  Hypericum perforatum
periclymenum honeysuckle (Greek)
  Lonicera periclymenum
permixtus much mixed

perralderianus named for a French naturalist, Henri de la Perraudière (1831–1861)

   Epimedium perralderianum

persicifolius with leaves like *Prunus persica* (peach tree)

   Campanula persicifolia

COMMON DESCRIPTIVE TERMS

persicus from Iran (Persia)

Cyclamen persicum

Fritillaria persica

Morina persica

Parrotia persica

---

persimilis very similar (e.g. to another species)

   Crataegus persimilis 'Prunifolia'

perspicuus transparent

perulatus with conspicuous bud-scales (perules)

   Enkianthus perulatus

peruvianus Peruvian

   Scilla peruviana (named by Linnaeus in error – it actually comes from the Mediterranean

---

COMMON DESCRIPTIVE TERMS

petiolaris with a (long) leaf stalk (petiole)

Helichrysum petiolare

Hydrangea anomala subsp. *petiolaris*

Primula petiolaris

Tilia 'Petiolaris'

---

petraeus growing among rocks
   Quercus petraea
petrophilus rock-loving
   Epacris petrophila
phaeus dusky
   Geranium phaeum
phello- cork
   Euonymus phellomanus
philadelphicus from Philadelphia
   Erigeron philadelphicus
philippinensis from the Philippines
   Lilium philippinensis
phillyreoides like *Phillyrea*
   Quercus phillyreoides
phlogopappus with seeds like *Phlox*
   Olearia phlogopappa
phoeniceus Phoenician; purple-red
   (from the Phoenician purple dye
   made from the mollusc
   Murex)
   Verbascum phoeniceum
phu rotten-smelling; acrid
   Valeriana phu 'Aurea'
phyllocephalus with a leafy head
   Carex phyllocephala
physalodes like *Physalis*
   Nicandra physalodes
picturatus embellished; variegated
   Crocus vernus 'Picturatus'
pictus (literally) painted; vividly
   colored
   Acer pictum
pileatus with a cap
   Lonicera pileata

VALERIANA PHU

COMMON DESCRIPTIVE TERMS

pilosus with long soft hairs, shaggy
Dipsacus pilosus
Genista pilosa
Luzula pilosa
Papaver pilosum

---

pilosissimus very shaggy
   Heuchera pilosissima
pilulifer bearing little balls
   (small globular fruits)
   Carex pilulifera
pimeleoides like the Australian
   evergreen shrub *Pimelea*
   Hebe pimeleoides

pimpinellifolius with pinnate leaves
  like the umbelliferous plant
  Pimpinella
  Rosa pimpinellifolia
pinaster wild pine
  Pinus pinaster
pinguifolius with fat leaves
  Hebe pinguifolia
pinifolius with leaves like pine
pinnatifidus pinnately divided
  Quercus dentata 'Pinnatifida'
pinnatisectus pinnately cut
  Erigeron pinnatisectus

PINNATIFIDUS

COMMON DESCRIPTIVE TERMS
pinnatus pinnate
Epimedium pinnatum
Lavandula pinnata
Mahonia pinnata
Santolina pinnata

---

piperitus like pepper
  Mentha × *piperita*
pisifer (literally) bearing peas
  Chamaecyparis pisifera
planifolius with flat leaves
  Iris planifolia
planipes with a flat stalk or foot
  Euonymus planipes
planiscapus with a flat or even scape
  (leafless stem)
  Ophiopogon planiscapus
plantagineus like *Plantago* (plantain)
  Hosta plantaginea

platanifolius with leaves like *Platanus*
  (plane tree)
  Ranunculus platanifolius
planus flat
  Eryngium planum
platanoides like *Platanus*
  Acer platanoides
platy- broad, flat
platyanthus with broad flowers
  Geranium platyanthum
platyglossus with a broad tongue
  Phyllostachys platyglossa
platypetalus with broad (or flat)
  petals
  Epimedium platypetalum

COMMON DESCRIPTIVE TERMS
platyphyllus, platyphyllos with
  broad (or flat) leaves
Galanthus platyphyllus
Lilium auratum var. *platyphyllum*
Limonium platyphyllum
Tilia platyphyllos

---

pleniflorus with double (full) flowers
  Kerria japonica 'Pleniflora'

plenus double (flowers); full (see also page 81, *flore pleno*)
  Clematis 'Purpurea Plena Elegans'
plicatus folded or pleated
  Viburnum plicatum
plinianus named for the 1st-century AD Roman scholar Pliny the Elder
  Arundo pliniana
plumarius feathery
  Dianthus plumarius
plumbaginoides like *Plumbago*
  Ceratostigma plumbaginoides

page 81, *flore pleno*

COMMON DESCRIPTIVE TERMS

plumosus feathered
Gymnocarpium dryopteris 'Plumosum'
Muscari comosum 'Plumosum'
Sambucus racemosa 'Plumosa Aurea'

pluricaulis with several stems
  Sedum pluricaule
poculiformis cup-shaped
  Galanthus nivalis Poculiformis Group

CULTIVAR NAMES
Gardeners and Plantsmen

THYMUS PULEGIOIDES 'BERTRAM ANDERSON'
HELLEBORUS × *HYBRIDUS* 'HELEN BALLARD'
CROCUS CHRYSANTHUS 'E.A. BOWLES'
GERANIUM MACULATUM 'BETH CHATTO'
HEUCHERA 'HELEN DILLON'
FUCHSIA CHARLIE DIMMOCK ('FONCHA')
FORSYTHIA 'BEATRIX FARRAND'
ARTEMISIA LUDOVICIANA 'VALERIE FINNIS'
PENSTEMON 'MARGERY FISH'
MAHONIA × *MEDIA* 'LIONEL FORTESCUE'
PENSTEMON 'GEOFF HAMILTON'
OENOTHERA 'PENELOPE HOBHOUSE'
ACER PALMATUM 'COLLINGWOOD INGRAM'
VINCA MINOR F. *ALBA* 'GERTRUDE JEKYLL'
ROSA 'LAWRENCE JOHNSTON'
COLCHICUM AUTUMNALE 'NANCY LINDSAY'

GAZANIA 'CHRISTOPHER LLOYD'
NARCISSUS 'CEDRIC MORRIS'
PULMONARIA 'LEWIS PALMER'
MECONOPSIS CAMBRICA 'FRANCES PERRY'
ARTEMISIA ARBORESCENS 'FAITH RAVEN'
VIOLA 'VITA'
DIANTHUS 'LADY SALISBURY'
BERGENIA 'ERIC SMITH'
FUCHSIA 'GEOFFREY SMITH'
PRIMULA AURICULA 'ANNE SWITHINBANK'
ROSA GRAHAM THOMAS ('AUSMAS')
ASTER NOVI-BELGII 'PERCY THROWER'
DIANTHUS 'ALAN TITCHMARSH'
VIOLA 'TONY VENISON'
GERANIUM × *OXONIANUM* 'ROSEMARY VEREY'
SCABIOSA CAUCASICA 'MISS WILLMOTT'

podagricus swollen at the base (literally 'gouty')
   Jatropha podagrica
podophyllus with stalked leaves
   Rodgersia podophylla
poeticus, poetarum relating to (usually Classical) poets
   Narcissus poeticus
pogonanthus with bearded flowers
   Geranium pogonanthum
polifolius gray-leaved
   Andromeda polifolia
poluninianus named for Oleg Polunin (1914–1985), the British botanist, author and plant collector
   Saxifraga poluniniana
poly- many (see below)
polyacanthus with many thorns
   Opuntia polyacantha
polyandrus with many anthers
   Phytolacca polyandra
polyanthus with many flowers
   Jasminum polyanthum
polycarpus with many fruits
polychromus many-colored
   Euphorbia polychroma
polymorphus with many forms
   Persicaria polymorpha
polyneurus with many veins
   Primula polyneura
polyphyllus with many leaves
   Paris polyphylla
polytrichus with many hairs
   Draba polytricha

pomifer bearing apples
ponderosus heavy
   Pinus ponderosa

COMMON DESCRIPTIVE TERMS
ponticus from Pontus, an area south of the Black Sea, in Asia Minor
Artemisia pontica
Daphne pontica
Fritillaria pontica
Quercus pontica
Rhododendron ponticum

---

populifolius with leaves like *Populus* (poplar)
   Cistus populifolius
porphyrophyllus with purple leaves
   Sambucus nigra f. *porphyrophylla*
populneus of poplars
   Hoheria populnea
portenschlagianus named for Franz von Portenschlag-Ledermayer (1777–1827), an Austrian botanist
   Campanula portenschlagiana
poscharskyanus named for Gustav Poscharsky (1832–1914), a German gardener
   Campanula poscharskyana
potaninii named for Grigori Potanin (1835–1920), a Russian naturalist and explorer
   Indigofera potaninii
potentilloides like *Potentilla*
   Geranium potentilloides

CULTIVAR NAMES
Foreign Expressions

P

PAPILLON (*French*) BUTTERFLY
(*IRIS SIBIRICA* 'PAPILLON')

PARELMOER (*Dutch*)
MOTHER OF PEARL
(*GAULTHERIA MUCRONATA* 'PARELMOER')

PERLE D'AZUR (*French*) AZURE PEARL
(*CLEMATIS* 'PERLE D'AZUR')

PERLMUTTERSCHALE (*German*)
MOTHER OF PEARL
(*PLATYCODON GRANDIFLORUS*
'PERLMUTTERSCHALE')

PETIT FAUCON (*French*)
LITTLE FALCON
(*CLEMATIS* PETIT FAUCON
('EVISIX'))

PLUIE DE FEU (*French*) RAIN OF FIRE
(*HEUCHERA* 'PLUIE DE FEU')

POLARSOMMER (*German*)
ARCTIC SUMMER
(*VERBASCUM BOMBYCIFERUM*
'POLARSOMMER')

PORZELLAN (*German*)
PORCELAIN
(*NEPETA* 'PORZELLAN')

PRÄRIENACHT (*German*)
PRAIRIE NIGHT
(*MONARDA* 'PRÄRIENACHT')

PREZIOSA (*Italian*) PRECIOUS
(*HYDRANGEA* 'PREZIOSA')

PRIMAVERA (*Italian*) SPRING
(*CAMELLIA JAPONICA* 'PRIMAVERA')

PRINZ HEINRICH (*German*)
PRINCE HENRY
(*ANEMONE* × *HUPEHENSIS* VAR. *JAPONICA*
'PRINZ HEINRICH')

PÜNKTCHEN (*German*)
LITTLE DOT
(*MISCANTHUS SINENSIS* 'PÜNKTCHEN')

PURPURLANZE (*German*)
PURPLE LANCE
(*ASTILBE CHINENSIS* VAR. *TAQUETII*
'PURPURLANZE')

COMMON DESCRIPTIVE TERMS

praecox precocious, developing early
Chimonanthus praecox
Clematis 'Praecox'
Cytisus × *praecox*
Hydrangea paniculata 'Praecox'
Prunus incisa 'Praecox'
Rhododendron 'Praecox'
Stachyurus praecox

praemorsus as if bitten off
praestans distinguished, excellent
   Tulipa praestans
praeteritus past
praetermissus neglected, overlooked,
   omitted
   Dactylorhiza praetermissa
praetextus fringed, bordered
prasinus green like a leek

WHAT'S IN A NAME?

NURSERIES AND NURSERYMEN

backhouseanus James Backhouse (1794–1869), English nurseryman

beesianus Bees, nursery and seed supplier in Cheshire, UK

burkwoodii Arthur (1888–1951) and Albert Burkwood, nurserymen at Kingston upon Thames, Surrey, UK

durandii Durand Frères, French nursery

fraseri John Fraser (1750–1811), London nurseryman and plant collector in North America

frikartii Carl Ludwig Frikart (1879-1964), Swiss nurseryman

jackmanii George Jackman (1801–1869) and his son, British clematis breeders in Woking, Surrey, UK

lawsonianus Charles Lawson (1794–1873), Scottish nurseryman who raised Lawson's cypress from seed

lemoinei Victor Lemoine (1823–1911) and his son Emile (1862–1942), French nurserymen

lizei Lizé Frères, nursery in Nantes, France

soulangeanus Etienne Soulange-Bodin (1774–1846), French horticulturist

sprengeri Karl Sprenger (1846–1917), German nurseryman working in Italy

standishii John Standish (1814–1875), British nurseryman

vanhouttei Louis Van Houtte (1810–1876), Belgian nurseryman,

veitchii, veitchianus Veitch & Sons, 19th-century nurseries in Exeter and London, UK

vilmorinii Vilmorin-Andrieux, French nursery and seed supplier

---

COMMON DESCRIPTIVE TERMS

pratensis of meadows

Cardamine pratensis (lady's smock)

Geranium pratense (meadow cranesbill)

Lathyrus pratensis

Pulsatilla pratensis

---

primulifolius with leaves like *Primula*

Campanula primulifolia

primuloides like *Primula*

Mimulus primuloides

princeps princely, most distinguished

Artemisia princeps

prismaticus prism-shaped

Iris prismatica

proboscideus with a proboscis or snout

Arisarum proboscideum

procerus high, tall

Ulmus procera (English elm)

COMMON DESCRIPTIVE TERMS

procumbens prostrate

Asarina procumbens

Fuchsia procumbens

Gaultheria procumbens

Juniperus procumbens

---

procurrens spreading, running

Arabis procurrens

proliferus free-flowering; or reproducing by offshoots

Primula prolifera

prolificus prolific, fruitful
  Hypericum prolificum
propinquus related, neighboring
  Phyllostachys propinqua
prostratus prostrate
  Veronica prostrata
proteiflorus with flowers like *Protea*
  Eryngium proteiflorum
prunifolia with leaves like *Prunus*
  Crataegus persimilis 'Prunifolia'
przewalskii named for a Russian
  explorer and naturalist, Nikolai
  Przewalski (1839–1888)
  Ligularia przewalskii
pseud-, pseudo- false (see below)
pseudacorus like ("false") *Acorus*
  (sweet flag)
  Iris pseudacorus
pseudoacacia like ("false") *Acacia*
  Robinia pseudoacacia
pseudocamellia like ("false") *Camellia*
  Stewartia pseudocamellia
pseudocyperus like ("false") *Cyperus*
  Carex pseudocyperus
pseudodictamnus like ("false")
  Dictamnus
  Ballota pseudodictamnus
pseudonarcissus like ("false") *Narcissus*
  Narcissus pseudonarcissus
pseudoplatanus like ("false") *Platanus*
  (plane)
  Acer pseudoplatanus (sycamore)
psilostemon with smooth stamens
  Geranium psilostemon

psittacinus like a parrot
  Alstroemeria psittacina
ptarmicus, ptarmicoides sneeze-
  inducing
  Achillea ptarmica
  Aster ptarmicoides
puberulus slightly downy
  Helenium puberulum

COMMON DESCRIPTIVE TERMS
pubescens, pubiger downy, with
  soft hair
Betula pubescens
Epimedium pubigerum
Primula × *pubescens*
Syringa pubescens

---

pudicus shy
  Mimosa pudica

COMMON DESCRIPTIVE TERMS
pulcher, pulchellus beautiful, pretty
Coleonema pulchrum
Correa pulchella
Crocus pulchellus
Deutzia pulchra
Dodecathon pulchellum
Gaillardia pulchella
Geranium pulchrum
Heuchera pulchella

---

pulcherrimus very beautiful
  Dierama pulcherrimum
pulchra see *pulcher*

DIGITALIS PURPUREA

pulegius, pulegioides derived
  from Latin *pulex* (flea),
  indicating flea-repellent qualities
  in aromatic plants
  Mentha pulegium (Pennyroyal)
  Thymus pulegioides
pullus dark in color
  Campanula pulla

---

pulverulentus dusty
Cistus × *pulverulentus*
Eucalyptus pulverulenta
Primula pulverulenta
Sambucus nigra 'Pulverulenta'

---

pulvinaris, pulvinatus like a cushion
  Myosotis pulvinaris

pumilus dwarf
Astilbe chinensis var. *pumila*
Cortaderia selloana 'Pumila'
Ficus pumila
Iris pumila
Lilium pumilum
Pinus pumila

---

punctatus spotted
Anthemis punctata subsp. *cupaniana*
Campanula punctata
Lysimachia punctata
Phyllostachys nigra var. *punctata*

---

pungens piercing, pungent, ending
  in a hard sharp point
  Elaeagnus pungens
puniceus purplish crimson
  Clianthus puniceus

---

purpurascens purplish, becoming
  purple; **purpuratus** clad in purple;
  purpureus purple
Bergenia purpurascens
Clematis 'Purpurea Plena Elegans'
Corylus maxima 'Purpurea'
Digitalis purpurea
Echinacea purpurea
Eupatorium purpureum
Foeniculum vulgare 'Purpureum'
Osmanthus heterophyllus 'Purpureus'
Weigela florida 'Foliis Purpureis'

purpusii named for German plant-collecting brothers Carl (1853–1941) and Josef (1860–1932) Purpus
  Lonicera × *purpusii*
pustulatus blistered or pimply
  Begonia pustulata 'Argentea'

COMMON DESCRIPTIVE TERMS
pygmaeus pygmy, dwarf, very small
Borago pygmaea
Chamaecyparis obtusa 'Pygmaea'
Lewisia pygmaea
Nymphaea 'Pygmaea Helvola'
Penstemon hirsutus var. *pygmaeus*

---

pyramidalis pyramid-shaped
  Campanula pyramidalis

COMMON DESCRIPTIVE TERMS
pyrenaicus, pyrenaeus from the Pyrenees (on the borders of France and Spain)
Fritillaria pyrenaica
Geranium pyrenaicum
Hepatica nobilis var. *pyrenaica*
Horminum pyrenaicum
Lilium pyrenaicum
Ornithogalum pyrenaicum
Quercus pyrenaica

---

pyrethrifolius with leaves like Pyrethrum (now *Tanacetum*)
  Leptinella pyrethrifolia

CULTIVAR NAMES
Some American States
Canna 'Alaska'
Pelargonium 'Arizona'
Fremontodendron 'California Glory'
Hedera helix 'Carolina Crinkle'
Nymphaea 'Colorado'
Lilium 'Connecticut King'
Primula auricula 'Dakota'
Canna 'Delaware'
Rhododendron 'Florida'
Cuphea llavea 'Georgia Scarlet'
Camellia japonica 'Hawaii'
Pseudotsuga menziesii 'Idaho Gem'
Morus 'Illinois Everbearing'
Nymphaea 'Indiana'
Paeonia lactiflora 'Kansas'
Iris 'Kentucky Bluegrass'
Phlox divaricata 'Louisiana Purple'
Magnolia 'Maryland'
Arctostaphylos uva-ursi 'Massachusetts'
Philadelphus 'Minnesota Snowflake'
Hemerocallis 'Missouri Beauty'
Rosa 'Nevada'
Geranium sanguineum 'New Hampshire Purple'
Iris 'Oregon Skies'
Fuchsia 'Tennessee Waltz'
Fuchsia 'Texas Longhorn'
Pinus banksiana 'Wisconsin'
Canna 'Wyoming'

Q

quadrangularis, quadrangulatus with
four angles
  Chimonobambusa quadrangularis
  Fraxinus quadrangulata
quadratus square; in fours; in four
  Restio quadratus
quadridentatus with four teeth
quadrifolius with four leaves
  or leaflets
  Paris quadrifolia
quadripinnatus four times pinnate
  Lophosoria quadripinnata
quamash from a Native American
  word meaning "sweet"
  Camassia quamash
quarciticus like quartz
quercifolius with leaves like
  Quercus (oak)
  Hydrangea quercifolia
quinatus in fives
  Akebia quinata
quinquefolius with five leaves
  Parthenocissus quinquefolia
quitoensis from Quito, Ecuador
  Solanum quitoense
quinquelobatus with five lobes
  Pelargonium quinquelobatum
quintuplinervius with five veins
  Meconopsis quintuplinervia
quotidianus everyday, common

CULTIVAR NAMES
Nurseries and Plant Breeders

HELLEBORUS × HYBRIDUS ASHWOOD
  GARDEN HYBRIDS
ROSA PAT AUSTIN ('AUSMUM')'
LOBELIA 'BEES' FLAME'
DIASCIA 'BLACKTHORN APRICOT'
DICENTRA 'ADRIAN BLOOM'
IRIS 'BROADLEIGH ROSE'
GERANIUM 'SUE CRÛG'
CALAMAGROSTIS × ACUTIFLORA
  'KARL FOERSTER'
PULMONARIA SACCHARATA 'GLEBE
  COTTAGE BLUE'
DAPHNE 'VALERIE HILLIER'
POTENTILLA FRUTICOSA 'HOPLEYS
  ORANGE'
GERANIUM MACRORRHIZUM
  'INGWERSEN'S VARIETY'
MACLEAYA MICROCARPA 'KELWAY'S
  CORAL PLUME'
MALUS × PURPUREA 'LEMOINEI'
VIBURNUM OPULUS 'NOTCUTT'S
  VARIETY'
PRUNUS DOMESTICA (PLUM) 'RIVERS'S
  EARLY PROLIFIC'
SAXIFRAGA 'RIVERSLEA'
ESCALLONIA 'SLIEVE DONARD'
ASTRANTIA MAJOR 'SUNNINGDALE
  VARIEGATED'
DIGITALIS PURPUREA 'SUTTON'S
  APRICOT'
CLEMATIS 'JOHN TREASURE'
ECHINOPS RITRO 'VEITCH'S BLUE'
SPIRAEA JAPONICA 'ANTHONY
  WATERER'
ROSA 'HARRY WHEATCROFT'

Apple *Malus* hybrids
Apricot *Prunus armeniaca*
Banana *Musa*
Blackberry *Rubus*
Black currant *Ribes nigrum*
Blueberry *Vaccinium corymbosum*
Boysenberry *Rubus* 'Boysen'
Bullace *Prunus domestica* ssp. *insititia*
Canteloupe *Cucumis melo* subsp. *melo*
Cherry *Prunus avium*
Chokeberry *Prunus virginiana*
Cranberry *Vaccinium macrocarpon*
Damson plum *Prunus insititia*
  varieties
Date *Phoenix dactylifera*
Fig *Ficus carica*
Gooseberry *Ribes* × *hirtellum*
Grape *Vitis vinifera*
Grapefruit *Citrus* × *paradisi*
Greengage *Prunus domestica*
  varieties
Guava *Psidium guajava*
Jostaberry *Ribes* × *nidigrolaria*
Kiwi fruit *Actinidia deliciosa*
Lemon *Citrus limonia*
Lime *Citrus aurantifolia*
Loganberry *Rubus* 'Logan'
Loquat *Eriobotrya japonica*
Mango *Mangifera indica*
Melon *Cucumis melo*
Mulberry, black *Morus nigra*
Mulberry, red *Morus rubra*
Nectarine *Prunus persica* var.
  nectarina
Orange, sweet *Citrus sinensis*
Papaya (paw-paw) *Carica papaya*
Passion fruit *Passiflora edulis*
Peach *Prunus persica*

Pear *Pyrus communis*
Persimmon *Diospyros virginiana*
Pineapple *Ananas comosus*
Plum *Prunus* × *domestica*
Pomegranate *Punica granatum*
Prickly pear *Opuntia*
Quince *Cydonia oblonga*

PEAR

Raspberry *Rubus idaeus*
Redcurrant *Ribes rubrum*
Rhubarb *Rheum* × *cultorum*
Satsuma *Citrus unshui*
Sour cherry *Prunus cerasus*
Strawberry *Fragaria*
Tangerine *Citrus reticulata*
Tomatillo *Physalis ixocarpa*
Watermelon *Citrullus lanatus*

R

raddeanus named for Gustav Radde (1831–1903), a German naturalist

   Campanula raddeana

radiatus with rays; radiating

radicans with rooting stems

   Campsis radicans

radula a scraper or file

   Pelargonium 'Radula'

ramiflorus flowering on branches

ramosissimus much branched

   Tamarix ramosissima

ramulosus twiggy

   Olearia ramulosa

ranunculoides like *Ranunculus*

   Anemone ranunculoides

raphanifolius with leaves like *Raphanus* (radish)

   Cardamine raphanifolia

rapunculoides like a little turnip

   Campanula rapunculoides

rariflorus with scattered flowers

reclinatus bent back or down

   Phoenix reclinata

rectifolius with erect leaves

rectus upright

   Clematis recta

recurvus, recurvatus recurved, curved backwards

   Narcissus poeticus var. *recurvus*

redivivus revived

   Lunaria rediviva

reducta reduced

   Sorbus reducta

refractus bent back

refulgens shining

regalis royal; fit for a king

   Lilium regale

Quaking-grass *Briza*
Quamash *Camassia*
Queen Anne's lace *Anthriscus sylvestris*
Quince *Cydonia oblonga*
Ragged robin *Lychnis flos-cuculi*
Ragwort *Senecio*
Ramsons *Allium ursinum*
Rangoon creeper *Quisqualis indica*
Redbud *Cercis canadensis*
Red campion *Silene dioica*
Red-hot poker *Kniphofia*
Red valerian *Centranthus ruber*
Reed *Phragmites*
Reedmace *Typha*
Restharrow *Ononis*
Ribbon grass *Phalaris*
Rock cress *Arabis*
Rock jasmine *Androsace*
Rock purslane *Calandrinia umbellata*
Rock samphire *Crithmum maritimum*
Rock-rose *Cistus, Helianthemum*
Rocky Mountain juniper *Juniperus scopulorum*
Rose *Rosa*
Rose of Sharon *Hypericum*
Rosebay willowherb *Chamerion angustifolium*
Rosemary *Rosmarinus officinalis*

ROWAN

Royal fern *Osmunda regalis*
Rowan *Sorbus aucuparia*
Rubber plant *Ficus elastica*
Rue *Ruta graveolens*
Rush *Juncus*
Russian olive *Elaeagnus*
Russian sage *Perovskia atriplicifolia*
Russian vine *Fallopia baldschuanica*
Rye *Elymus*

---

reginae of the queen; *reginae olgae* named for Queen Olga of Greece (1851–1926)
   Galanthus reginae-olgae
   Strelitzia reginae
regius royal
   Juglans regia
regularis regular, uniform

rehderi, rehderianus named for Alfred Rehder (1863–1949), a dendrologist at the Arnold Arboretum in Massachusetts
   Clematis rehderiana
remotus remote, scattered
reniformis kidney-shaped
   Pelargonium reniforme

repandens, repandus with wavy or turned-up edges

Cyclamen repandum

Taxus baccata 'Repandens'

replicatus folded back

COMMON DESCRIPTIVE TERMS

repens, reptans creeping

Ajuga reptans

Coprosma repens

Gypsophila repens

Mazus reptans

Melinis repens

Ononis reptans

Polemonium reptans

requienii named for Esprit Requien (1788–1851), a French naturalist

Mentha requienii (Corsican mint)

resinifer, resinosus resinous

reticulatus netted

Iris reticulata

retinodes tenacious, retaining

Acacia retinodes

retroflexus bent back

retusus with a rounded or blunt tip

Daphne tangutica Retusa Group

revolutus rolled or turned back

Erythronium revolutum

rex king

Begonia rex

rhaeticus from the Rhaetian Alps (Switzerland/Austria)

Geum × *rhaeticum*

rhamnoides like *Rhamnus* (buckthorn)

Hippophae rhamnoides

rhizomatosus rhizomatous

Epimedium rhizomatosum

rhodopensis from the Rhodope Mountains in Bulgaria

Haberlea rhodopensis

rhombeus, rhombicus, rhombiformis rhomboidal, diamond-shaped

Hedera rhombea

rhombifolius with diamond-shaped leaves

Cissus rhombifolia

rhytidophyllus with wrinkled leaves

Viburnum rhytidophyllum

rigens, rigidus rigid, stiff; **rigescens, rigidulus** rather stiff

Diascia rigescens

Euphorbia rigida

Gazania rigens

Hebe rigidula

Leontodon rigens

Polystichum rigens

Verbena rigida

---

rigidifolius with stiff leaves

rimosus cracked

ringens open-mouthed, gaping, wide open

Mimulus ringens

riparius of riverbanks

Carex riparia

ritualis ritual, of ceremonies

Kniphofia ritualis

rivalis, rivularis growing near brooks

Cirsium rivulare 'Atropurpureum'

Geum rivale (water avens)

riversleaianum named for Prichard's Riverslea nursery at Christchurch, Dorset, UK

Geranium × *riversleaianum*

rivinianus after Augustus Rivinus, the Latinized name of A. Bachmann (1652–1722), a German botanist

Viola riviniana (common dog violet)

robbiae named for Mary Anne Robb (1829–1912); she is reputed to have brought *Euphorbia amygdaloides* var. *robbiae* back from Turkey in her hat-box: hence its nickname, Mrs Robb's bonnet

robinsonianus (see panel below)

WILLIAM ROBINSON (1838–1935)

William Robinson began his career as a gardener in Ireland before moving to England, where he became one of the most influential plantsmen of his day. A passionate advocate of naturalistic gardening, he founded the periodical *The Garden*, and his books *The Wild Garden* (1870) and *The English Flower Garden* (1883) remain classics. Plant names associated with him include *Anemone nemorosa* 'Robinsoniana'. *Clematis* 'Gravetye Beauty' and *Geranium himalayense* 'Gravetye' are named for his home, Gravetye Manor, in West Sussex. His head gardener there was clematis expert Ernest Markham.

Quisqualis from Latin *quis?* (what?), and *qualis?* (what kind?)

Ranunculus from a Latin diminutive of *rana*, a frog

Reseda from Latin *resedare*, to heal

Rhaphiolepis from Greek *rhaphis*, needle, and *lepis*, scale

Rhodochiton from Greek *rhodo*, red, and *chiton*, a tunic or cloak

Rhododendron from Greek *rhodon*, rose, and *dendron*, tree

Ribes from Arabic *ribas*, acid

Robinia named for Jean Robin (1550–1629), French royal gardener

Rodgersia named for John Rodgers (1812–1882), American naval officer

Romneya named for Thomas Romney Robinson (1792–1882), Irish astronomer

Rosmarinus from Latin *ros*, dew, and *marinus*, maritime

Rudbeckia named for Olof Rudbeck (1630–1702), Swedish botanist

robur oakwood, hardwood; strength
   Quercus robur

COMMON DESCRIPTIVE TERMS

robustus robust, strong

Eremurus robustus

Fargesia robusta

Grevillea robusta

Malus × robusta

Taxus cuspidata 'Robusta'

romanus Roman

rooperi named for Edward Rooper (1818–1854), a British soldier serving in South Africa
   Kniphofia rooperi

rosa-sinensis Chinese rose
   Hibiscus rosa-sinensis

COMMON DESCRIPTIVE TERMS

roseus, rosea like a rose, rose-colored

Alcea rosea

Centranthus ruber 'Roseus'

Deutzia × rosea

Erodium × variabile 'Roseum'

Primula rosea

Rhodiola rosea

Wisteria floribunda 'Rosea'

QUERCUS ROBUR

CULTIVAR NAMES
Foreign Expressions
R

RAKET (*Dutch*) ROCKET
(*POPULUS ALBA* 'RAKET')

RAUBRITTER (*German*)
ROBBER KNIGHT
(*ROSA* 'RAUBRITTER')

REGENBOGEN (*German*) RAINBOW
(*HELIANTHEMUM* 'REGENBOGEN')

REINE DU JOUR (*French*)
QUEEN OF THE DAY
(*PHLOX MACULATA* 'REINE DU JOUR')

REINE ROUGE (*French*) RED QUEEN
(*MENTHA* × *PIPERITA* 'REINE ROUGE')

RIJNSTROOM (*Dutch*) RIVER RHINE
(*GEUM* 'RIJNSTROOM')

RÖDE KLOKKE (*Flemish*) RED BELL
(*PULSATILLA VULGARIS* 'RÖDE KLOKKE')

ROODKAPJE (*Dutch*) RED CAP
(*DIANTHUS* 'ROODKAPJE')

ROSA ERFÜLLUNG (*German*)
PINK ZENITH
(*ASTER AMELLUS* 'ROSA ERFÜLLUNG')

ROSAKÖNIGIN (*German*)
PINK QUEEN
(*HELIANTHEMUM* 'ROSAKÖNIGIN')

ROSENKUPPEL (*German*) ROSY DOME
(*ORIGANUM* 'ROSENKUPPEL')

ROSENPOKAL (*German*) ROSY
GOBLET
(*ARTEMISIA* 'ROSENPOKAL')

ROSENROT (*German*) ROSE RED
(*PERSICARIA CAMPANULATA* 'ROSENROT')

ROSENSCHLEIER (*German*)
ROSY VEIL
(*ARTEMISIA* 'ROSENSCHLEIER')

ROTBLUM (*German*) RED FLOWER
(*BERGENIA* 'ROTBLUM')

ROTFUCHS (*German*) RED FOX
(*VERONICA SPICATA* 'ROTFUCHS')

ROTGOLD (*German*) RED GOLD
(*HELENIUM* 'ROTGOLD')

ROTKÄPPCHEN (*German*)
LITTLE RED RIDING HOOD
(*PRUNELLA GRANDIFLORA*
'ROTKÄPPCHEN')

ROTKEHLCHEN (*German*) ROBIN
(*HYDRANGEA MACROPHYLLA*
'ROTKEHLCHEN')

ROTKOPF (*German*) RED HEAD
(*SEMPERVIVUM* 'ROTKOPF')

ROTKUGEL (*German*) RED BALL
(*ORIGANUM* 'ROTKUGEL')

ROTSILBER (*German*) RED SILVER
(*MISCANTHUS SINENSIS* 'ROTSILBER')

ROTSTIEL (*German*) RED STEM
(*ATHYRIUM FILIX-FEMINA* 'ROTSTIEL')

ROTSTRAHLBUSCH (*German*)
RED SUNBEAM BUSH
(*PANICUM VIRGATUM*
'ROTSTRAHLBUSCH')

RUBINZWERG (*German*)
RUBY DWARF
(*HELENIUM* 'RUBINZWERG')

CULTIVAR NAMES
Personal Names
R

HEUCHERA 'RACHEL'
FUCHSIA 'RALPH'S DELIGHT'
PRIMULA FLORINDAE 'RAY'S RUBY'
VIOLA 'REBECCA'
HEUCHERA 'ROBERT'
SEMPERVIVUM 'ROBIN'
NARCISSUS 'ROGER'
MISCANTHUS SINENSIS 'ROLAND'
CANNA 'ROSA'
ERICA CARNEA 'ROSALIE'
ALSTROEMERIA 'LITTLE MISS ROSALIND'
PIERIS JAPONICA 'ROSALINDA'
PHLOX MACULATA 'ROSALINDE'
CLEMATIS 'FAIR ROSAMOND'
SIDALCEA 'ROSANNA'
IRIS 'BROADLEIGH ROSE'
ROSA 'ROSEMARY ROSE'
ACHILLEA 'ROSIE'
HYDRANGEA MACROPHYLLA 'ROSITA'
OSTEOSPERMUM 'CANNINGTON ROY'
MALUS 'RUDOLPH'
FUCHSIA 'RUFUS'
HELLEBORUS FOETIDUS 'RUTH'
GERANIUM ROZANNE ('GERWAT')

rosmarinifolius with leaves like
　　Rosmarinus (rosemary)
　　Ozothamnus rosmarinifolius
rostratus beaked
rosularis with rosettes
　　Plantago major 'Rosularis'
rotatus shaped like a wheel

COMMON DESCRIPTIVE TERMS
rotundifolius with round leaves
Bellis rotundifolia
Campanula rotundifolia
Lathyrus rotundifolius
Ligustrum japonicum 'Rotundifolium'
Origanum rotundifolium
Pellaea rotundifolia
Prostanthera rotundifolia
Tithonia rotundifolia

rotundus round
rubellus light red

COMMON DESCRIPTIVE TERMS
ruber red
Acer rubrum
Alnus rubra
Astrantia major 'Rubra'
Atriplex hortensis var. *rubra*
Centranthus ruber
Epimedium × *rubrum*
Escallonia rubra
Filipendula rubra
Fritillaria imperialis 'Rubra'
Imperata cylindrica 'Rubra'
Pulmonaria rubra
Pulsatilla rubra
Quercus rubra

rubescens reddish, reddening
　　Acer rubescens
rubiginosus rusty
　　Rosa rubiginosa

rubra see *ruber*

rubrifolius with red leaves
   Plantago major 'Rubrifolia'

rubromarginatus edged with red
   Phyllostachys rubromarginata

rufinervis with red veins
   Acer rufinerve

rufus, rufescens reddish
   Fargesia rufa

rugosus, rugulosus wrinkled
   Rosa rugosa

runcinatus with teeth pointing
   towards the base
   Persicaria runcinata

COMMON DESCRIPTIVE TERMS

rupestris rock-loving
Erodium rupestre
Leptospermum rupestre
Potentilla rupestris
Sedum rupestre

---

rupicola rock-dweller
   Penstemon rupicola

rupifragus rock-breaking
   Papaver rupifragum

ruscifolius with leaves like *Ruscus*
   (butcher's broom)
   Coriaria ruscifolia

russelianus named for John Russell
   (1766–1839), 6th Duke of Bedford
   Phlomis russeliana

russicus from Russia
   Echium russicum

WHAT'S IN A NAME?

COLOR: YELLOW AND GOLD

auratus, aureatus decorated with gold
aureopictus (literally) gold-painted
aureus gold, golden
canarinus canary yellow
cerinus waxy yellow
chrys-, chryso- gold
chrysographes marked with gold
citrinus lemon yellow
croceus saffron yellow
flavens yellow
flavescens, flavicans, flavidus yellowish
flavissimus very yellow
flavovirens yellowish green
flavus pure, pale yellow
fulvus, fulvellus, fulvescens, fulvidus
   tawny yellow, yellowish brown
helvolus grayish yellow
icterinus jaundice yellow
isabellinus tawny yellow
luridus dirty yellow
luteolus, lutescens pale yellow
luteus yellow
ochraceus brownish yellow
stramineus like straw, straw-colored
sulphureus sulphur yellow
vitellinus egg-yolk yellow
xanth-, xantho- yellow
xanthinus yellow

rusticanus, rusticus rural
   Armoracia rusticana
Magnolia × *soulangeana* 'Rustica
   Rubra'

ruthenicus from Ruthenia, a region
   of Russia (and used more generally
   to mean Russian)
   Echinops ritro subsp. *ruthenicus*

S

sabatius from Savona, on the
   Ligurian coast of north-west Italy
   Convolvulus sabatius

saccatus like a bag; with sacs
   Plectranthus saccatus

saccharatus, saccharinus sweet, sugary
   Acer saccharinum
   Pulmonaria saccharata

saccharum sugar cane
   Acer saccharum

sachalinensis from the island of
   Sakhalin, off the east coast of Russia
   Lilium sachalinense

sagittalis, sagittatus arrow-shaped
   Genista sagittalis

sagittifolius with arrow-shaped leaves
   Hedera hibernica 'Sagittifolia'

salicarius like *Salix* (willow)
   Lythrum salicaria (purple
   loosestrife)

COMMON DESCRIPTIVE TERMS

salicifolius with leaves like willow

Pyrus salicifolia 'Pendula'

Aucuba japonica f. *longifolia*
   'Salicifolia'

Buphthalmum salicifolium

Cotoneaster salicifolius

Hebe salicifolia

Magnolia salicifolia

CORNUS SANGUINEA

salignus like willow
   Callistemon salignus

salinus salty, growing in salty places

salsillus salted

saluenensis from the region of
   Nu Jiang (the Salween river) in
   Yunnan, China, and Burma
   Nomocharis saluenensis

salviifolius with leaves like *Salvia*
   Cistus salviifolius

sambucinus like *Sambucus* (elder)

samius from the Greek island
   of Samos
   Phlomis samia

sancti-johannis St. John
   Anthemis sancti-johannis

sanctus holy

sanguineus bloody, blood-red
Cornus sanguinea
Geranium sanguineum
Heuchera sanguinea
Ribes sanguineum

sapidus tasty, savoury
sarajevensis from Sarajevo
   Knautia sarajevensis
sarcocaulis with fleshy stems
   Crassula sarcocaulis
sardiniensis from the Mediterranean
   island of Sardinia

sargentii, sargentianus named for
   the American dendrologist Charles
   Sprague Sargent (1841–1927), first
   director of the Arnold Arboretum
   in Massachusetts
Hydrangea aspera subsp. *sargentiana*
Lilium sargentiae
Magnolia sargentiana var. *robusta*
Malus toringo subsp. *sargentii*
Prunus sargentii
Rhododendron sargentianum
Sorbus sargentiana

sarmaticus from Sarmatia (an old
   name for a region covering part
   of eastern Poland, Belarus and
   the Ukraine)
   Campanula sarmatica

sarmentosus with runners
   Androsace sarmentosa
sarniensis from Guernsey,
   Channel Islands
   Nerine sarniensis

CULTIVAR NAMES
Personal Names
S

Rosa Sally's Rose ('Canrem')
Liriope muscari 'Samantha'
Kniphofia 'Samuel's Sensation'
Hamamelis vernalis 'Sandra'
Streptocarpus 'Sarah'
Hemerocallis 'Sebastian'
Primula auricula 'Sheila'
Tulipa 'Shirley'
Fuchsia 'Siobhan'
Polemonium 'Sonia's Bluebell'
Fuchsia 'Sophie's Silver Lining'
Sequoiadendron giganteum 'Little Stan'
Fuchsia 'Sophie Louise'
Vaccinium corymbosum 'Stanley'
Campanula poscharskyana 'Stella'
Erodium 'Stephanie'
Hedychium densiflorum 'Stephen'
Iris sibirica 'Steve'
Primula auricula 'Susannah'
Lonicera periclymenum 'Sweet Sue'
Magnolia 'Susan'
Primula 'Sunshine Susie'
Campanula carpatica 'Suzie'
Narcissus 'Suzy'
Iris 'Broadleigh Sybil'
Camellia japonica 'Sylvia'

CULTIVAR NAMES
Colors: White

Bergenia 'Bressingham White'

Buddleia davidii 'White Profusion'

Calluna vulgaris 'White Lawn'

Campanula lactiflora 'White Pouffe'

Clematis 'White Moth'

Cortaderia selloana 'White Feather'

Dianthus 'Haytor White'

Echinacea purpurea 'White Swan'

Erica carnea 'Springwood White'

Erythronium californicum 'White Beauty'

Geranium clarkei 'Kashmir White'

Gypsophila fastigiata 'White Festival'

Hydrangea macrophylla 'Lanarth White'

Iris 'White City'

Lamium maculatum 'White Nancy'

Lathyrus latifolius 'White Pearl'

Lilium longiflorum 'White American'

Narcissus 'White Lion'

Paeonia lactiflora 'White Wings'

Pelargonium 'White Boar'

Penstemon 'White Bedder'

Phlox paniculata 'White Admiral'

Pieris japonica 'White Rim'

Rhododendron 'Loder's White'

Sorbus 'White Wax'

Viburnum tinus 'French White'

COMMON DESCRIPTIVE TERMS

sativus sown, planted, cultivated
Castanea sativa (sweet chestnut)
Coriandrum sativum (coriander)
Crocus sativus (saffron crocus)
Lathyrus sativus
Medicago sativa (alfalfa, lucerne)

---

saxatilis found among rocks
  Primula saxatilis
saxifragus stone-breaking
  Petrorhagia saxifraga
saximontanus from the Rocky Mountains, North America
  Aquilegia saximontana
saxosus stony, growing among stones
  Gentiana saxosa
scaber, scabrosus rough, gritty
  Eccremocarpus scaber
scabiosifolius with leaves like *Scabiosa* (scabious)
  Patrinia scabiosifolia
scabriusculus slightly rough or gritty
  Fuchsia scabriuscula
scalaris like a ladder
  Sorbus scalaris

COMMON DESCRIPTIVE TERMS

scandens climbing
Celastrus scandens
Cobaea scandens
Dicentra scandens
Hibbertia scandens
Senecio scandens

scandicus, scandinavicus from
Scandinavia
  Primula scandinavica
scariosus shriveled
sceleratus harmful
schillingii named for the British
plantsman Tony Schilling
  Euphorbia schillingii
schizo- split, divided
schoenoprasum (literally) rush-like
leek
  Allium schoenoprasum (chives)
schubertii named for Gotthilf von
Schubert (1780–1860), a German
naturalist and plant collector
  Allium schubertii
scilloides like *Scilla*
  Puschkinia scilloides var. *libanotica*
scilloniensis from the Isles of Scilly,
England
  Olearia × *scilloniensis*
scirpoides like *Scirpus* (club rush)
  Equisetum scirpoides
sclero- hard
scolopendrius millipede
  Asplenium scolopendrium
scoparius a broom or sweeper
  Cytisus scoparius
scopulinus little rock
  Erigeron scopulinus
scopulorum of rocks, cliffs or crags
  Juniperus scopulorum
scorodonius of garlic
  Teucrium scorodonia

WHAT'S IN A NAME?

PLANT HUNTERS AND COLLECTORS

armandii as *davidii*, below
davidii, davidianum Abbé Jean Pierre
Armand David (1826–1900)
douglasii, douglasianus David
Douglas (1799–1834)
drummondii James (1786–1863) and
Thomas (1793–1835) Drummond
endressii Philip Endress (1806–1831)
fargesii Paul Farges (1844–1912)
farreri Reginald Farrer (1880–1920)
forrestii George Forrest (1873–1932)
fortunei Robert Fortune (1812–
1880)
giraldianus, giraldii Giuseppe Giraldi
(1848–1901)
haastii Sir Johann von Haast
(1824–1887)
jeffreyi John Jeffrey (1826–1854)
lancasteri Roy Lancaster
lindheimeri Ferdinand Lindheimer
(1802–1879)
lyallii David Lyall (1817–1895)
mariesii Charles Maries (1851–
1902)
ogisui Mikinori Ogisu
purpusii Carl (1853–1941) and Josef
(1860–1932) Purpus
sieboldianus, sieboldii Philipp von
Siebold (1796–1866)
turczaninowii Nicolai Turczaninov
(1796–1864)
wardii Frank Kingdon Ward (1885–
1958)
whittallii Edward Whittall (1851-
1917)
wilsonianus, wilsonii E.H. ("Chinese")
Wilson (1876–1930)

Saffron crocus *Crocus sativus*
Sagebrush *Artemisia*
St. John's wort *Hypericum*
Sallow *Salix caprea*
Sandwort *Arenaria*
Scarborough lily *Cyrtanthus elatus*
Scotch thistle *Onopordum acanthium*
Scots pine *Pinus sylvestris*
Sea buckthorn *Hippophae rhamnoides*
Sea holly *Eryngium*
Sea lavender *Limonium platyphyllum*
Sea pink *Armeria maritima*
Sedge *Carex*
Shasta daisy *Leucanthemum* × *superbum*
Shepherd's purse *Capsella bursa-pastoris*
Shoo-fly plant *Nicandra physalodes*
Shuttlecock fern *Matteuccia struthiopteris*
Silver birch *Betula pendula*
Skullcap *Scutellaria*
Smoke bush *Cotinus coggygria*
Snakebark maple *Acer capillipes*; *Acer davidii*
Snakeshead fritillary *Fritillaria meleagris*
Snapdragon *Antirrhinum*
Snowball tree *Viburnum opulus* 'Roseum'
Snowberry *Symphoricarpos*
Snowdrop *Galanthus*
Snow-in-summer *Cerastium tomentosum*

Snowy mespilus *Amelanchier*
Soft shield fern *Polystichum setiferum*
Solomon's seal *Polygonatum multiflorum*
Southernwood *Artemisia abrotanum*
Spanish broom *Spartium junceum*
Speedwell *Veronica*
Spider flower *Cleome*
Spider plant *Chlorophytum comosum*
Spindle *Euonymus europaeus*
Spleenwort *Asplenium*
Spotted laurel *Aucuba japonica*
Spring snowflake *Leucojum vernum*
Spruce *Picea*
Spurge *Euphorbia*
Spurge laurel *Daphne laureola*
Squill *Scilla*
Star-of-Bethlehem *Ornithogalum umbellatum*
Statice *Limonium*
Stock *Matthiola*
Stonecrop *Sedum*
Strawberry tree *Arbutus*
Sugar maple *Acer saccharum*
Sunflower *Helianthus annuus*
Swan River daisy *Brachyscome*
Sweet alyssum *Lobularia maritima*
Sweet briar *Rosa rubiginosa*
Sweet cicely *Myrrhis odorata*
Sweet pea *Lathyrus odoratus*
Sweet rocket *Hesperis matronalis*
Sweet sultan *Amberboa*
Sweet William *Dianthus barbatus*
Sweet woodruff *Galium odoratum*

SHEPHERD'S PURSE

scorpioides like a scorpion
   Myosotis scorpioides
scoticus Scottish, from Scotland
   Daboecia cantabrica subsp. *scotica*
scutellaroides like *Scutellaria*
   Solenostemon scutellaroides (coleus)
sectus cut
   Carex secta
secunda secund (arranged on one
   side only)
   Echeveria secunda var. *glauca*
sedifolius with leaves like *Sedum*
   Aster sedifolius
seguieri, seguierianus named for
   J.F. Séguier (1703–1784), a French
   botanist
   Euphorbia seguieriana
selloanus named for Friedrich Sello
   (1789–1831), a German naturalist
   and plant collector
   Cortaderia selloana
semiplenus semi-double
   Camassia leichtlinii 'Semiplena'
semperflorens always flowering
   Begonia semperflorens

COMMON DESCRIPTIVE TERMS

semervirens evergreen

Buxus sempervirens
Cupressus sempervirens
Helictotrichon sempervirens
Iberis sempervirens
Lonicera sempervirens
Sequoia sempervirens

CULTIVAR NAMES
Anniversaries

CLEMATIS ANNIVERSARY ('PYNOT')
IRIS SIBIRICA 'ANNIVERSARY'
DAHLIA 'ANNIVERSARY BALL'
IRIS 'ANNIVERSARY CELEBRATION'
FUCHSIA 'DIAMOND CELEBRATION'
FUCHSIA 'GOLDEN ANNIVERSARY'
HOSTA 'GOLDEN ANNIVERSARY'
LAMIUM MACULATUM GOLDEN
   ANNIVERSARY ('DELLAM')
ROSA 'GOLDEN ANNIVERSARY'
ROSA GOLDEN CELEBRATION
   ('AUSGOLD')
PELARGONIUM 'GOLDEN WEDDING'
RHODODENDRON 'GOLDEN
   WEDDING'
ROSA HAPPY ANNIVERSARY
   ('BEDFRANC')
ROSA PEARL ANNIVERSARY
   ('WHITSTON')
ROSA RUBY ANNIVERSARY
   ('HARBONNY')
ROSA RUBY CELEBRATION
   ('PEAWINNER')
ASTRANTIA 'RUBY WEDDING'
CAMELLIA × WILLIAMSII 'RUBY
   WEDDING'
FUCHSIA 'RUBY WEDDING'
LEPTOSPERMUM SCOPARIUM 'RUBY
   WEDDING'
ROSA 'RUBY WEDDING'
BUDDLEIA 'SILVER ANNIVERSARY'
CAMELLIA JAPONICA 'SILVER
   ANNIVERSARY'
ROSA SILVER ANNIVERSARY ('POULARI')
ROSA 'SILVER WEDDING'

CULTIVAR NAMES
Strange but True
S

Narcissus 'Satsuma'

Monarda 'Scorpion'

Pinus sylvestris 'Scrubby'

Malus domestica (apple) 'Scrumptious'

Pinus strobus 'Sea Urchin'

Platycodon grandiflorus 'Sentimental Blue'

Iris 'Serengeti Spaghetti'

Rosa Sexy Rexy ('Macrexy')

Astrantia major subsp. *involucrata* 'Shaggy'

Paeonia 'Shaggy Dog'

Geranium maculatum 'Shameface'

Iris 'Shampoo'

Malus domestica 'Sheep's Nose'

Geranium sanguineum 'Shepherd's Warning'

Juniperus scopulorum 'Skyrocket'

Pelargonium 'Small Fortune'

Narcissus 'Small Talk'

Primula auricula 'The Sneep'

Dahlia 'Sneezy'

Primula auricula 'Snooty Fox'

Fuchsia 'Snow White' (and 'Bashful', 'Doc', 'Dopey', 'Grumpy', 'Happy', 'Sleepy' and 'Sneezy'!)

Dianthus barbatus 'Sooty'

Dianthus 'Sops-in-Wine'

Penstemon 'Sour Grapes'

Phlox paniculata 'Speed Limit'

Hemerocallis 'Spiderman'

Juniperus communis 'Spotty Spreader'

Iris 'Stairway to Heaven'

Sanguisorba tenuifolia 'Stand Up Comedian'

Iberis sempervirens 'Starkers'

Magnolia 'Star Wars'

Omphalodes cappadocica 'Starry Eyes'

Primula auricula 'Stormin Norman'

Hemerocallis 'Strawberry Fields Forever'

Plantago lanceolata 'Streaker'

Hosta 'Striptease'

Malus domestica 'Stub Nose'

Saxifraga 'Sugar Plum Fairy'

Papaver orientale 'Sultana'

Leucanthemum × *superbum* 'Sunny Side Up'

Iris 'Superstition'

Phormium 'Surfer'

Quercus palustris 'Swamp Pygmy'

---

sempervivoides like *Sempervivum* (houseleek)

senescens growing old

  Allium senescens

sensibilis, sensitivus sensitive

  Onoclea sensibilis

senticosus thorny

septem- seven (see below)

septemfidus divided into seven

  Gentiana septemfida

septemlobus with seven lobes

  Kalopanax septemlobus

septentrionalis northern (from
the seven stars of the Plough
constellation)
Betula albosinensis var.
septentrionalis
serbicus from Serbia
Ranunculus serbicus
sericeus silky
Daphne sericea
sericifer silk-bearing

COMMON DESCRIPTIVE TERMS
serotinus late
Dianthus serotinus
Lonicera periclymenum 'Serotina'
Populus × *canadensis* 'Serotina'
Prunus serotina

---

serratus serrated, saw-toothed;
serratifolius with serrated leaves;
serrula a small saw; **serrulatus**
with small saw-like teeth
Hydrangea serrata
Penstemon serrulatus
Photinia serratifolia
Prunus serrula
Zelkova serrata

---

sessilis sessile, stalkless
Trillium sessile
sessiliflorus with sessile flowers
Libertia sessiliflora
sessilifolius with sessile leaves
Lobelia sessilifolia

setaceus bristly
Asparagus setaceus
setchuenensis from Sichuan, China
Deutzia setchuenensis
setifer bearing bristles
Polystichum setiferum
setosus bristly
Iris setosa
setulosus with small bristles
Crassula setulosa
sexstylosus with six styles
Hoheria sexstylosa

COMMON DESCRIPTIVE TERMS
sibericus, sibiricus from Siberia
Claytonia sibirica
Cornus alba 'Sibirica'
Iris sibirica
Ligularia sibirica
Nepeta sibirica
Scilla siberica

---

sibthorpianus, sibthorpii named for
the English botanist Humphrey
Sibthorp (1713–1797) and his son
John (1758–1796)
Fritillaria sibthorpiana
Primula vulgaris subsp. *sibthorpii*
siculum Sicilian, from Sicily
Nectaroscordum siculum
sieberi named for the Prague
naturalist Franz Sieber (1789–
1844)
Crocus sieberi

GENERAL NAMES

Santolina from Latin *sanctum linum,* holy flax

Saponaria from Latin *sapo,* soap

Sarcococca from Greek *sarco-,* flesh, and *kokkos,* berry

Saxifraga from Latin *saxum,* rock, and *frangere,* to break

Schizanthus from Greek *schizo,* to divide, and *anthos,* flower

Schizostylis from Greek *schizo,* to divide, and *stylis,* style

Scutellaria from Latin *scutella,* a small dish

Sedum from Latin *sedere,* to sit

Sempervivum from Latin *semper,* always, and *vivus,* alive

Senecio from Latin *senex,* old man

Shibataea named for Keita Shibata (1877–1949), Japanese botanist

Skimmia from the Japanese name *Shikimi*

Stachyurus from Greek *stachys,* spike, and *oura,* tail

Stewartia named for John Stuart (1713–1792), 3rd Earl of Bute and British Prime Minister. Unfortunately Linnaeus misspelled his name

Stokesia named for Dr. Jonathan Stokes (1755–1831), English botanical author

Streptocarpus from Greek *streptos,* twisted, and *karpos,* fruit

Symphoricarpos from Greek *symphorein,* bear together, and *karpos,* fruit

Syringa from Greek *syrinx,* pipe

sieboldianus, sieboldii named for Philipp von Siebold (1796–1866), a German doctor who had a special interest in the plants of Japan and introduced many into Europe

Acer sieboldianum

Clematis florida var. *sieboldiana*

Dryopteris sieboldii

Hosta sieboldiana

Magnolia sieboldii

Primula sieboldii

Viburnum sieboldii

sikkimensis from Sikkim in the eastern Himalayas

Allium sikkimensis

Euphorbia sikkimensis

Malus sikkimensis

Musa sikkimensis

Primula sikkimensis

sikikianus from the Japanese island of Shikoku

siliceus growing in sand

silvaticus, silvestris of woods, growing wild (see also *sylvaticus*)

silvicola an inhabitant of woods

similis similar

Lonicera similis var. *delavayi*

simplex simple, unbranched

Actaea simplex

simplicicaulis with unbranched stems

Centaurea simplicicaulis

CULTIVAR NAMES
Foreign Expressions

S

SANGO-KAKU (*Japanese*) CORAL SHELL
(*ACER PALMATUM* 'SANGO-KAKU')

SATSUKI (*Japanese*) AZALEA
(*PELARGONIUM* 'SATSUKI')

SCHARLACHGLUT (*German*)
SCARLET GLOW
(*ROSA* 'SCHARLACHGLUT ')

SCHNEEHAUBE (*German*) SNOW CAP
(*ARABIS ALPINA* SUBSP.
CAUCASICA 'SCHNEEHAUBE')

SCHNEEWITTCHEN (*German*)
SNOW WHITE
(*ERIGERON* 'SCHNEEWITTCHEN')

SCHWEFELBLÜTE (*German*)
FLOWERS OF SULPHUR
(*ACHILLEA* 'SCHWEFELBLÜTE')

SEEIGEL (*German*) SEA URCHIN
(*FESTUCA GLAUCA* 'SEEIGEL')

SEMPRE AVANTI (*Italian*)
ALWAYS IN FRONT
(*NARCISSUS* 'SEMPRE AVANTI')

SHIROFUJI (*Japanese*)
MOUNT FUJI WHITE
(*HYDRANGEA SERRATA* 'SHIROFUJI')

SHIROTAE (*Japanese*) SNOW WHITE
(*PRUNUS* 'SHIROTAE')

SILBERFEDER (*German*)
SILVER FEATHER
(*MISCANTHUS SINENSIS* 'SILBERFEDER')

SILBERLICHT (*German*) SILVER LIGHT
(*BERGENIA* 'SILBERLICHT')

SILBERLOCKE (*German*) SILVER CURL
(*ABIES KOREANA* 'SILBERLOCKE')

SILBERSCHMELZE (*German*)
MOLTEN SILVER
(*ERICA* × *DARLEYENSIS*
'SILBERSCHMELZE')

SINEE DOZHD (*Russian*) BLUE RAIN
(*CLEMATIS* 'SINEE DOZHD')

SOLEIL D'OR (*French*) GOLDEN SUN
(*PYRACANTHA* 'SOLEIL D'OR')

SOMMERSCHNEE (*German*)
SUMMER SNOW
(*ANAPHALIS TRIPLINERVIS*
'SOMMERSCHNEE')

SONNENKIND (*German*) SUN CHILD
(*COREOPSIS* 'SONNENKIND')

SONNENWENDE (*German*) SOLSTICE
(*OENOTHERA FRUTICOSA* SUBSP. *GLAUCA*
'SONNENWENDE')

SOUVENIR DE... (*French*)
MEMORY OF...
(*ROSA* 'SOUVENIR DU DOCTEUR
JAMAIN')

SPITZENTÄNZERIN (*German*)
BALLERINA
(*HELIOPSIS HELIANTHOIDES* VAR. *SCABRA*
'SPITZENTÄNZERIN')

STELLA DE ORO (*Italian*) GOLD STAR
(*HEMEROCALLIS* 'STELLA DE ORO')

STRAUSSENFEDER (*German*)
OSTRICH FEATHER
(*ASTILBE* 'STRAUSSENFEDER')

simplicifolius with simple (i.e. not divided or lobed) leaves
 Meconopsis simplicifolia
simplicissimus completely undivided or unbranched

CULTIVAR NAMES
Weddings

ALSTROEMERIA 'BLUSHING BRIDE'

LATHYRUS LATIFOLIUS 'BLUSHING BRIDE'

LAVATERA × *CLEMENTII* 'BLUSHING BRIDE'

GERANIUM DALMATICUM 'BRIDAL BOUQUET'

NARCISSUS 'BRIDAL CROWN'

IRIS SIBIRICA 'BRIDAL JIG'

DIANTHUS 'BRIDAL VEIL'

FUCHSIA 'BRIDESMAID'

PELARGONIUM 'BRIDESMAID'

RHODODENDRON 'BRIDESMAID'

FUCHSIA 'HAPPY WEDDING DAY'

HYDRANGEA PANICULATA 'OCTOBER BRIDE'

CLEMATIS 'THE BRIDE'

EXOCHORDA × *MACRANTHA* 'THE BRIDE'

GAURA LINDHEIMERI 'THE BRIDE'

GERANIUM VERSICOLOR 'THE BRIDE'

GLADIOLUS 'THE BRIDE'

PRUNUS INCISA 'THE BRIDE'

NARCISSUS 'TROUSSEAU'

CAMPANULA PUNCTATA 'WEDDING BELLS'

CHRYSANTHEMUM 'WEDDING DAY'

ROSA 'WEDDING DAY'

COMMON DESCRIPTIVE TERMS

sinensis, sinicus Chinese
 Buxus sinica var. *insularis*
 Citrus sinensis (orange tree)
 Corylopsis sinensis
 Geranium sinense
 Magnolia sieboldii subsp. *sinensis*
 Miscanthus sinensis
 Nyssa sinensis
 Wisteria sinensis

sinuatus, sinuosus wavy-edged
 Limonium sinuatum
sino- Chinese
sitchensis from Sitka, Alaska
 Picea sitchensis
smilacinus like *Smilax*
 Disporum smilacinum
sobolifer with creeping stems that form roots
 Jovibarba sobolifera ("hen and chickens" houseleek)
socialis growing in colonies
 Ledebouria socialis
solandri named for Daniel Solander (1736–1782), a biologist who traveled with Captain Cook on the *Endeavour*
 Olearia solandri
solaris sun-loving
soldanellus like a small coin
 Carex soldanella
solidus solid, dense
 Corydalis solida

somnifer sleep-bringing
    Papaver somniferum
sonchifolius with leaves like *Sonchus*
    (sow-thistle)
    Francoa sonchifolia
songaricus from Dzungaria in north-
    west China, bordering Kazakhstan
    Clematis songarica
soulangeanus named for Etienne
    Soulange-Bodin (1774–1846),
    a French horticulturist
    Magnolia × *soulangeana*
spathaceus with a spathe
    Salvia spathacea
spathulatus spoon-shaped
    Moraea spathulata
spathulifolius with spoon-shaped
    leaves
    Sedum spathulifolium

COMMON DESCRIPTIVE TERMS

speciosus showy, splendid
Chaenomeles speciosa
Colchicum speciosum
Crocus speciosus
Lilium speciosum
Ribes speciosum
Tropaeolum speciosum

spectabilis spectacular
Dicentra spectabilis
Lampranthus spectabilis
Primula spectabilis
Sedum spectabile

WHAT'S IN A NAME?

COLOR: BLUE AND PURPLE

amethystinus violet-colored
atropurpureus dark purple
azureus sky blue
betinus purple like beet
caeruleus, coeruleus bright, deep
  blue
caesius light grayish blue, lavender
  blue
cobaltinus cobalt blue
coelestinus sky blue
cyaneus, cyanus clear, bright blue
ianthinus violet-blue
indigoticus deep, dark blue
lilacinus lilac-colored
lividus leaden blue-gray
ostrinus rich purple
pavoninus peacock blue
porphyro-, porphyreus purple
purpurascens purplish, becoming
  purple
purpuratus clad in purple
purpureus purple
tyrius purple
violaceus violet

spectatus beheld; esteemed
spelunca cave
    Microlepia speluncae
-spermus -seeded
sphaericus spherical
sphaerocarpus with globose fruits
sphaerocephalus with globose heads
    Allium sphaerocephalon
sphegodes like a wasp
    Ophrys sphegodes
sphen- wedge-shaped

COMMON DESCRIPTIVE TERMS

spicatus spicate, bearing a spike
Hedychium spicatum
Liatris spicata
Liriope spicata
Mentha spicata (spearmint)
Veronica spicata

spicifer spike-bearing
spiciformis spike-shaped
spiculatus with fine points
spilophaeus dark-spotted
    Hieracium spilophaeum
spina-christi Christ's thorn
    Paliurus spina-christi

CULTIVAR NAMES
Cities of the World

FUCHSIA 'CITY OF ADELAIDE'
GLADIOLUS 'AMSTERDAM'
KNIPHOFIA 'ATLANTA'
CONVALLARIA MAJALIS 'BERLIN GIANT'
CLEMATIS INTEGRIFOLIA 'BUDAPEST'
GREVILLEA 'CANBERRA GEM'
HIBISCUS ROSA-SINENSIS 'CASABLANCA'
HEMEROCALLIS 'CHICAGO APACHE'
IRIS 'CORDOBA'
PANICUM VIRGATUM 'DALLAS BLUES'
PERSICARIA AFFINIS 'DARJEELING RED'
PAEONIA LACTIFLORA 'DRESDEN'
ASTILBE 'DÜSSELDORF'
CLEMATIS 'DUCHESS OF EDINBURGH'
CLEMATIS 'GOTHENBURG'
IRIS 'GRANADA GOLD'
HYDRANGEA MACROPHYLLA 'HAMBURG'
PENNISETUM ALOPECUROIDES 'HAMELN'
CLEMATIS 'HELSINGBORG'
AMARYLLIS BELLADONNA 'JOHANNESBURG'
CANNA 'KANSAS CITY'
FUCHSIA 'LONDON 2000'
DIANTHUS 'LONDON POPPET'

CLEMATIS 'VILLE DE LYON'
CANNA 'MADRAS'
LAVANDULA STOECHAS 'MADRID BLUE'
NARCISSUS 'MEXICO CITY'
TULIPA 'MONTE CARLO'
MALUS PUMILA 'MONTREAL BEAUTY'
OSTEOSPERMUM 'NAIROBI PURPLE'
IRIS SIBIRICA 'OTTAWA'
CLEMATIS 'ETOILE DE PARIS'
HEDERA HELIX 'PITTSBURGH'
CANNA 'CITY OF PORTLAND'
PRIMULA AURICULA 'PRAGUE'
ASTRANTIA MAJOR 'ROMA'
CANNA 'SINGAPORE GIRL'
COLUMNEA 'STAVANGER'
IRIS 'STOCKHOLM'
CANNA 'STRASBOURG'
CANNA 'STUTTGART'
MENTHA SPICATA 'TASHKENT'
HYDRANGEA MACROPHYLLA 'TOKYO DELIGHT'
ARGYRANTHEMUM 'VANCOUVER'
NARCISSUS 'VERONA'
TULIPA 'YOKOHAMA'
COREOPSIS VERTICILLATA 'ZAGREB'

spinosus, spinifer thorny; ***spinulifer***
with little spines; ***spinalbus*** with
white spines

Acanthus spinosus

Androsace spinulifera

Cleome spinosa

Desfontainea spinosa

Eryngium spinalba

Prunus spinosa

---

spiralis spiral
   Cryptomeria japonica 'Spiralis'

splendens brilliant
   Salvia splendens

splendidum bright, brilliant, splendid
   Helichrysum splendidum

spooneri named for Herman Spooner
   (1878–1976), a botanist at Veitch
   & Sons' nurseries (see page 204)
   Clematis spooneri

sprengeri named for Karl Sprenger
   (1846–1917), a German
   nurseryman working in Italy
   Tulipa sprengeri

spurius false
   Iris spuria

squalidus dirty
   Leptinella squalida

squamatus, squamosus scaly
   Oxalis squamata

squarrosus rough, scurfy; with
   protruding scales
   Chamaecyparis pisifera 'Squarrosa'

Stellatus

standishii named for John
   Standish (1814–1875), founder
   of Sunningdale Nurseries, in
   Berkshire, UK
   Lonicera standishii

stans upright
   Clematis stans

stellatus stellate, starry, star-shaped
   Magnolia stellata

stellerianus named for Georg Steller
   (1709–1746), a German naturalist
   Artemisia stelleriana

stellulatus rather starlike
   Olearia stellulata

sten-, steno- narrow (see below)

stenantherus with narrow anthers

stenocephalus with a narrow head
   Ligularia stenocephala

---

stenophyllus with narrow leaves

Berberis × *stenophylla*

Cistus × *stenophyllus*

Eremurus stenophyllus

Hebe stenophylla

Iris stenophylla

---

stenopterus with narrow wings
  Pterocarya stenoptera
sternianus, sternii named for Sir
  Frederick Stern (1884–1967),
  British plantsman, gardener
  and author
  Cotoneaster sternianus
  Helleborus × *sternii*
stewartii named for Laurence Stewart
  (1877–1934), Keeper of the Royal
  Botanic Garden Edinburgh, Scotland
  Digitalis stewartii
stimulosus with stings or prickles
  Phyllostachys stimulosa

stipularis, stipulatus with (large)
  stipules
  Gillenia stipulata
stoechas from the Iles d'Hyères, off
  the French Mediterranean coast
  Lavandula stoechas
stolonifer with rooting runners
  Phlox stolonifera
stragulus, stragulatus mat-forming
  Gentiana stragulata
stramineus like straw, straw-colored
  Gentiana straminea
strepto- twisted (see below)
streptocarpus with twisted fruits
streptophyllus with twisted leaves

COMMON DESCRIPTIVE TERMS

striatus striped; **striatulus** rather
  stripy
Aloe striatula
Geranium sanguineum var. *striatum*
Polygonatum × *hybridum* 'Striatum'
Sisyrinchium striatum

strictus upright, erect, tight
Agave stricta
Babiana stricta
Crataegus monogyna 'Stricta'
Juniperus chinensis 'Stricta'

---

strigillosus
  with short, flattened bristles
strigosus bristly
  Hydrangea aspera subsp. *strigosa*

strobilaceus scaly like a pine-cone

strobilifer bearing cones

struthiopteris ostrich fern
    Matteuccia struthiopteris

studiosorum of scholars
    Androsace studiosorum

stygianus of the River Styx of classical
    mythology
    Euphorbia stygiana

stylosus with a conspicuous or large
    style
    Phuopsis stylosa

styracifluus flowing with gum
    Liquidambar styraciflua

suaveolens fragrant, smelling sweetly
    Mentha suaveolens

sub- almost, somewhat, not
    completely (see below)

subalpinus growing below the
    timber line
    Hebe subalpina

subcrenulatus somewhat scalloped
    Eucalyptus subcrenulata

suberectus somewhat erect

subhirtellus somewhat hairy
    Prunus × *subhirtella*

subulatus shaped like an awl
    Callistemon subulatus

succulentus juicy, fleshy
    Oxalis succulenta

suecicus Swedish
    Cotoneaster × *suecicus*

suffruticosus somewhat shrubby
    Buxus sempervirens 'Suffruticosa'

sulphureus sulphur yellow
    Epimedium × *versicolor*
    'Sulphureum'

COMMON DESCRIPTIVE TERMS

superbus superb

Chaenomeles × *superba*

Leucanthemum × *superbum*

Lilium superbum

Salvia × *superba*

---

suspensus hanging
    Forsythia suspensa

COMMON DESCRIPTIVE TERMS

sylvaticus, sylvestris of woods,
    or growing wild

Fagus sylvatica

Geranium sylvaticum

Luzula sylvatica

Malus sylvestris

Malva sylvestris

Nicotiana sylvestris

Nyssa sylvatica

Pinus sylvestris

Tulipa sylvestris

---

syriacus from Syria
    Hibiscus syriacus

syringanthus with flowers like *Syringa*
    (lilac)
    Lonicera syringantha

szechuanicus from Sichuan, China
    Betula szechuanica

T

tabularis, tabuliformis flat
like a board
Aeonium tabuliforme
Blechnum tabulare
taiwanensis, taiwanianus
from Taiwan
Angelica taiwaniana
tamariscifolius with leaves like
Tamarix (tamarisk)
Juniperus sabina 'Tamariscifolia'

CULTIVAR NAMES
Famous Writers

DIANTHUS 'JANE AUSTEN'
FUCHSIA 'ALAN AYCKBOURN'
RHODODENDRON 'BALZAC'
NARCISSUS 'BARRETT BROWNING'
ROSA 'ROBERT BURNS'
FUCHSIA 'LORD BYRON'
RHODODENDRON 'CORNEILLE'
HOSTA 'EMILY DICKINSON'
HOSTA 'ROBERT FROST'
CLEMATIS VICTOR HUGO
NARCISSUS 'KEATS'
RHODODENDRON 'SAPPHO'
TULIPA 'SHAKESPEARE'
PELARGONIUM 'SHELLEY'
SEMPERVIVUM 'VIRGIL'
HELIANTHEMUM 'VOLTAIRE'
PELARGONIUM 'WORDSWORTH'

---

tanacetifolius with leaves like
Tanacetum (tansy)
Crataegus tanacetifolia
tanguticus from the region of the
Tangut people in north-west China
Daphne tangutica
tardiflorus late-flowering
Hosta tardiflora
tardivus, tardus late
Hydrangea paniculata 'Tardiva'
Tulipa tarda
tarentinus from Taranto in Italy
Myrtus communis subsp. *tarentina*
tartareus with a crumbly or rough
surface
tasmanicus from Tasmania
Gaultheria tasmanica
tasmanii named for the Dutch
explorer Abel Tasman (1603–
1659), who discovered Tasmania
Davallia tasmanii
tataricus, tartaricus from Tatary
(Tartary), an old name for a region
of central Asia/European Russia
Lonicera tatarica
tatsienensis from Kangding
(Tatsienlu) in Sichuan, China
Delphinium tatsienense
tauricus from the Crimea
Asphodeline tauricus
taurinus from the region around
Turin (Torino), Italy
taxifolius with leaves like *Taxus* (yew)
Juniperus taxifolius

Tacamahac *Populus balsamifera*
Tamarisk *Tamarix*
Tansy *Tanacetum vulgare*
Teasel *Dipsacus fullonum*
Tenby daffodil *Narcissus obvallaris*
Texas bluebonnet *Lupinus subcarnosus*
Thorn-apple *Datura stramonium*
Three-cornered leek *Allium triquetrum*
Thrift *Armeria maritima*
Thyme *Thymus*
Tickseed *Coreopsis*
Toad lily *Tricyrtis*
Toadflax *Linaria*
Toothache tree *Zanthoxylum americanum*
Torch lily *Kniphofia*
Traveler's joy *Clematis vitalba*
Tree fern *Dicksonia antarctica*
Tree heath *Erica arborea*
Tree mallow *Lavatera × clementii*
Tree of heaven *Ailanthus altissima*
Trout lily *Erythronium*
Trumpet vine *Campsis*
Tulip tree *Liriodendron tulipifera*
Tupelo *Nyssa*
Turtlehead *Chelone*
Twinflower *Linnaea borealis*

Valerian *Centranthus, Valeriana*
(Vegetables, see page 113)
Venus flytrap *Dionaea muscipula*
Vervain *Verbena officinalis*
Vine *Vitis vinifera*
Violet *Viola*
Viper's bugloss *Echium vulgare*
Virginia creeper *Parthenocissus quinquefolia*

TANSY

---

tectorum of roofs
　Sempervivum tectorum
tenax tenacious, holding fast, tough
　Phormium tenax
tenellus rather delicate
　Prunus tenella
tenuicaulis with a thin stem
　Persicaria tenuicaulis

tenuiculmis with thin culms (stalks)
　Carex tenuiculmis

COMMON DESCRIPTIVE TERMS

tenuifolius with thin leaves
Gypsophila tenuifolia
Paeonia tenuifolia
Philadelphus tenuifolius
Pittosporum tenuifolium

COLOR: RED AND ORANGE

calendulinus orange like pot marigold
(*Calendula*)

capsicinus bright red, like a pepper
(*Capsicum*)

capucinus orange-red, like nasturtium
(*Tropaeolum*)

cardinalis cardinal red

carmesinus crimson

carneus flesh-colored

cerasinus cherry red

coccineus deep carmine red

corallinus coral-colored

cruentus bloody

erubescens reddening, blushing

erythro- red

flammeus; flammeolus flame-colored

fuscoruber dark red

igneus fiery red

incarnatus flesh-colored

kermesinus carmine, purplish red

lateritius brick red

miniatus the color of red lead

phoeniceus purplish red

puniceus purplish crimson

rhodo- light red

roseus, rosea like a rose, rose-colored

rubellus light red

ruber red

rubescens reddish, reddening

rubiginosus rusty

rufus, rufescens reddish

sanguineus bloody, dull red

vermiculatus vermilion

tenuis thin, fine, slender

tenuissimus very thin
  Stipa tenuissima

terebinthus turpentine

teres cylindrical

terminalis terminal; of boundaries
  Pachysandra terminalis

ternatus in threes
  Choisya ternata

terniflorus with flowers in threes

ternifolius with three leaves or leaflets
  Gentiana ternifolia

terrestris terrestrial, growing in the
  ground

tessellatus checkered
  Indocalamus tessellatus

testaceus terracotta-colored
  Carex testacea

testudinarius tortoise-like

tetra- four

tetragonus with four angles
  Chamaecyparis obtusa 'Tetragona
  Aurea'

tetrandrus with four anthers
  Tamarix tetrandra

tetraphyllus with four leaves or
  leaflets
  Oxalis tetraphylla

tetrapterus four-winged
  Sophora tetraptera

teucrioides like *Teucrium*

texanus, texensis from Texas
  Clematis texensis

thapsus former name of a town
  in Sicily
  Verbascum thapsus (great mullein)

thessalus from Thessalia in Greece
  Fritillaria thessala

thibetanus, thibeticus, tibetanus, tibeticus from Tibet
Clematis tibetana
Gentiana tibetica
Helleborus thibetanus
Primula tibetica

thomsonii named for Thomas Thomson (1817–1878), a Scottish doctor and botanist working in India

thunbergii named for the Swedish botanist Carl Thunberg (1743–1828)
Berberis thunbergii
Fritillaria thunbergii
Geranium thunbergii
Hemerocallis thunbergii

thuringiacus from Thuringia in Germany
Lavatera thuringiaca
thymifolius thyme-leaved
Fuchsia thymifolia
thyrsiflorus with flowers in a thyrse (a type of flowerhead, like lilac or horse-chestnut)
Ceanothus thyrsiflorus
thyrsoides like a thyrse (see above*)*
Campanula thyrsoides
tibetanus, tibeticus (see panel above)

tinctorius used in dyeing
Anthemis tinctoria
Carthamus tinctorius
Genista tinctoria
Impatiens tinctoria
Indigofera tinctoria

tingens dyeing, a dyer
Euonymus tingens
tingitanus from Tangier
Lathyrus tingitanus

tomentosus tomentose, woolly
Cerastium tomentosum
Galactites tomentosa
Paulownia tomentosa
Pelargonium tomentosum
Philadelphus tomentosus
Tilia tomentosa

tommasinianus named for an Italian botanist, Muzio de' Tommasini (1794–1879)
Crocus tommasinianus
topiaria of or for topiary
Hebe topiaria
torminalis curing gripe or colic
Sorbus torminalis
torosus, torulosus cylindrical with bulges or contractions at intervals
torquatus twisted round; with a collar
Helleborus torquatus

CULTIVAR NAMES
Strange but True
T

Juniperus scopulorum 'Tabletop'

Ligustrum ovalifolium 'Taff's Indecision'

Geranium phaeum 'Taff's Jester'

Pennisetum orientale 'Tall Tails'

Iris sibirica 'Temper Tantrum'

Malus domestica (apple) 'Ten Commandments'

Hosta 'Thumb Nail'

Fuchsia 'Thunderbird'

Pinus thunbergii 'Thunderhead'

Lavandula 'Tickled Pink'

Iris 'Tickle Me'

Miscanthus sinensis 'Tiger Cub'

Begonia 'Tiger Paws'

Geranium 'Tiny Monster'

Narcissus 'Tittle-tattle'

Kniphofia 'Toffee Nosed'

Primula auricula 'Tomboy'

Pelargonium 'Tomcat'

Fuchsia 'Tom Thumb' (and his family 'Lady Thumb', 'Son of Thumb' and 'Baby Thumb')

Narcissus 'Topolino'

Corydalis 'Tory MP'

Iris 'To the Point'

Narcissus 'Toto'

Kniphofia hirsuta 'Traffic Lights'

Primula auricula 'Trouble'

Narcissus 'Tuesday's Child'

Olearia traversii 'Tweedledum'

Malus domestica 'Twenty Ounce'

---

tortuosus, tortus, tortilis tortuous, winding

  Fagus sylvatica 'Tortuosa Purpurea'

trachelius curing throat ailments

  Campanula trachelium

tradescantii named for John Tradescant (1570–1638) and his son John (1608–1662), English plant collectors and royal gardeners

  Aster tradescantii

tragophyllus with goat-like leaves

  Lonicera tragophylla

tranquillans calming

  Hibanobambusa tranquillans

transsilvanicus, transylvanicus from Transylvania, Romania

  Hepatica transsilvanica

transitorius passing, transitory

  Malus transitoria

tremulus trembling, quivering

  Populus tremula

triacanthos three-thorned

  Gleditsia triacanthos

triandrus with three stamens

  Narcissus triandrus

triangularis three-angled

  Kniphofia triangularis

tricho- hair (see below)

trichocarpus with hairy fruits

  Populus trichocarpa

trichocaulon with a hairy stem
  Hypericum trichocaulon
trichophyllus with hairy leaves
  Leucojum trichophyllum
trichotomum with divisions in threes
  Clerodendron trichotomum
trichorhizum with hairy rhizomes

COMMON DESCRIPTIVE TERMS
tricolor three-colored
Convolvulus tricolor
Fagus sylvatica 'Tricolor'
Fuchsia magellanica var. *gracilis*
  'Tricolor'
Hydrangea macrophylla 'Tricolor'
Ipomoea tricolor
Ligustrum lucidum 'Tricolor'
Salvia officinalis 'Tricolor'
Viola tricolor

---

tricornis with three horns
tricuspidatus three-pointed
  Parthenocissus tricuspidata
trifidus divided or cleft into three
  Carex trifida
triflorus three-flowered
  Acer triflorum

COMMON DESCRIPTIVE TERMS
trifolius, trifoliatus three-leaved
Cardamine trifolia
Gillenia trifoliata
Menyanthes trifoliata (bogbean)
Ptelea trifoliata

WHAT'S IN A NAME?

PATTERNS AND MARKINGS

albomaculatus white-spotted
albovariegatus white-variegated
argenteoguttatus silver-spotted
argenteomarginatus silver-edged
argenteovariegatus silver-variegated
astictus without spots
aureomaculatus gold-spotted
aureomarginatus gold-edged
aureoreticulatus gold-veined
erythrostictus with red spots
fasciatus banded, striped
guttatus spotted
irroratus (literally) sprinkled with
  dew; finely spotted
luteovenosus with yellow veins
maculatus, maculifer spotted, blotchy
marginalis, marginatus with a distinct
  margin, edge or border
marmoratus marbled
melanostictus spotted with black
monostictus with one spot
nigropunctatus black-spotted
non-scriptus unmarked
ocellatus, oculatus with an eye
picturatus embellished; variegated
punctatus spotted
reticulatus netted
rubromarginatus edged with red
rufinervis with red veins
spilophaeus dark-spotted
striatus striped; *striatulus* rather
  stripy
tessellatus checkered
variegatus variegated
viridistriatus green-striped
zebrinus striped
zonalis, zonatus with a distinct band
  of a different color

CULTIVAR NAMES
Some English Counties

JUNIPERUS COMMUNIS 'BERKSHIRE'

ROSA 'CHESHIRE LIFE'

ERICA VAGANS 'CORNISH CREAM'

LONICERA NITIDA 'CUMBRIAN CALYPSO'

FUCHSIA 'DEVONSHIRE DUMPLING'

KNIPHOFIA 'DORSET SENTRY'

FUCHSIA 'HAMPSHIRE BLUE'

MALUS DOMESTICA (APPLE) 'HEREFORDSHIRE BEEFING'

CAMPANULA 'KENT BELLE'

FUCHSIA 'FLAT JACK O'LANCASHIRE'

ROSA LINCOLNSHIRE POACHER ('GLAREABIT')

VERBASCUM 'NORFOLK DAWN'

ROSA NORTHAMPTONSHIRE ('MATTDOR')

ROSA A SHROPSHIRE LAD ('AUSLED')

DAPHNE × *BURKWOODII* 'SOMERSET'

DAHLIA 'SUFFOLK PUNCH'

RHODODENDRON 'SURREY HEATH'

LAVANDULA × *INTERMEDIA* 'SUSSEX'

CLEMATIS 'WARWICKSHIRE ROSE'

LATHYRUS ODORATUS 'WILTSHIRE RIPPLE'

ROSA WORCESTERSHIRE ('KORLALON')

CLEMATIS 'YORKSHIRE PRIDE'

trifurcatus three-pronged
  Azorella trifurcata
trilobus, trilobatus three-lobed
  Malus trilobata
trimestris of three months
  Lavatera trimestris

trinervis three-veined
trionum "of the Wain" (the constellation comprising Ursa Major and Ursa Minor)
  Hibiscus trionum
tripartitus divided into three parts
  Eryngium × *tripartitum*
tripetalus with three petals
  Magnolia tripetala
triphyllus three-leaved
  Aloysia triphylla
tripinnatus thrice pinnate
triplinervis with three veins
  Anaphalis triplinervis
tripteris three-winged
  Coreopsis tripteris
triquetrus three-cornered
  Allium triquetrum

COMMON DESCRIPTIVE TERMS
tristis sad; **tristulis** rather sad
Betula pendula 'Tristis'
Fritillaria affinis var. *tristulis*
Gladiolus tristis
Pelargonium triste

---

triternatus thrice ternate
  Clematis × *triternata*
trullifolius with scoop-shaped leaves
  Anemone trullifolia
truncatus truncated, cut off
tuberculatus tuberculate, covered with small warty nodules
  Echium tuberculatum

COMMON DESCRIPTIVE TERMS

tuberosus tuberous

Allium tuberosum (Chinese chives)
Asclepias tuberosa
Geranium tuberosum
Hermodactylus tuberosus
Oxalis tuberosa
Tropaeolum tuberosum

tubiformis tube-shaped
   Fritillaria tubiformis
tubulosus like a small pipe or tube
   Clematis tubulosa
tulipifer tulip-bearing
   Liriodendron tulipifera
tumidissinodus with very swollen nodes
   Chimonobambusa tumidissinoda
tuolumnensis from Tuolumne County, California (from a Native American name)
   Erythronium tuolumnense
turbinatus shaped like a spinning-top
   Aesculus turbinata

COMMON DESCRIPTIVE TERMS

turkestanicus from Turkestan

Acer turkestanicum
Dianthus turkestanicus
Salvia turkestanica
Tulipa turkestanica

typhoides like *Typha* (bulrush)
   Kniphofia typhoides

GENUS NAMES
T, U

Taraxacum from Persian *talkh chakok*, bitter herb
Taxodium from Latin *Taxus*, yew, and Greek *eidos*, resemblance
Thunbergia named for Carl Thunberg (1743–1828), Swedish botanist and plant collector
Tiarella diminutive of Greek *tiara*, crown
Tolmiea named for Dr. William Tolmie (1812–1886), Scottish doctor and botanist in Canada
Torreya named for Dr. John Torrey (1796–1873), leading American botanist
Trachelospermum from Greek *trachelos*, neck, and *sperma*, seed
Trachycarpus from Greek *trachys*, rough, and *karpos*, fruit
Tradescantia named for the John Tradescants, father and son (see page 198)
Tragopogon from Greek *tragos*, goat, and *pogon*, beard
Tricyrtis from Greek *tri-*, three, and *kyrtos*, humped
Trifolium from Latin *tri-*, three, and *folium*, leaf
Trillium from Latin *tri-*, three
Tropaeolum from Latin *tropaeum*, trophy
Tulipa from Turkish *tulbend*, turban
Ursinia named for Johannes Ursinus (1608–1667), German botanical writer
Uvularia from Latin *uvula*, the lobe at the back of the palate

U

ucranicus from the Ukraine
  Scabiosa ucranica
uliginosus of marshy, wet places
  Salvia uliginosa
ulmarius like *Ulmus* (elm)
  Filipendula ulmaria (meadowsweet)

COMMON DESCRIPTIVE TERMS
umbellatus umbelliferous
Butomus umbellatus
Calandrinia umbellata
Elaeagnus umbellata
Iberis umbellata (candytuft)
Ornithogalum umbellatum
Rhaphiolepis umbellata

---

umbraculifer umbrella-bearing
  Pinus densiflora 'Umbraculifera'
umbrosus growing in shade
  Saxifraga umbrosa
uncinatus hooked or barbed
  Clematis uncinata

COMMON DESCRIPTIVE TERMS
undulatus wavy
Asplenium scolopendrium Undulatum
  Group
Hosta undulata
Mahonia × *wagneri* 'Undulata'
Nerine undulata

---

unedo "I eat one"
  Arbutus unedo
unguicularis clawed
  Iris unguicularis
unifolius with one leaf
  Allium unifolium
uniflorus with one flower
  Ipheion uniflorum
uplandicus from Uppland, Sweden
  Symphytum × *uplandicum*
urbanus, urbium urban, of towns
  Saxifraga × *urbium*
urniger with urn-shaped fruits
  Eucalyptus urnigera
urophyllus with leaves like an ox's tail
  Clematis urophylla
ursinus bearlike; also northern (from
  the constellation Ursa Major, the
  Great Bear or the Plough)
  Allium ursinum

CULTIVAR NAMES
Strange but True
U, V

PINUS BANKSIANA 'UNCLE FOGY'
JUNCUS 'UNICORN'
PELARGONIUM 'URCHIN'
PHLOX PANICULATA 'UTOPIA'
CLEMATIS 'THE VAGABOND'
PIERIS JAPONICA 'VALLEY VALENTINE'
PINUS FLEXILIS 'VANDERWOLF'S
  PYRAMID'
ARMERIA MARITIMA 'VINDICTIVE'
PELARGONIUM 'VOODOO'

ARBUTUS UNEDO

urticifolius with leaves like *Urtica*
  (nettle)
  Clematis urticifolia
uruguayensis from Uruguay
  Azara uruguayensis
utahensis from Utah
  Penstemon utahensis
usitatissimus very useful
  Linum usitatissimum
utilis useful
  Betula utilis
uva-crispa curly grape
  Ribes uva-crispa (gooseberry)
uvarius like grapes
  Kniphofia uvaria
uva-ursi bear's grape
  Arctostaphylos uva-ursi
uva-vulpis fox's grape
  Fritillaria uva-vulpis

CULTIVAR NAMES
Foreign Expressions
T, U, V

TAUBE (*German*) DOVE
(*HYDRANGEA MACROPHYLLA* 'TAUBE')

TIEFROT (*German*) DEEP RED
(*LOBELIA* 'FAN TIEFROT')

TOITS DE PARIS (*French*)
ROOFS OF PARIS
(*PHLOX PANICULATA* 'TOITS DE PARIS')

TRÈS COUPÉ (*French*) MUCH CUT
(*HEDERA HELIX* 'TRÈS COUPÉ')

TRIOMPHE DE ... (*French*)
TRIUMPH OF ...
(*HELIANTHUS* 'TRIOMPHE DE GAND')

TRISTESSE (*French*) SADNESS
(*SEMPERVIVUM* 'TRISTESSE')

UKIGUMO (*Japanese*)
FLOATING CLOUD
(*ACER PALMATUM* 'UKIGUMO')

VEILCHENBLAU (*German*)
VIOLET BLUE
(*ROSA* 'VEILCHENBLAU')

VEILCHENKÖNIGIN (*German*)
VIOLET QUEEN
(*ASTER AMELLUS* 'VEILCHENKÖNIGIN')

VOIE LACTÉE (*French*)
THE MILKY WAY
(*PHILADELPHUS* 'VOIE LACTÉE')

VORLÄUFER (*German*)
FORERUNNER
(*MISCANTHUS SINENSIS* 'VORLÄUFER')

VUURBAAK (*Dutch*) LIGHTHOUSE
(*HYACINTHUS ORIENTALIS* 'VUURBAAK')

V

vacciniifolius with leaves like
  Vaccinium
  Persicaria vacciniifolia
vagans, vagensis wandering; widely
  distributed
  Erica vagans
  Sorbus × *vagensis*
valdivianus from Valdivia in Chile
  Berberis valdiviana
valentinus from Valencia, Spain
  Coronilla valentina
validus strong, robust, powerful
  Lobelia valida
vanhouttei named for a Belgian
  nurseryman, Louis Van Houtte
  (1810–1876)
  Spiraea × *vanhouttei*
variabilis, varians, variatus variable
  Erodium × *variabile*

COMMON DESCRIPTIVE TERMS
variegatus variegated
Aloe variegata
Iris pallida 'Variegata'
Miscanthus sinensis 'Variegatus'
Pleioblastus variegatus
Rhamnus alaternus 'Variegata'

---

variifolius with variable leaves
  Eryngium variifolium

COMMON DESCRIPTIVE TERMS
veitchii, veitchianus named for
  Veitch & Sons, a famous 19th-
  century nursery founded by John
  Veitch (1752–1839) and run by
  five generations of the Veitch
  family in Exeter and London, UK
Abies veitchii
Ligularia veitchii
Paeonia veitchii
Sasa veitchii
Saxifraga veitchiana

---

velatus covered, concealed
vellerius fleecy
velutinus velvety
  Fraxinus velutina
venenatus, venenosus poisonous
venetus from Venice
  Lathyrus venetus
venosus veined, prominently veined
  Clematis 'Venosa Violacea'
ventricosus (literally) pot-bellied;
  with a swelling
  Hosta ventricosa

COMMON DESCRIPTIVE TERMS
venustus lovely, charming, pleasing
Adiantum venustum
Eryngium venustum
Filipendula rubra 'Venusta'
Fuchsia venusta
Hosta venusta
Penstemon venustus

WHAT'S IN A NAME?

PLACES

MANY LATIN AND LATINIZED PLACE-NAMES, SUCH AS *AMERICANUS*, *ITALICUS* AND *GERMANICUS*, NEED NO EXPLANATION. THE FOLLOWING LIST GIVES A SAMPLE OF DESCRIPTIVE TERMS DERIVED FROM SOME LESS OBVIOUS ONES.

aegypticus, aegyptiacus Egypt

aethiopicus, aethiopis Ethiopia; also used to mean South African

afer, afra, afrum; africanus Africa

anatolicus Anatolia, Turkey

ancyrensis Ankara, Turkey

asturiensis Asturias, Spain

atticus Attica or Athens, Greece

baeticus Andalucia, Spain

berolinensis Berlin, Germany

bonariensis Buenos Aires, Argentina

bucarius, bucharicus Bokhara, Turkestan

byzantinus Istanbul (formerly Byzantium), Turkey

calabricus Calabria, Italy

canadensis Canada or the north-eastern USA

canariensis Gran Canaria or the Canary Islands

cantabricus Cantabria in Spain

capensis the Cape (of Good Hope), meaning South Africa

caucasicus Caucasia, former Soviet Union

cornubiensis Cornwall, England

creticus Crete

cyprius Cyprus

damascenus Damascus, Syria

etruscus Tuscany, Italy

fennicus Finland

florentinus Florence, Italy

fluminensis Rio de Janeiro

formosanus Taiwan (Formosa)

georgicus Georgia (Caucasus)

groenlandicus Greenland

ibericus the Iberian peninsula

illyricus Illyria (the Adriatic coast of Croatia and Dalmatia)

japonicus, niponicus, nipponicus Japan

libani, libanotis, libanoticus Lebanon

lusitanicus Portugal

lutetianus Paris, France

magellanicus the southern tip of South America, around the Straits of Magellan

monacensis Munich, Germany

monspeliensis, monspessulanus Montpellier, France

narbonensis Narbonne, France

norvegicus Norway

novae-zelandiae New Zealand

numidicus Algeria

oxonianus, oxoniensis Oxford, England

pedemontanus Piedmont, Italy

pekinensis Beijing, China

ponticus Pontus, Asia Minor

ruthenicus Ruthenia, a region of Russia (and used more generally to mean Russian)

sabatius Savona, on the Ligurian coast of north-west Italy

sarniensis Guernsey, Channel Islands

siculus Sicily

sinensis, sinicus China

sitchensis Sitka, Alaska

syriacus Syria

valentinus Valencia, Spain

tarentinus Taranto, Italy

tauricus the Crimea

yedoensis, yesoensis, yezoensis Tokyo

veris, vernalis, vernus of spring

Crocus vernus

Gentiana verna

Hamamelis vernalis

Lathyrus vernus

Leucojum vernum

Omphalodes verna

Primula veris

Pulsatilla vernalis

vernicosus varnished

   Eucalyptus vernicosa

verrucosus warty

   Euonymus verrucosus

verruculosus with little warts

   Berberis verruculosa

PRIMULA VERIS

versicolor in various colors

Brugmansia versicolor

Epimedium × *versicolor*

Geranium versicolor

Iris versicolor

Lupinus versicolor

Oenothera versicolor

Oxalis versicolor

verticillatus verticillate; in whorls

   Coreopsis verticillata

WHAT'S IN A NAME?

COLOR: GREEN

aeruginosus blue-green
(the color of verdigris)

atrovirens dark green

chlorinus yellow-green

chloro- clear green

elaio- olive green

flavovirens yellowish green

glaucus, glaucescens dull green
to grayish blue

olivaceus olive green, brownish
green

prasinus leek green

smaragdinus emerald green, clear
bright green

thalassicus sea green

virens verdant green

virescens greenish, becoming green

viridescens greenish

viridis green (general)

viridissimus very green

viridulus greenish

xanthochlorus yellowish green

verus true; standard
  Aloe vera
vescus small, feeble
  Fragaria vesca
vesicarius relating to the bladder;
  a remedy for bladder ailments
  Eruca vesicaria
vestitus covered or clothed
  Polystichum vestitum
vialii named for Paul Vial (1855–
  1917), a French missionary
  Primula vialii
viburnifolius with leaves like
  Viburnum
viburnoides like *Viburnum*
  Pileostegia viburnoides
victoriae-reginae Queen Victoria
  Agave victoriae-reginae
vigilis watchful, alert
  Diascia vigilis

COMMON DESCRIPTIVE TERMS

villosus softly hairy
Androsace villosa
Hydrangea aspera Villosa Group
Mentha × *villosa*
Pennisetum villosum
Soldanella villosa

---

vilmorinii named for Vilmorin-
  Andrieux, a long-established
  French nursery and seed
  supplier
  Sorbus vilmorinii

viminalis, vimineus with long, thin
  shoots; like osiers
  Salix viminalis (osier)
vinciflorus with flowers like *Vinca*
vinealis of vines or vineyards
  Allium vineale

VITIS VINIFERA

vinifer wine-producing
  Vitis vinifera (grape vine)

---

virens green
virescens greenish, becoming green
  Galanthus nivalis 'Virescens'
virgatus twiggy
  Corokia × *virgata*

---

viridapice with green tips
  Galanthus nivalis 'Viridapice'

---

viridistriatus green-striped
  Pleioblastus viridistriatus
viscosus sticky, viscous
  Rhododendron viscosum
vitalba white vine
  Clematis vitalba
vitellinus egg-yolk yellow
  Salix alba subsp. *vitellina*
viticella little vine
  Clematis viticella
vitifolius with leaves like *Vitis* (vine)
  Abutilon × *vitifolium*
volubilis winding, revolving
vomitorius causing vomiting
  Ilex vomitoria
vulcanicus of volcanoes, growing
  on a volcano
  Fuchsia vulcanica

Common descriptive terms

vulgaris common
Aquilegia vulgaris (columbine)
Calluna vulgaris (heather)
Echium vulgare (viper's bugloss)
Filipendula vulgaris (dropwort)
Foeniculum vulgare (fennel)
Leucanthemum vulgare (oxeye daisy)
Origanum vulgare (wild marjoram)
Polypodium vulgare (common
  polypody)
Primula vulgaris (primrose)
Pulsatilla vulgaris (Pasque flower)
Syringa vulgaris (lilac)
Thymus vulgaris (common thyme)

GENUS NAMES
V, W, X, Y, Z

Valeriana from Latin *valere*,
  to be well
Veronicastrum from *Veronica* and
  Latin -*astrum*, which denotes an
  incomplete resemblance
Vesicaria from Latin *vesica*, bladder
Vinca from Latin *vincire*, to wind
  around or bind
Waldsteinia named for Count
  Franz Waldstein-Wartenburg
  (1759–1823), Austrian botanist
  and author
Washingtonia named for George
  Washington (1732–1799), first
  President of the USA
Weigela named for Christian
  Weigel (1748–1831), German
  botanist
Wisteria named for Caspar Wistar
  (1761–1818), American professor
Xerochrysum from Greek *xeros*, dry,
  and *chrysos*, gold
Yucca from a Caribbean word
  meaning cassava or manioc
Zantedeschia named for Francesco
  Zantedeschi (1797–1873), Italian
  priest and physicist
Zephyranthes from Greek *zephyros*,
  the west wind, and *anthos*, flower
Zinnia named for Johann Zinn
  (1727–1759), German botanist

vulnerarius of wounds; for wounds
  Anthyllis vulneraria
vulpinus of foxes
  Carex vulpina

W

waldsteinii named for an Austrian botanist, Count Franz Waldstein-Wartenburg (1759–1823)
  Cardamine waldsteinii

COMMON DESCRIPTIVE TERMS

wallichianus, wallichii named for Nathaniel Wallich (1786–1854), a Danish botanist and doctor who specialized in the flora of India
  Dryopteris wallichiana
  Euphorbia wallichii
  Geranium wallichianum
  Lilium wallichianum
  Meconopsis wallichii
  Persicaria wallichii
  Pinus wallichiana
  Selinum wallichianum
  Strobilanthes wallichii

---

wardii (see panel above right)
warleyensis named for Warley Place, Essex, UK, once famous as the lavish garden of Ellen Willmott (see *willmottianus*, page 212)
  Epimedium × *warleyense*
warscewiczii named for a Polish plant collector, Joseph Warszczewicz (1812–1866)
  Canna warscewiczii

FRANK KINGDON WARD (1885–1958)

Carrying the tradition of the great plant hunters into the 1950s, Englishman Kingdon Ward was the last in a 300-year line. Beginning when he was a schoolmaster in Shanghai, he explored the remoter reaches of the Far East for nearly 50 years, introducing many rhododendrons, lilies, gentians, primulas and the beautiful Tibetan blue poppy, *Meconopsis betonicifolia*. Plants commemorating him include *Cotoneaster wardii* and *Rhododendron wardii*. *Primula florindae* and *Lilium mackliniae* are named for his first and second wives respectively.

watereri named for members of several generations of the Waterer family – owners, from the 18th to the 20th century, of a leading nursery firm based at Bagshot and Woking in Surrey, UK
  Cotoneaster × *watereri*

WHAT'S THE LATIN NAME?
W, X, Y, Z

Wake-robin *Trillium*
Wallflower *Erysimum*
Walnut *Juglans*
Water avens *Geum rivale*
Water lily
   Nymphaea
Water mint
   Mentha aquatica
Water soldier
   Stratiotes aloides
Water violet
   Hottonia palustris
Wattle *Acacia*
Wayfaring-tree
   Viburnum lantana
Wellingtonia
   Sequoiadendron
   giganteum
Welsh poppy
   Meconopsis
   cambrica
Whitebeam
   Sorbus aria
Wild marjoram
   Origanum vulgare
Wild service tree *Sorbus torminalis*
Willow *Salix*
Windflower *Anemone*
Wingnut *Pterocarya*
Winter aconite *Eranthis hyemalis*
Winter heliotrope *Petasites fragrans*

Winter jasmine *Jasminum nudiflorum*
Winter sweet *Chimonanthus praecox*
Winter's bark *Drimys winteri*
Winter-flowering cherry *Prunus*
   × *subhirtella*
   'Autumnalis'
Wire-netting bush
   Corokia cotoneaster
Witch-hazel
   Hamamelis
Wood anemone
   Anemone nemorosa
Wood sorrel *Oxalis*
   acetosella
Woodbine *Lonicera*
   periclymenum
Woodruff *Asperula*;
   Galium odoratum
Woodrush *Luzula*
   sylvatica
Wormwood
   Artemisia absinthium
Yarrow *Achillea*
   millefolium
Yellow archangel *Lamium galeobdolon*
Yellow loosestrife *Lysimachia vulgaris*
Yellow rattle *Rhinanthus minor*
Yellow wood *Cladrastis lutea*
Yew *Taxus baccata*
Yew, Irish *Taxus baccata* 'Fastigiata'
Yulan *Magnolia denudata*

WALNUT

weyrichii named for Heinrich
   Weyrich (1828–1868), a German
   botanist
wherryi named for American scientist
   Edgar Wherry (1885–1982)
   Tiarella wherryi

whittallii named for Edward
   Whittall (1851–1917), British
   Consul and merchant in Turkey,
   and a keen amateur botanist and
   plant collector
   Fritillaria whittallii

williamsii named for one of several
  botanists and collectors called
  Williams; perhaps the British
  botanist John Williams
  (1915–1991)
  Camellia × williamsii
willmottianus named for Miss Ellen
  Willmott (1858–1934), a keen
  amateur plantswoman who created
  an large and extravagant garden at
  Warley Place, Essex, UK
  Ceratostigma willmottianum
wilsonii (see panel below)
winteri named for Captain Winter,
  an Elizabethan seafarer
  Drimys winteri
wintonensis from Winchester,
  Hampshire, UK (usually applied to
  plants raised by Hillier Nurseries)
  × Halimiocistus wintonensis

CULTIVAR NAMES
Personal Names
W, X, Y, Z

Primula 'WANDA'

Galanthus plicatus 'WENDY'S
  GOLD'

Camellia japonica 'WILAMINA'

Rosa 'WILHELM'

Cardamine pratensis
  'WILLIAM'

Clematis 'WILLY'

Streptocarpus 'WINIFRED'

Linaria 'WINIFRID'S DELIGHT'

Malus domestica (APPLE)
  'WINSTON'

Chamaecyparis lawsoniana
  'YVONNE'

Fuchsia 'ZARA'

Primula auricula 'LADY ZOË'

Sempervivum 'ZORBA'

ERNEST HENRY WILSON (1876–1930)
Englishman Ernest Henry Wilson made his
first trip to China in 1899 for the nursery of
Veitch & Sons (see page 204). In a life full
of adventure, Wilson later traveled widely in
China and became one of the most prolific
of all plant hunters, introducing hundreds
of species to the Western world. In 1927 he
became Keeper of the Arnold Arboretum in
Massachusetts, but died three years later in a
car accident. "Chinese" Wilson introduced
such species as *Lilium regale* and *Kolkwitzia
amabilis* (his favorite). Plants commemorating
him include *Ilex × altaclerensis* 'Wilsonii', *Iris
wilsonii* and *Primula wilsonii*.

CULTIVAR NAMES
Foreign Expressions
W, X, Y, Z

WALDFEE (*German*) WOOD FAIRY
(*FUCHSIA* 'WALDFEE')

WÄLDLER (*German*)
WOODLANDER
(*LUZULA SYLVATICA* 'WÄLDLER')

WARSZAWSKA NIKE (*Polish*)
VICTORY OF WARSAW
(*CLEMATIS* 'WARSZAWSKA NIKE')

WEISSE GLORIA (*German*)
WHITE GLORIA
(*ASTILBE* 'WEISSE GLORIA')

WEISSE SCHWAN (*German*)
WHITE SWAN
(*PULSATILLA VULGARIS* 'WEISSE
SCHWAN')

WEISSER ZWERG (*German*)
WHITE DWARF
(*IBERIS SEMPERVIRENS* 'WEISSER
ZWERG')

WESTFALEN (*German*)
WESTPHALIA
(*HYDRANGEA PANICULATA* 'WESTFALEN')

WETTERFAHNE (*German*)
WEATHER VANE
(*MISCANTHUS SINENSIS* 'WETTERFAHNE')

WINDSPIEL (*German*) WIND PLAY
(*MOLINIA CAERULEA* SUBSP. *CAERULEA*
'WINDSPIEL')

WINTERMÄRCHEN (*German*)
WINTER FAIRY TALES
(*BERGENIA* 'WINTERMÄRCHEN')

WUNDER VON STÄFA (*German*)
WONDER OF STÄFA
(*ASTER* × *FRIKARTII* 'WUNDER
VON STÄFA')

YUKIKOMACHI (*Japanese*)
MORNING CLOUD
(*CLEMATIS* 'YUKIKOMACHI')

ZIGEUNERKNABE (*German*)
GYPSY BOY
(*ROSA* 'ZIGEUNERKNABE')

ZIMBELSTERN (*German*)
CYMBAL STAR
(*HELENIUM* 'ZIMBELSTERN')

ZWARTE SNOR (*Dutch*)
BLACK MOUSTACHE
(*FUCHSIA* 'ZWARTE SNOR')

ZWARTKOP (*Dutch*) BLACK HEAD
(*AEONIUM* 'ZWARTKOP')

ZWEIWELTENKIND (*German*)
CHILD OF TWO WORLDS
(*ARUNCUS DIOICUS* 'ZWEIWELTENKIND')

ZWERGELEFANT (*German*)
BABY ELEPHANT
(*MISCANTHUS SINENSIS*
'ZWERGELEFANT')

wisleyensis named for the Royal
Horticultural Society's garden
at Wisley, Surrey
Gaultheria × *wisleyensis*

wulfenii, wulfenianus named
for an Austrian botanist, Franz
von Wulfen (1728–1805)
Euphorbia characias subsp. *wulfenii*

X, Y, Z

xanth- yellow (see below)

xanthinus yellow
   Rosa xanthina

xanthocarpus with yellow fruit
   Sorbus aucuparia var. *xanthocarpa*

xanthocodon yellow bell
   Rhododendron cinnabarinum subsp.
   xanthocodon

CULTIVAR NAMES
Strange but True
W, X, Y, Z

NARCISSUS 'WALDORF ASTORIA'
PELARGONIUM 'WAYWARD ANGEL'
RHODODENDRON 'WEE BEE'
DIERAMA 'WESTMINSTER CHIMES'
GAURA LINDHEIMERI 'WHIRLING
   BUTTERFLIES'
FUCHSIA 'WIDOW TWANKY'
NARCISSUS 'WITCH DOCTOR'
CORNUS KOUSA 'WOLF EYES'
RHODODENDRON 'WOMBAT'
ROSA X-RATED ('TINX')
NARCISSUS 'XIT'
HEMEROCALLIS 'YABBA DABBA DOO'
RANUNCULUS FICARIA 'YAFFLE'
IRIS 'YO-YO'
LINARIA × *DOMINII* 'YUPPIE
   SURPRISE'
IRIS 'ZINC PINK'
IRIS 'ZIPPER'

---

xanthochlorus yellowish green
   Alchemilla xanthochlora

xiphium gladiolus; sword
   Iris xiphium

xylo- wood (see below)

xylocanthus with woody spines

xylocarpus with woody fruit
   Sinojackia xylocarpa

yakushimanus from Yaku-shima,
   a small island in southern Japan
   Rhododendron yakushimanum

COMMON DESCRIPTIVE TERMS
yedoensis, yesoensis, yezoensis from
   Tokyo
Cardamine yezoensis
Chrysanthemum yezoense
Geranium yesoense
Polemonium yezoense
Prunus × *yedoensis*

---

yuccifolium with leaves like *Yucca*
   Eryngium yuccifolium

COMMON DESCRIPTIVE TERMS
yunnanensis from Yunnan, China
Cardiocrinum giganteum var.
   yunnanense
Hedychium yunnanense
Lysimachia yunnanensis
Osmanthus yunnanensis
Pinus yunnanensis
Rhododendron yunnanense
Syringa yunnanensis

NATURAL FEATURES

aetnensis Mount Etna (Sicily)

aleuticus Aleutian Islands

alleghaniensis Allegheny Mountains (eastern USA)

altaicus Altai Mountains (Siberia/Kazakhstan/Mongolia/China)

amanus Amanus range (Turkey)

amazonicus River Amazon

amurensis Heilong Jiang (Amur river) (Russia/China)

andinus the Andes

antarcticus Antarctica

apenninus the Apennines (Italy)

atlanticus Atlas Mountains (N. Africa)

azoricus the Azores

balticus the area around the Baltic Sea

carpaticus Carpathian Mountains

cevennensis the Cévennes (France)

chathamicus the Chatham Islands

chiloensis Chiloé, an island off Chile

coum Kos (a Greek island)

dolomiticus the Dolomites (Italy)

emodensis, emodi the Himalayas

faeroensis Faeroe Isles

fuegianus Tierra del Fuego

karataviensis, karatavicus Karatau Mountains (Kazakhstan)

madagascariensis Madagascar

maderensis Madeira

megapotamicus (literally) big river: the Rio Grande (Brazil)

nootkatensis Nootka Sound (Canada)

olbius, olbiensis Iles d'Hyères (off the Mediterranean coast of France)

omeianus, omeiensis Emei Shan (Mount Omei, in Sichuan, China)

pyrenaicus, pyrenaeus the Pyrenees

rhodopensis Rhodope Mountains (Bulgaria)

sachalinensis Sakhalin island (east Asia)

saluenensis Nu Jiang (Salween river) (Burma/China)

scilloniensis Isles of Scilly (England)

tasmanicus Tasmania (Australia)

---

zabelii named after Hermann Zabel (1832–1912), a German tree expert
Eryngium × zabelii

zawadskii named after Alexander Zawadski (1798–1868), an Austrian scientist

---

COMMON DESCRIPTIVE TERMS

zebrinus striped
Malva sylvestris 'Zebrina'
Miscanthus sinensis 'Zebrinus'
Musa acuminata 'Zebrina'
Pinus wallichiana 'Zebrina'

zetlandicus from the Shetland Islands

zeylanicus from Sri Lanka (Ceylon)
Rhododendron arboreum subsp. *zeylanicum*

zonalis, zonatus with a distinct band of a different color
Pelargonium zonale

zoysii named after Karl von Zoys (1756–1800), an Austrian botanist
Campanula zoysii

zuluensis from the former kingdom of Zululand in southern Africa
Plectranthus zuluensis

GLOSSARY

A

Acuminate With a long point, tapering

Adpressed Lying close and flat against a surface

Alternate (of leaves) Borne singly at each node on opposite sides of the stem

Anther The pollen-bearing part of the stamen

Articulate Jointed

Auricle An ear-shaped projection or appendage

Axil The angle formed by a leaf or lateral branch with the stem, or of a vein with the midrib

B

Bifurcate Divided into two branches

Bipinnate Twice pinnate

Blade The expanded part of a leaf or petal

Bract A modified, usually reduced leaf at the base of a flower stalk

Bulbil A small bulb-like structure

C

Calyx The outer part of the flower, the sepals

Carpel Individual female part of a flower, comprising style, stigma and ovary

Catkin A normally dense spike or spike-like raceme of tiny, scaly-bracted flowers or fruits

Compound Composed of two or more similar parts

Corolla The inner, normally conspicuous part of a flower, the petals

Corymb A flat-topped or dome-shaped flowerhead with the outer flowers opening first

Crenate Toothed with shallow, rounded teeth; scalloped

Cultivar Distinct form not considered to warrant full botanical recognition, selected from either cultivated or wild plants and maintained in cultivation by propagation (example: *Heuchera* 'Plum Pudding')

Cuneate Wedge-shaped

Cuspidate Abruptly sharp pointed

Cyme A flat-topped or dome-shaped flowerhead with the inner flowers opening first

INFLORESCENCES
(SIMPLIFIED)

spike

raceme

panicle

corymb

umbel

cyme

*petal
(corolla)*

sepals (calyx)

stamen { *anther
filament* }

stigma

style } *pistil*

ovary

PARTS OF A SIMPLE FLOWER

pedicel

bract

node

internode

*axillary bud in
leaf axil*

peduncle

petiole

leaf blade

D

Decumbent Reclining, with ascending tips

Decurrent Extending down the stem

Decussate With x-shaped leaves at right angles to those below

Dehiscent Opening as seed vessels

Dioecious Bearing male and female flowers on different plants

Dissected Divided into many narrow segments

Distal Situated away from the point of attachment

Double (of flowers) With more than the usual number of petals, often with the style and stamens changed to petals

E

Elliptic Widest in the middle, narrowing equally at both ends

Entire Undivided and without teeth

Exstipulate Without stipules

F

Fastigiate With branches erect and close together

Fibrillose Having (or composed of) thin fibres, like the finest roots of a plant

Filament The stalk of a stamen

Fimbriate Fringed

Fistular Hollow like a pipe

Florets Small, individual flowers of a dense inflorescence

Forma (form; f.) Slightly differing variant of a species, ranked below varietas (var.). See also page 13

Fusiform Spindle-shaped

G

Genus In plant classification, the primary category, between family and species, grouping together species that have many characteristics in common. See also pages 11–12

Glabrous Hairless

Glaucous Covered with a bloom, bluish-white or silvery

H, I

Hybrid A plant resulting from a cross between different species

Inflorescence The flowering part of the plant

Internode The portion of stem between two nodes or joints

Involucre A whorl of bracts surrounding a flower or flower cluster

L

Lanceolate Lance-shaped

Lateral On or at the side

Leaflet Part of a compound leaf

Linear Long and narrow with nearly parallel margins

Lip One of the parts of an unequally divided flower

Lobe Any protruding part of an organ (as in leaf, corolla or calyx)

M, N, O

Midrib The central vein or rib of a leaf

Node The place on the stem where the leaves are attached; the joint

Oblong Longer than broad, with nearly parallel sides

Obovate Inversely ovate

Opposite (leaves) Borne two to each node, opposite each other.

Oval Broadest in the middle

Ovary The basal 'box' part of the pistil, containing the ovules

Ovate Broadest below the middle (like a hen's egg)

P

Palmate Lobed or divided in hand-like fashion, usually 5- or 7-lobed

Panicle A branching raceme

Pedicel The stalk of an individual flower in an inflorescence

Peduncle The stalk of a flower cluster or of a solitary flower

Perfoliate Having pairs of opposite leaves fused at the base, so the stem appears to pass through them

Perianth The calyx and corolla together; also used for a flower in which there is no distinction between corolla and calyx

Perule The covering of a seed or leaf-bud

Petal One of the separate segments of a corolla

Petiole The leaf-stalk

Pinnate With leaflets arranged on either side of a central stalk

Pistil The female reproductive part of a flower, comprising one or more carpels (ovary, style and stigma)

Pollen Spores or grains contained in the anther, containing the male element

R

Raceme A simple elongated inflorescence with stalked flowers

Rib A prominent vein in a leaf

Runner A trailing shoot taking root at the nodes

S

Scale A minute leaf or bract, or a flat gland-like appendage on the surface of a leaf, flower or shoot obovate   lanceolate   oblong   ovate   elliptic   oblanceolate   perfoliate

deltoid   subulate   filiform   acicular   linear   orbicular   rhomboidal   reniform

entire   ciliate   pectinate   cleft   lobed   dentate   denticulate   serrate   serrulate   doubly serrate   incised   crenate   crenulate   parted

acute   acuminate   aristate   cuspidate   mucronate   obtuse   retuse   emarginate

cuneate   attenuate   obtuse   cordate   auriculate   sagittate   hastate   truncate   oblique

pinnate

bipinnate

compound
palmate

trifoliolate   palmate

Scape A leafless stem of a flower or inflorescence

Secund Arranged on one side only

Sepal One of the segments of a calyx

Sessile Not stalked

Simple (of a leaf) Not compound; (of an inflorescence) unbranched

Sorus (plural sori) A cluster of spore-producing organs on the underside of a fern frond

Spathe A hoodlike bract surrounding a flower spike

Species In plant classification, a subdivision of a genus, grouping together individual plants with certain distinguishing characteristics. See also pages 11–12

Spine A sharp, pointed end of a branch or leaf

Stamen The male organ of a flower comprising filament and anther

Stigma The summit of the pistil, which receives the pollen, often sticky or feathery

Stipule Appendage (normally two) at the base of some petioles

Stolon A shoot at or below the surface of the ground that produces a new plant at its tip

Style The middle part of the pistil, often elongated, between the ovary and stigma

Subspecies (subsp.) In plant classification, a rank below species but above varietas (variety) and forma (form). See also page 13

T

Tendril A twining thread-like appendage

Terminal Located at the end of a stem or shoot

Ternate In threes

Thyrse A type of contracted flower panicle, like lilac or horse-chestnut

Tuberculate Having small wartlike projections

U, V, W

Umbelliferous Bearing umbels, flat-topped inflorescences in which the pedicels or peduncles all arise from the same point

Varietas (variety; var.) A variant of a species, occurring in the wild, and ranked below subspecies and above forma. See also page 13

Venation The arrangement of the veins

Verticillate Arranged in a whorl or ring

Whorl Three or more flowers or leaves arranged in a ring

INDEX

ACKNOWLEDGMENTS

David & Charles and OutHouse Publishing would like to thank the following organizations and individuals for their assistance in the preparation of this book: the Royal Horticultural Society for their help in finding and providing the portraits of plant hunters and plantsmen; the staff of the RHS Lindley Library for their patient and friendly help with research; Hillier for permission to use illustrations and botanical information from the *Hillier Gardener's Guide to Trees & Shrubs*, and for the photograph of Sir Harold Hillier; Ian Smith and Mike Park for assistance in sourcing illustrations; Dover Press for permission to use illustrations from the *Handbook of Plant and Floral Ornament from Early Herbals*; Yukari Paul for help in translating Japanese cultivar names; and Christopher Gordon for valuable assistance with proofreading.